PENCIL LEGENDS: PORTRAITS OF FAMOUS AMERICANS OF AFRICAN DESCENT

DRAWINGS BY
TIMOTHY E. POWELL

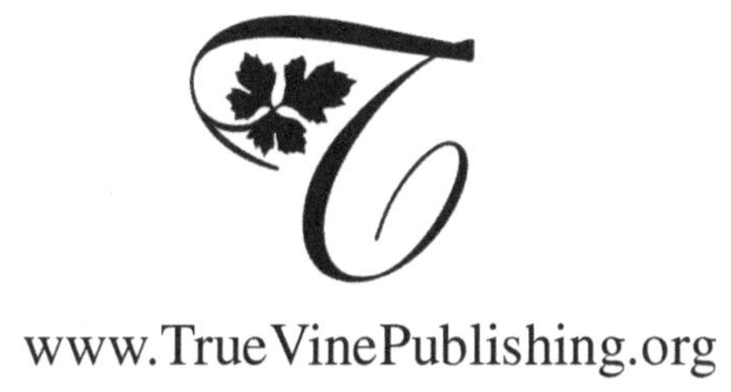

www.TrueVinePublishing.org

Pencil Legends
Timothy E. Powell

Published by
True Vine Publishing Co
810 Dominican Dr
Nashville, TN 37228
www.TrueVinePublishing.org

ISBN: 978-1-962783-66-8 Paperback

PREFACE

Drawing has been my lifelong passion. From my earliest days, I remember my first drawing—a portrait of President John F. Kennedy. This initial endeavor sparked a journey that has spanned decades, during which I have focused primarily on subjects of European descent. Recently, however, I have felt compelled to shine a light on some of the unsung heroes and renowned figures of African descent.

In creating this collection, my aim is to offer teachers, historians, parents, researchers, and students—from elementary school through college—a curated resource of richly detailed pencil portraits. My hope is to provide a singular, accessible source of inspiration and insight, eliminating the need to wade through countless online searches.

Throughout my artistic journey, I have remained devoted to the simplicity and precision of pencil work. This book reflects that commitment, showcasing a series of portraits that celebrate the impact and contributions of significant figures in a timeless medium.

This compilation is also a tribute to those who may have once felt marginalized or who believe it's too late to leave their mark. Having spent nearly 40 years working as a postal service worker, I have sought to demonstrate through this book that it's never too late to pivot and make a meaningful impact. May these portraits inspire readers to embrace their own creative passions and pursue their dreams, no matter where they are on their journey.

Cleveland, OH

TABLE OF CONTENTS

INTRODUCTION

The thought of compiling a collection of books showcasing my artwork was a distant dream until recently. It was during a visit to my brother and sister-in-law that fate intervened; I shared a few of my penciled etchings with them, igniting a spark that urged me to take action now rather than later. This unexpected moment of inspiration transformed my vision into a reality, compelling me to share my artistic journey with the world.

While I have created over 1,000 penciled portraits of Americans of African descent, only a select few are included in this book. To narrow the focus, I had to ask myself several critical questions; otherwise, this project risked becoming more of an encyclopedia than a curated collection of prominent individuals. For instance, should I concentrate solely on well-known figures, or include those who may be less popular yet still relevant? Although this book primarily celebrates Americans of African descent, I believe it would be incomplete without recognizing the contributions of a key Caucasian figure who played a crucial role in founding the NAACP. The final chapter, "Diverse Careers," showcases portraits from a broad spectrum of professions, including bishop, journalist, choreographer, and more.

I want to acknowledge the invaluable contributions of Wikipedia and various online platforms, which provided illustrations and factual information that enriched this book. The collaborative nature of these digital resources offered a wealth of diverse content. However, it's important to note that some information may not be entirely factual, as it has been sourced from these platforms. While I have made every effort to verify the accuracy of the material, I encourage readers to conduct their own research and consult additional sources for a more comprehensive understanding. I encourage readers to explore other platforms for further information and context.

I want to express my heartfelt thanks to my big brother, William Powell, for his constant support over the years. I also extend my gratitude to my sister-in-law, Norma, for her unwavering support and encouragement throughout the journey of constructing this book. Her insightful feedback from cover to cover for my ideas were instrumental in shaping the direction of this work. How to use this book? Here are a few creative ways to use a book with selected penciled drawings of famous Americans:

1. Use the drawings in classrooms to teach about African American history and culture. What were this person's key contributions, and how did they impact society?

2. Find famous quotes related to the depicted African Americans.

3. Use the drawings as prompts for storytelling, encouraging creativity and discussion around each figure's impact.

4. Consider gifting the book to schools or libraries for enriching educational resources and promoting cultural awareness in local institutions.

5. **Art Workshops**: Organize drawing workshops where participants replicate the styles of the sketches. Caption: "Fostering creativity and connection through art and history."

6. **Storytelling Events**: Use the drawings to inspire storytelling sessions in libraries or schools. Caption: "Bringing history to life through narrative and visual art."

7. **Interactive Projects**: Encourage students to create their own artwork inspired by the drawings. Caption: "Empowering young artists to interpret and express their understanding of cultural icons."

As you journey through this book and explore the many penciled illustrations, I encourage you to engage deeply with the content. Reflect on the themes presented, and seek further exploration of the untold history behind them. Let each penciled artwork spark your curiosity. Your engagement is key to unlocking the full potential of this experience!

Civil Rights Leaders

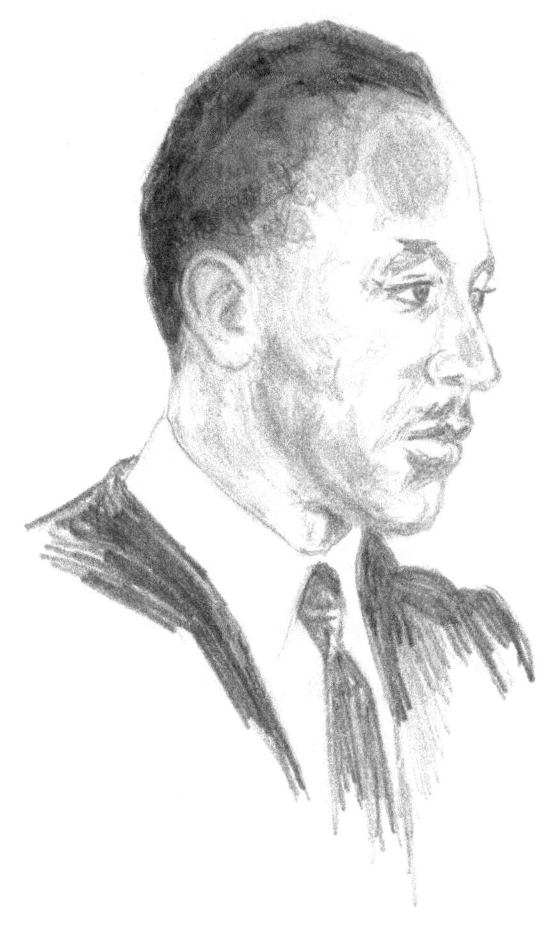

MARTIN LUTHER
KING Jr.

American orator, clergyman and civil rights leader

Nobel Peace Prize winner (1964)

1929 - 1968

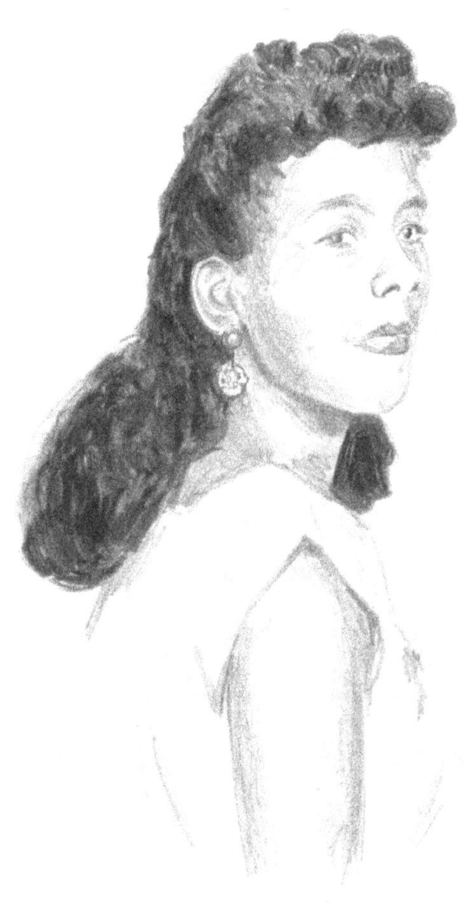

CORETTA SCOTT
KING
American author, singer, social and civil rights activist
widow of Martin Luther King Jr.

1927-2006

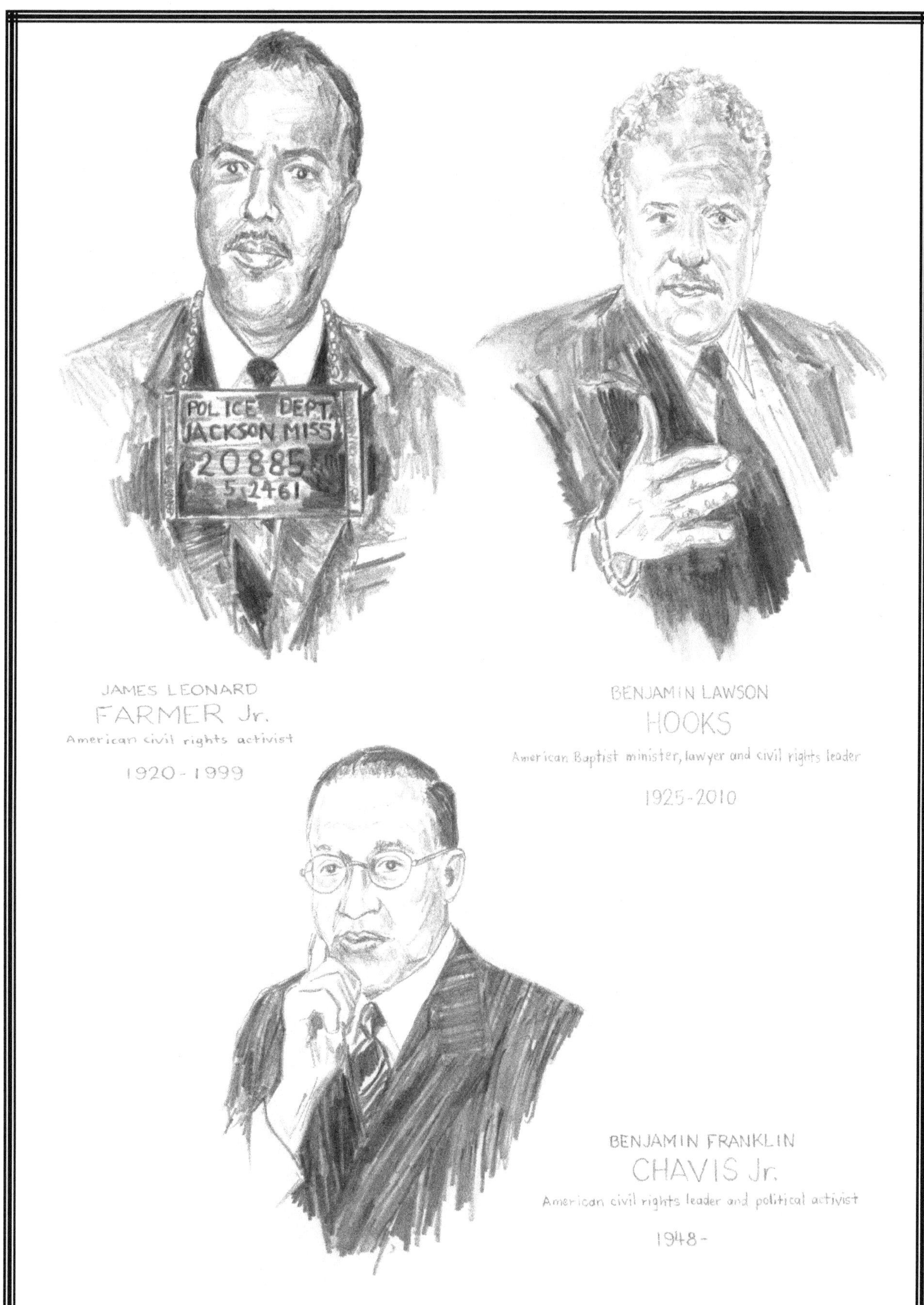

JAMES LEONARD
FARMER Jr.
American civil rights activist

1920 - 1999

BENJAMIN LAWSON
HOOKS
American Baptist minister, lawyer and civil rights leader

1925 - 2010

BENJAMIN FRANKLIN
CHAVIS Jr.
American civil rights leader and political activist

1948 -

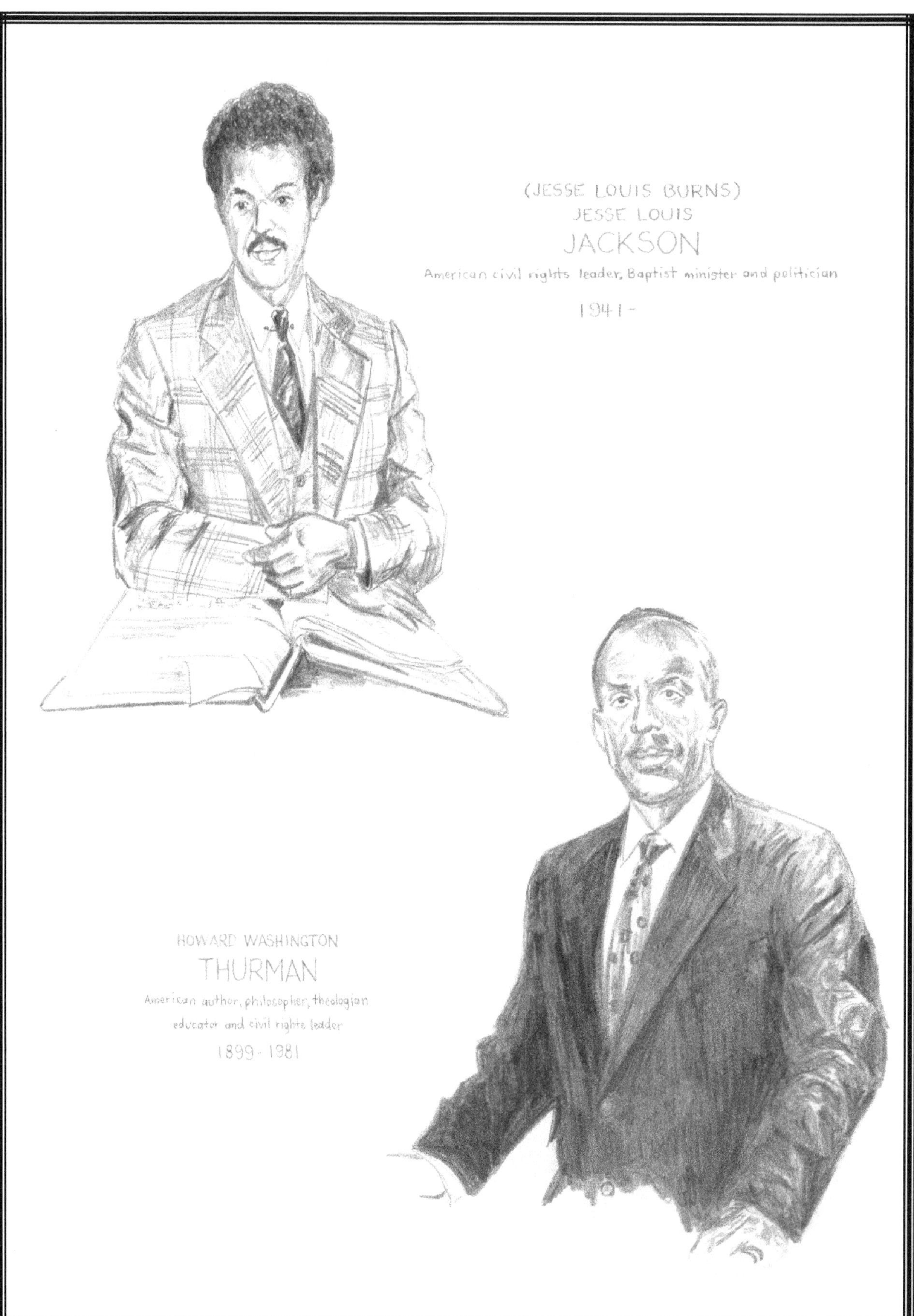

(JESSE LOUIS BURNS)
JESSE LOUIS
JACKSON
American civil rights leader, Baptist minister and politician
1941 -

HOWARD WASHINGTON
THURMAN
American author, philosopher, theologian
educator and civil rights leader
1899 - 1981

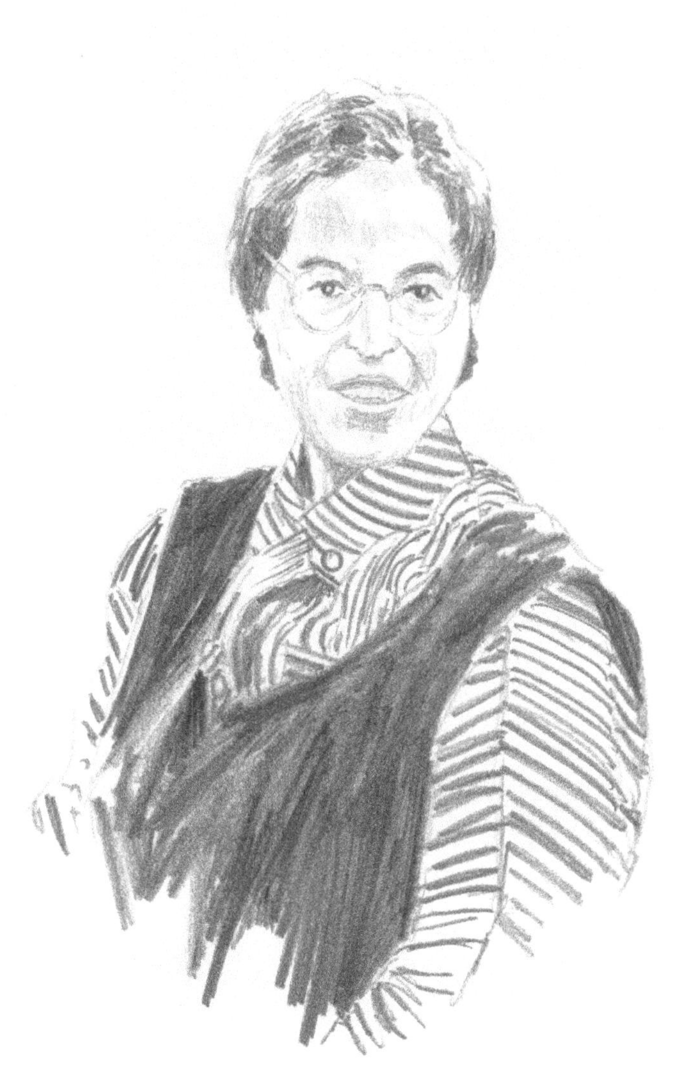

ROSE LEE
PARKS
American seamstress and civil rights activist

1913-2005

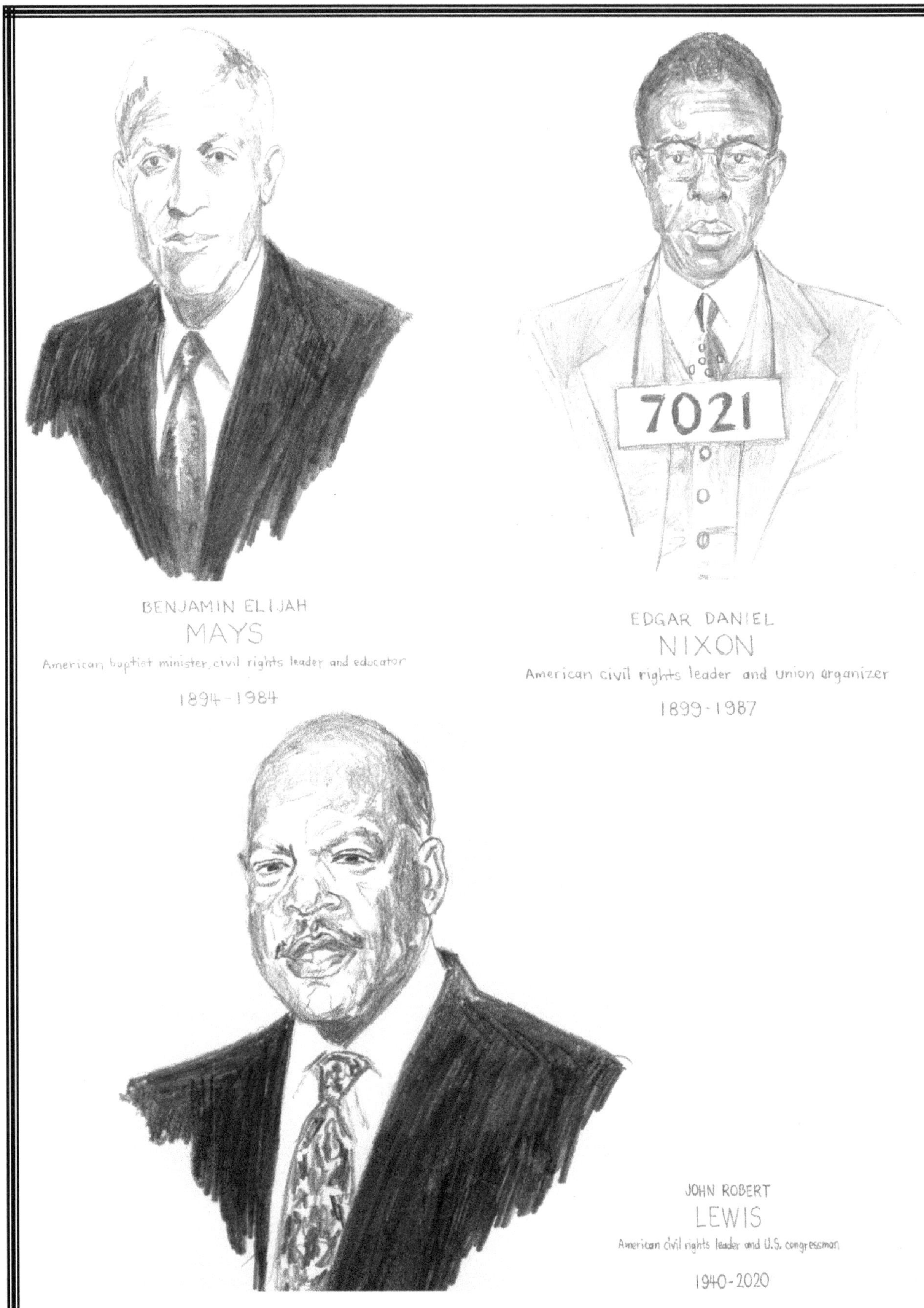

BENJAMIN ELIJAH
MAYS
American baptist minister, civil rights leader and educator

1894-1984

EDGAR DANIEL
NIXON
American civil rights leader and union organizer

1899-1987

JOHN ROBERT
LEWIS
American civil rights leader and U.S. congressman

1940-2020

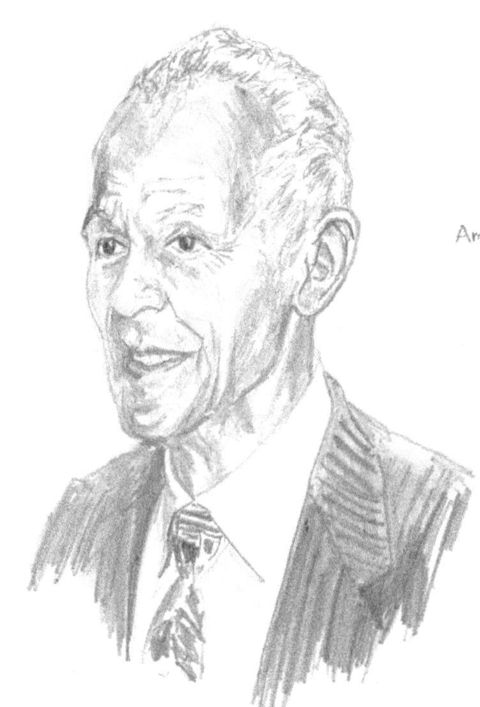

CORDY TINDELL
VIVIAN
American minister, author and civil rights activist

1924 - 2020

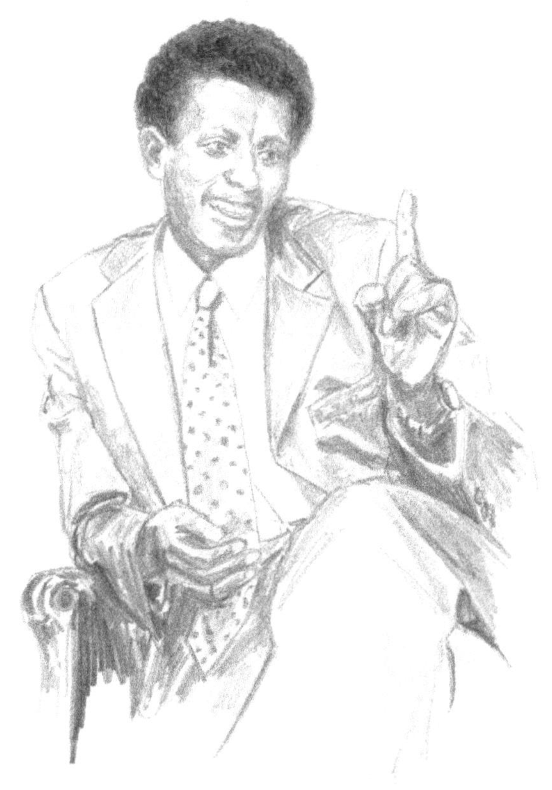

(KWAME TURE)
STOKELY
CARMICHAEL
Trinidadian-American civil rights and political activist

1941 - 1998

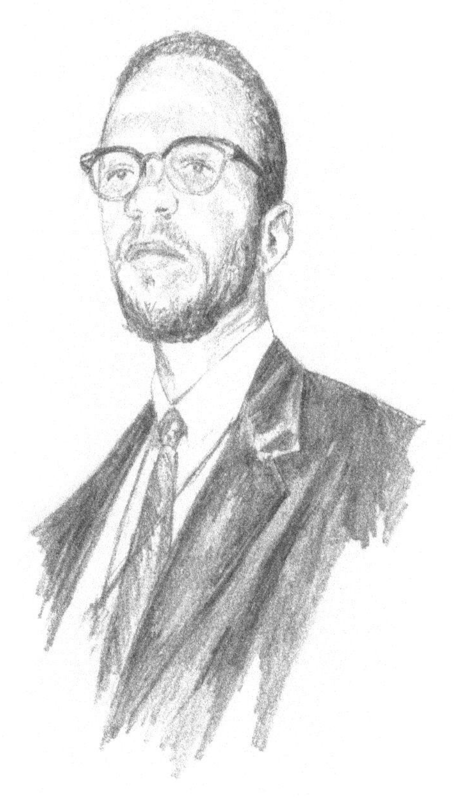

(MALCOLM LITTLE)
(EL-HAJJ MALIK EL-SHABAZZ)
MALCOLM X
American orator, militant and civil rights leader

1925 - 1965

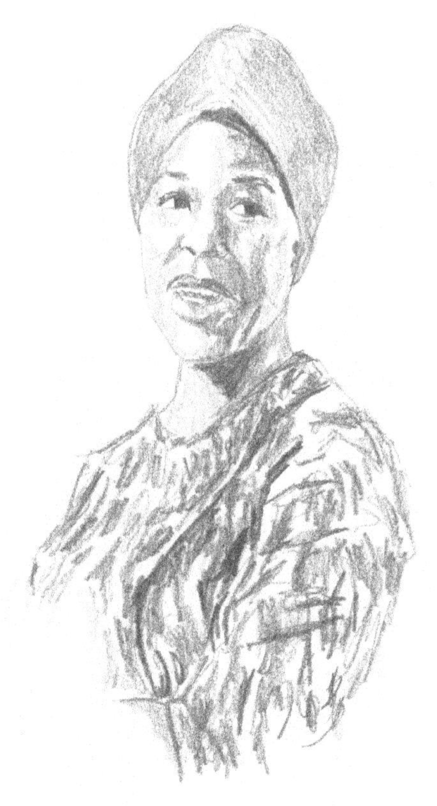

(BETTY DEAN SANDERS) (BETTY X)
BETTY
SHABAZZ
rican educator, civil rights advocate and wife of Malc

1934 - 1997

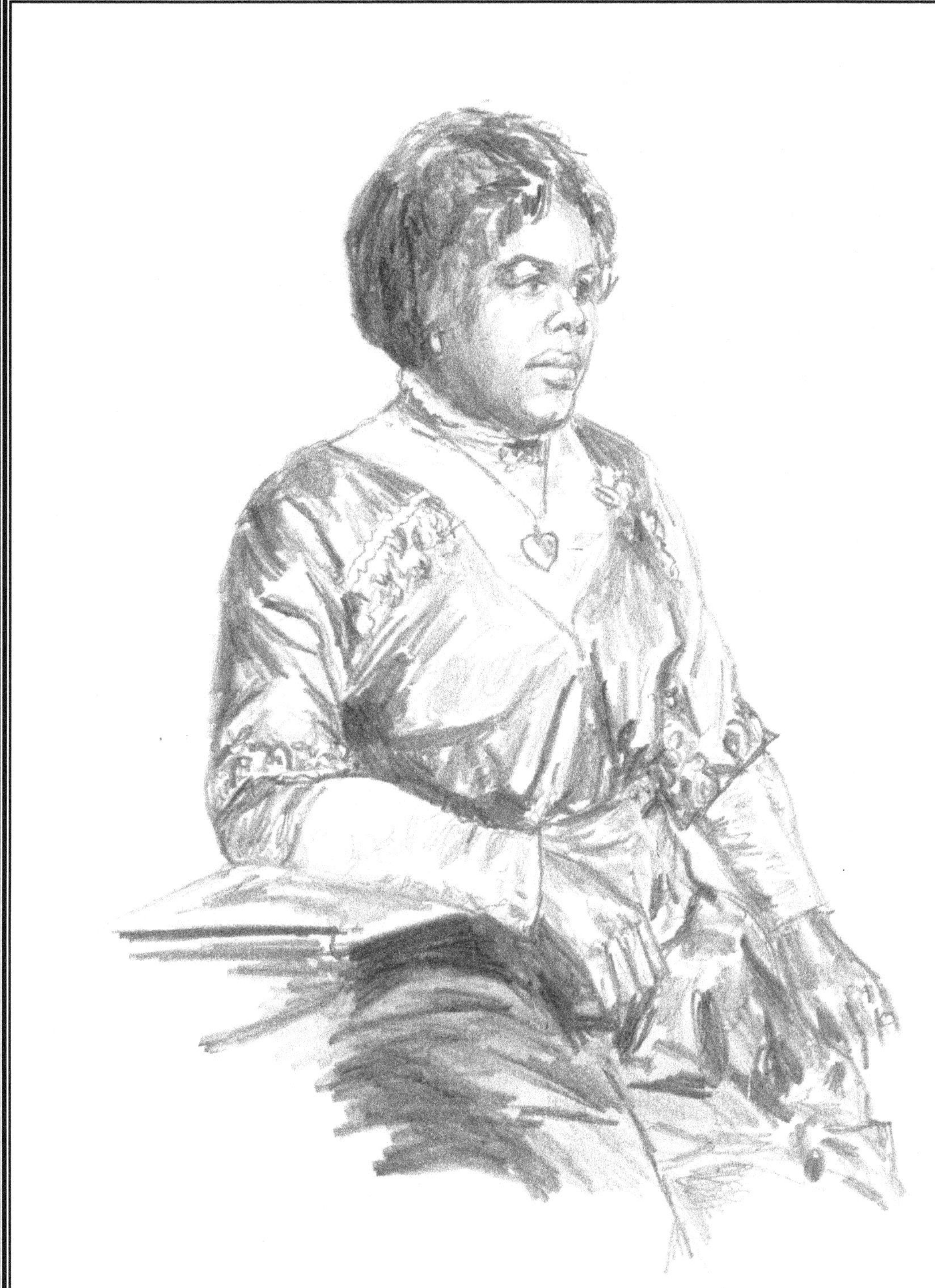

MARY JANE McLEOD
BETHUNE
American educator and civil rights leader

1875-1955

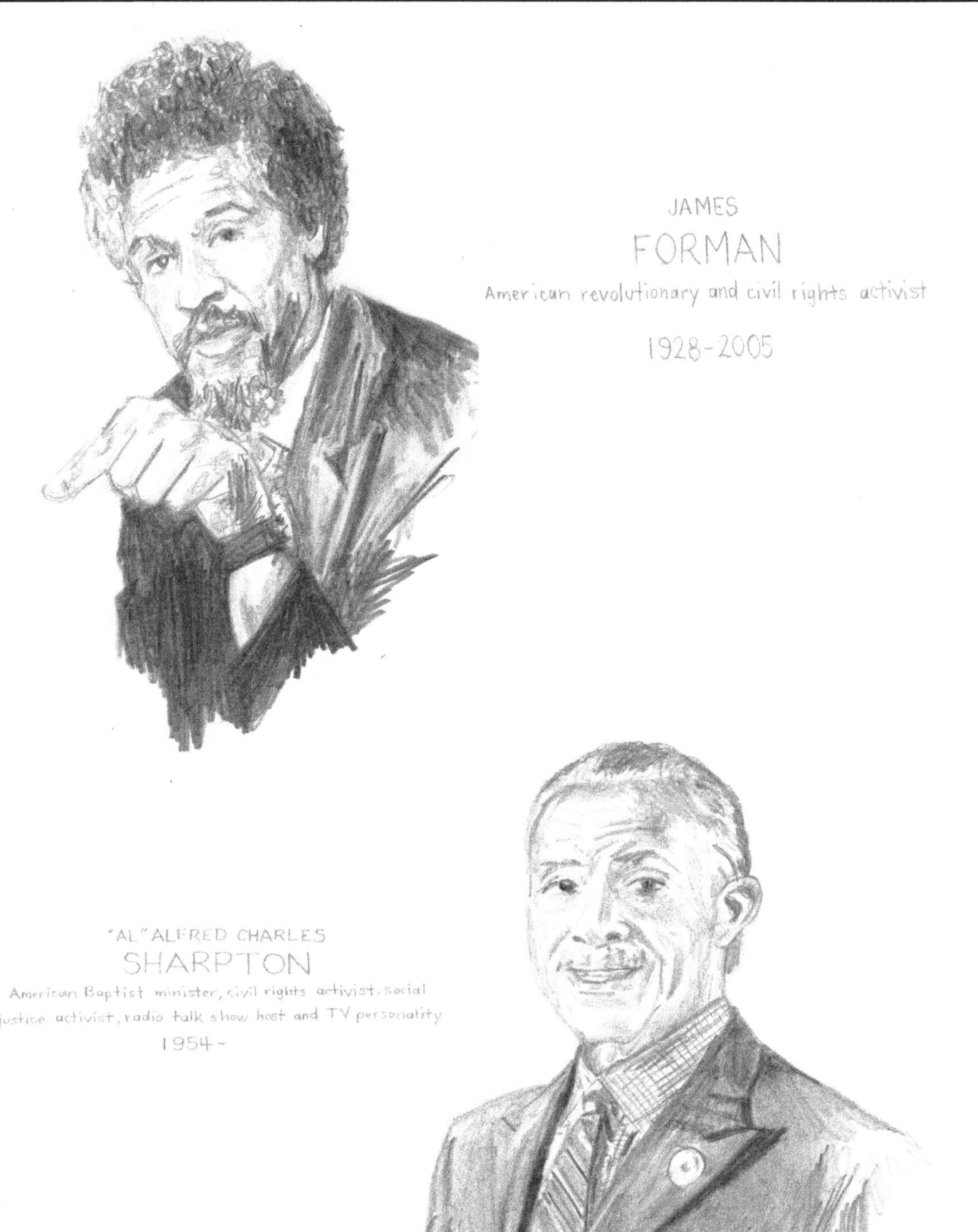

JAMES
FORMAN
American revolutionary and civil rights activist
1928-2005

"AL" ALFRED CHARLES
SHARPTON
American Baptist minister, civil rights activist, social
justice activist, radio talk show host and TV personality
1954-

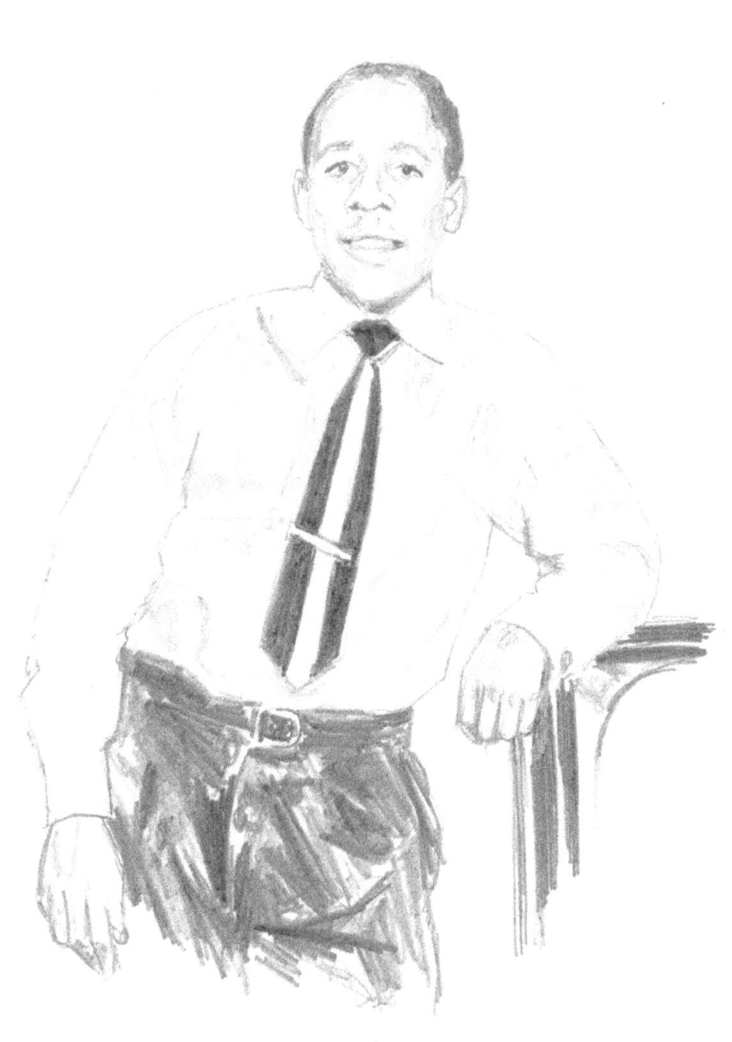

EMMETT LOUIS
TILL
American youth and murder victim that
triggered the American civil rights movement

1941 - 1955

Politicians

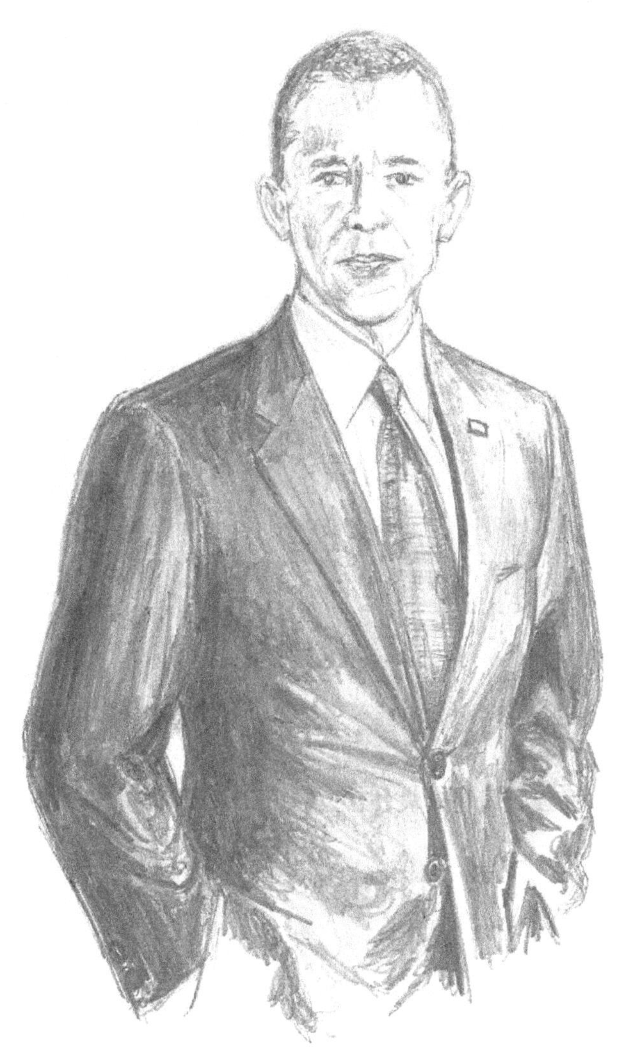

BARACK HUSSEIN
OBAMA

American lawyer, statesman and Nobel Peace Prize winner (2009)

President of the United States of America 2009-2017

1961 –

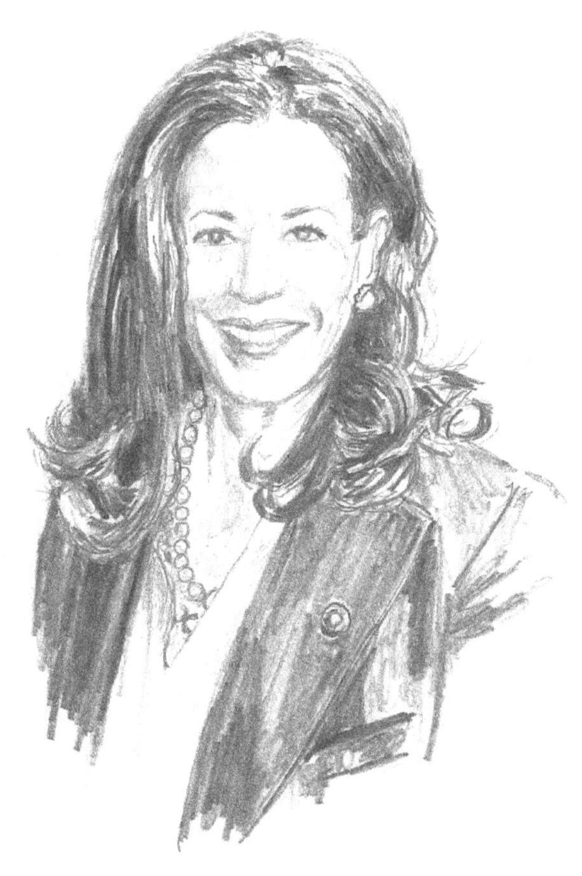

KAMALA DEVI
HARRIS
American politician, lawyer and
U.S. Vice-President 2021-2025

1964-

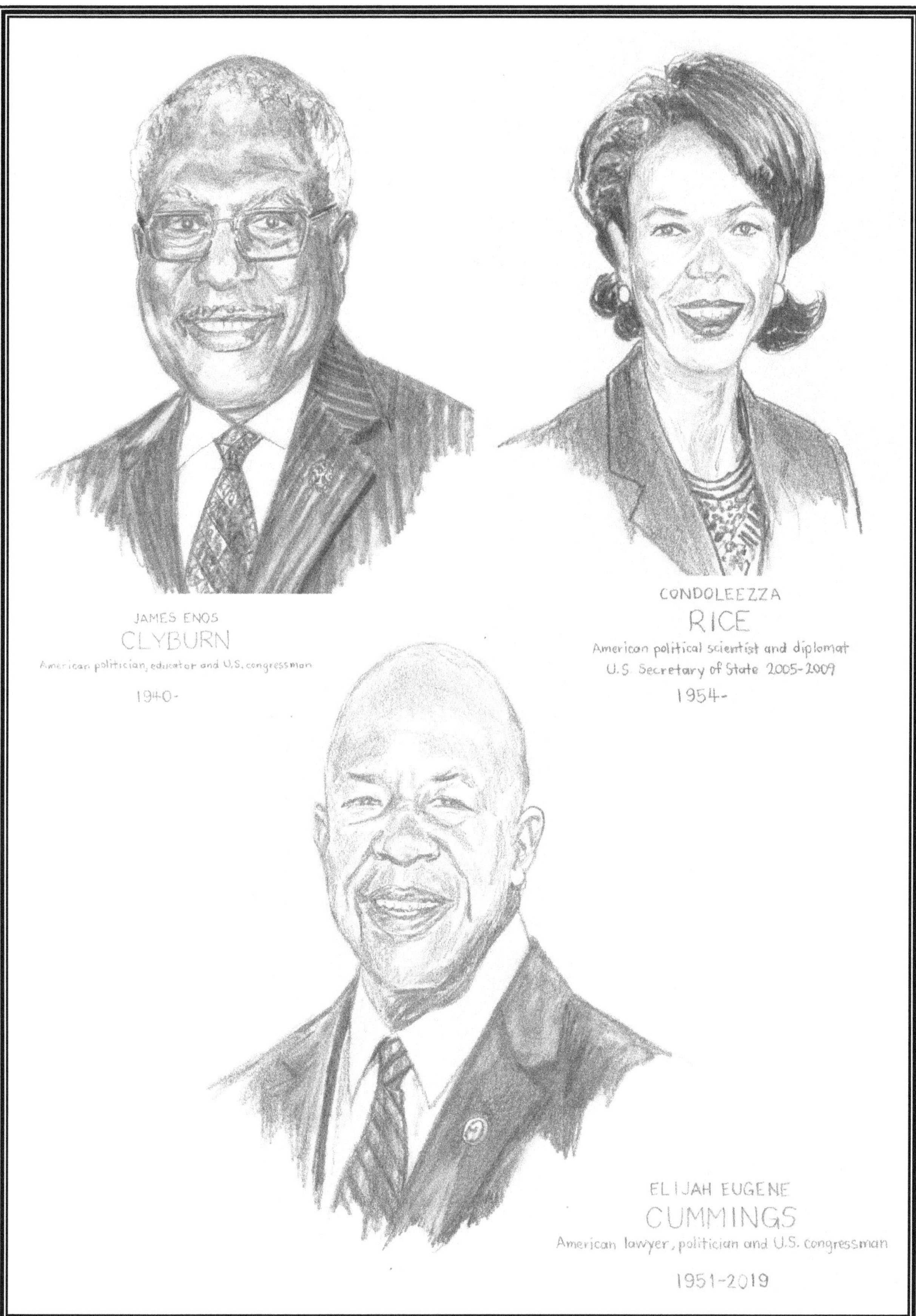

JAMES ENOS
CLYBURN
American politician, educator and U.S. congressman

1940-

CONDOLEEZZA
RICE
American political scientist and diplomat
U.S. Secretary of State 2005-2009

1954-

ELIJAH EUGENE
CUMMINGS
American lawyer, politician and U.S. congressman

1951-2019

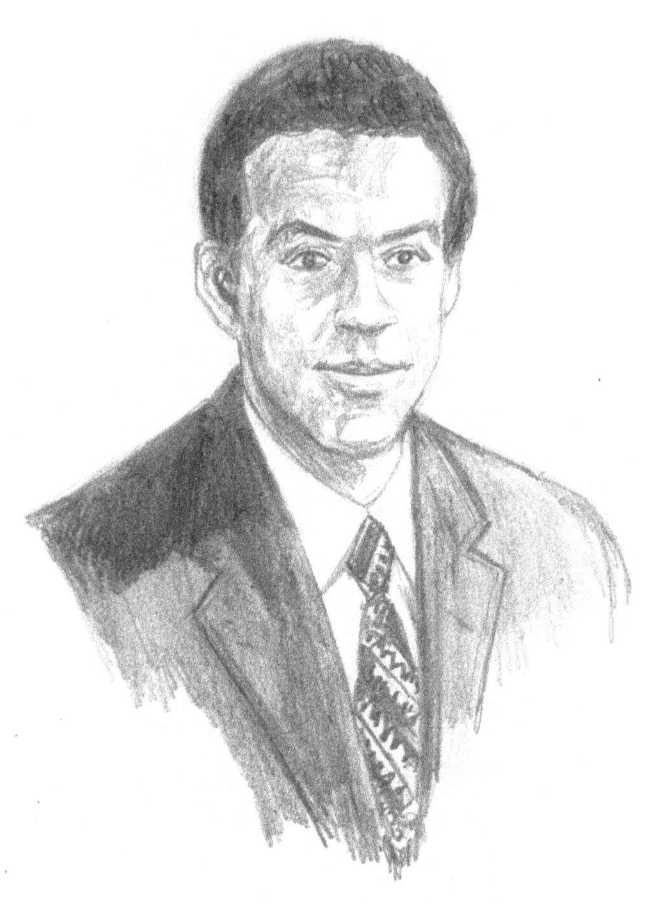

ANDREW JACKSON
YOUNG

American clergyman, politician, diplomat
civil rights activist and U.S. congressman,
Mayor of Atlanta, Georgia 1982-1990

1932-

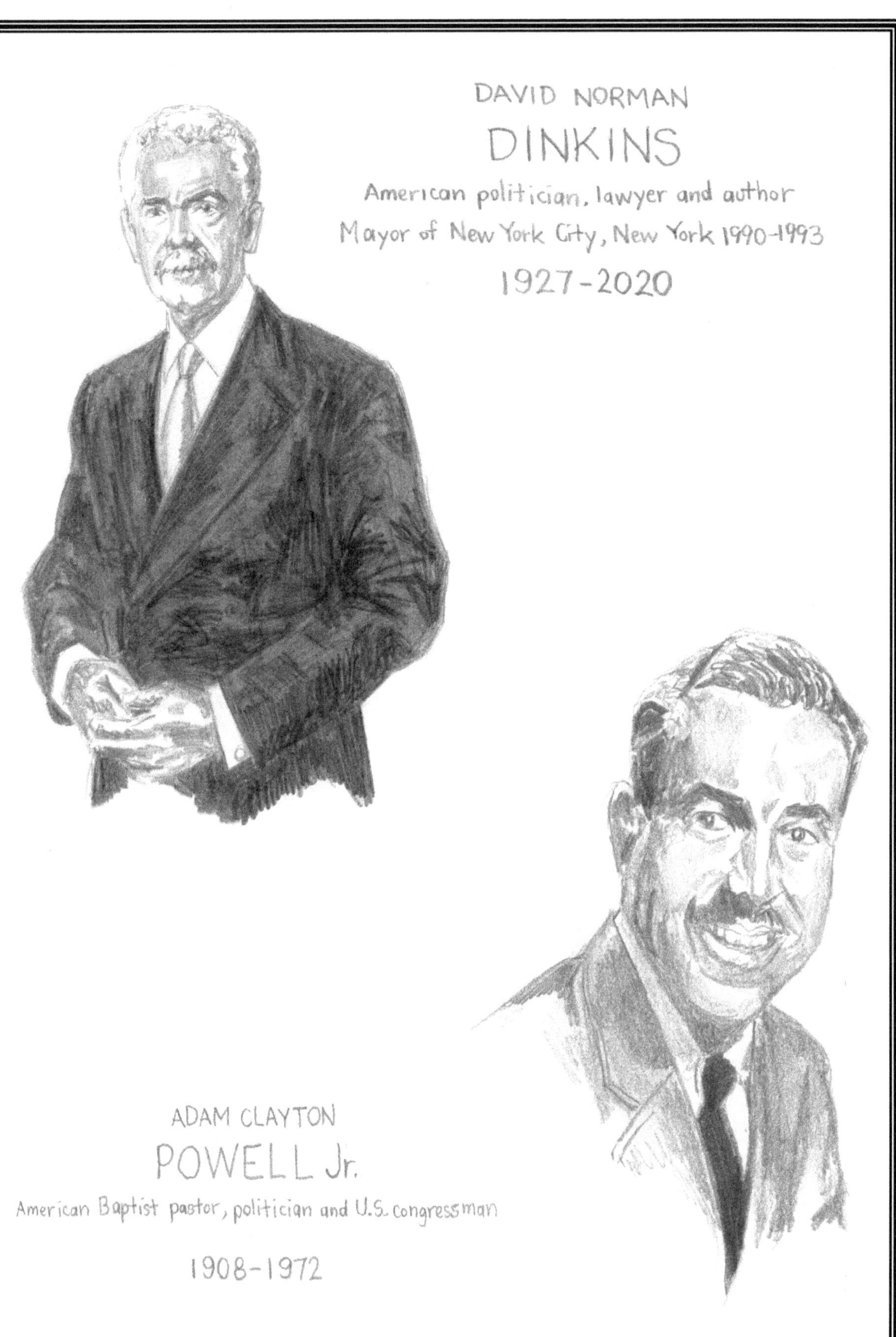

DAVID NORMAN
DINKINS
American politician, lawyer and author
Mayor of New York City, New York 1990-1993

1927-2020

ADAM CLAYTON
POWELL Jr.
American Baptist pastor, politician and U.S. congressman

1908-1972

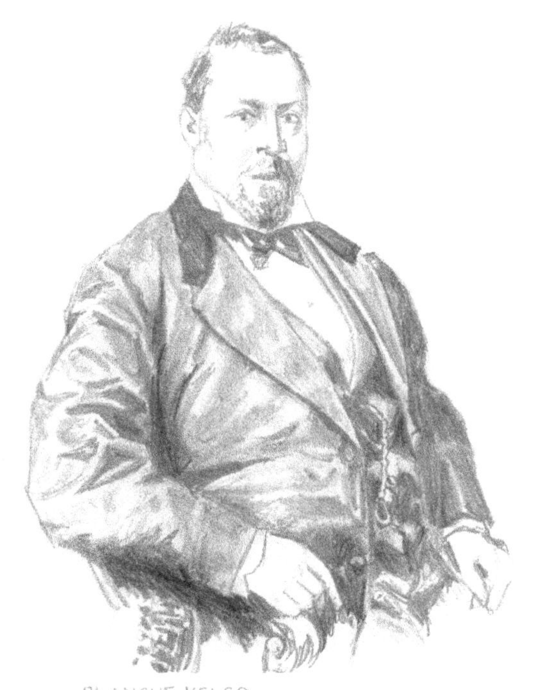

BLANCHE KELSO
BRUCE
American (born a slave) educator,
printer, politician and U.S. senator
1841 - 1898

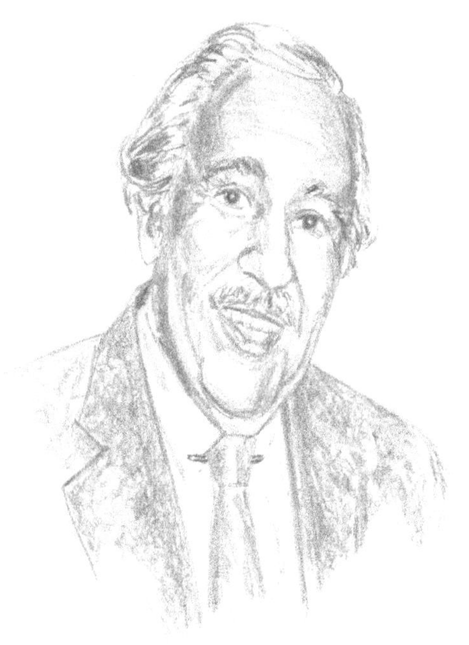

"CHARLIE" CHARLES BERNARD
RANGEL
American soldier, politician, lawyer and U.S. congressman
1930-

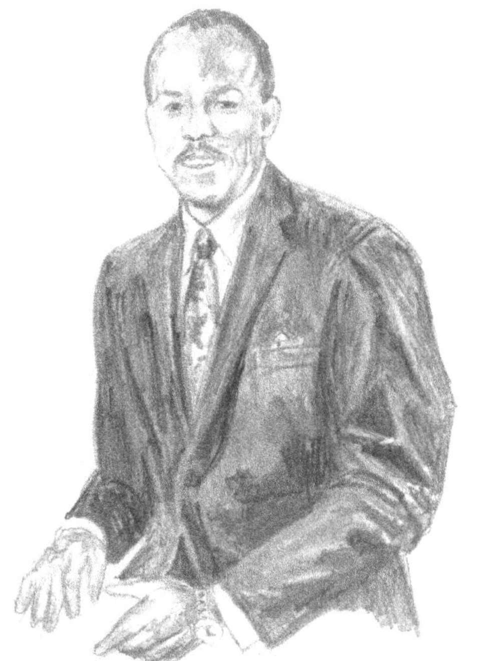

CARL BURTON
STOKES
American soldier, politician, diplomat and jurist
Mayor of Cleveland, Ohio 1968-1971

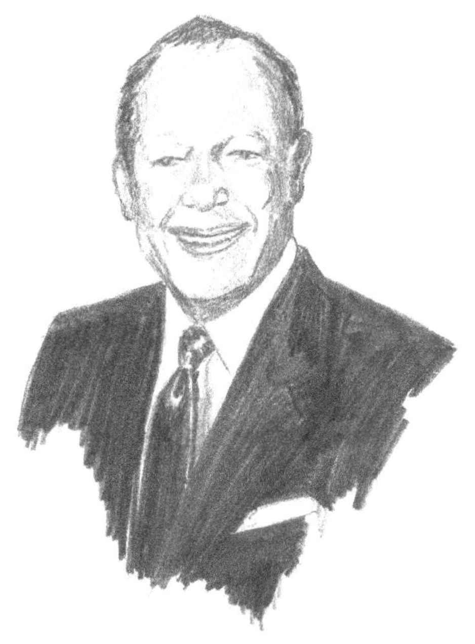

"TOM" THOMAS J.
BRADLEY
American politician
Mayor of Los Angeles, California 1973-1993
1917 - 1998

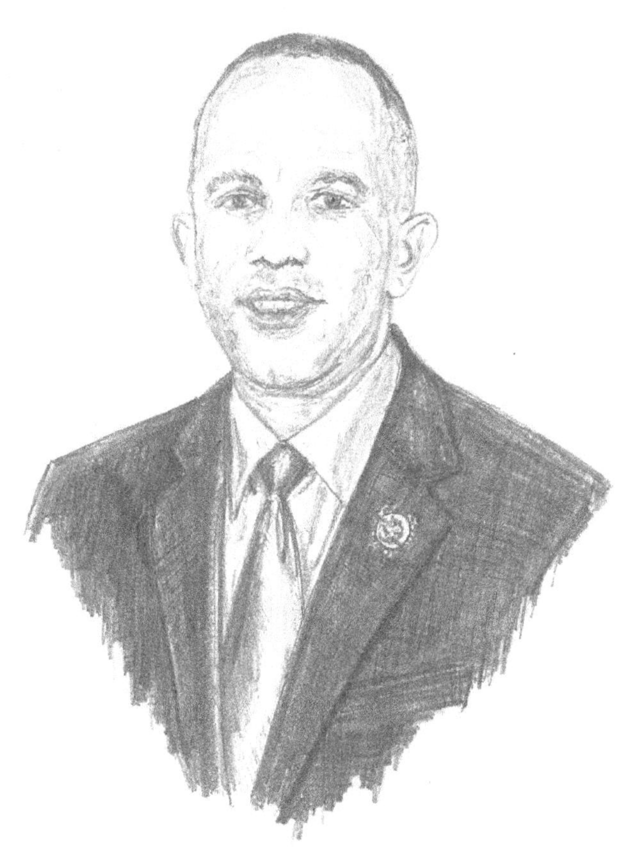

HAKEEN SEKOU
JEFFRIES
American politician, lawyer and U.S. congressman

1970-

Singers, Musicians, Composers

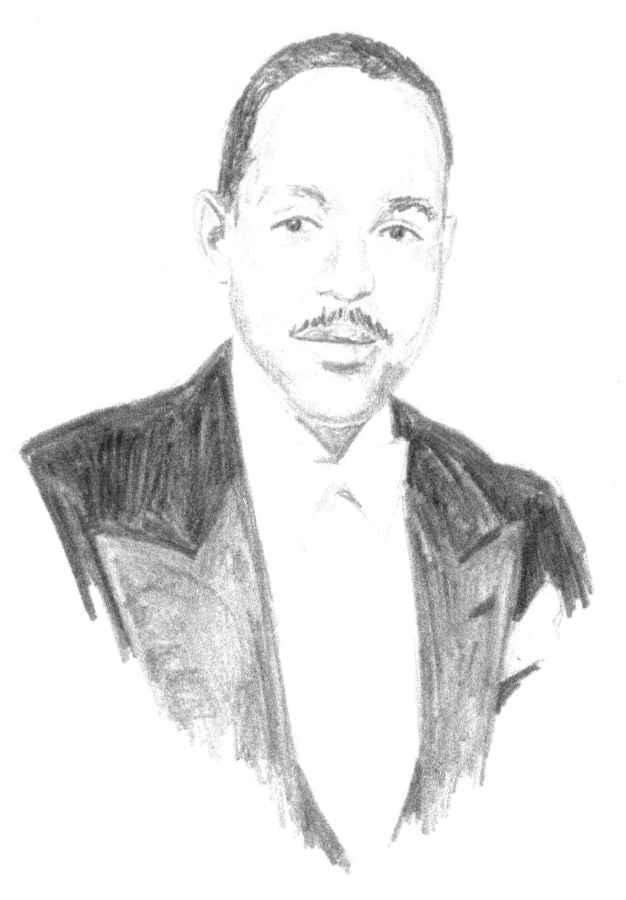

"BENNY" BENNETT LESTER
CARTER
American jazz musician and composer

1907-2003

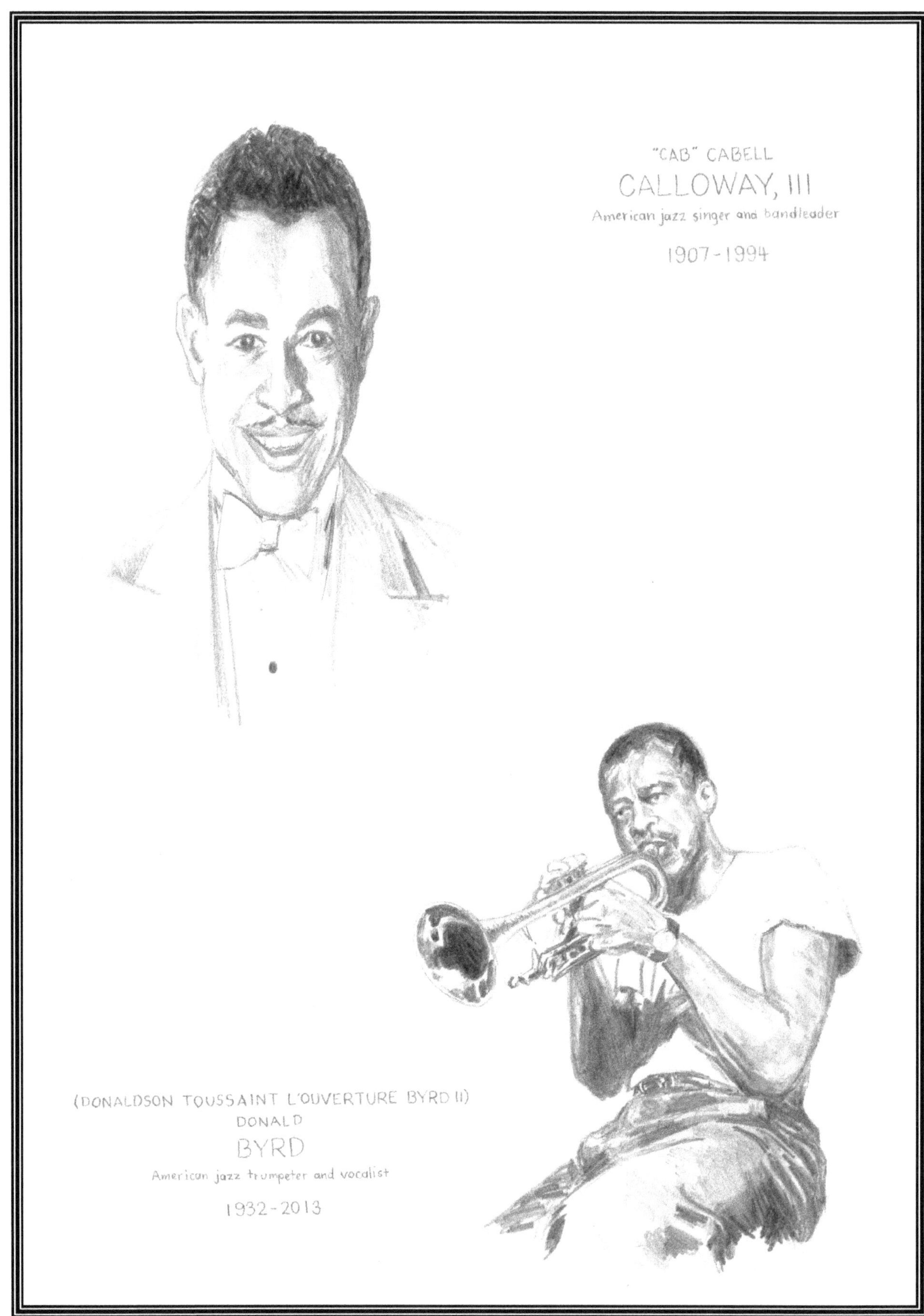

"CAB" CABELL
CALLOWAY, III
American jazz singer and bandleader

1907-1994

(DONALDSON TOUSSAINT L'OUVERTURE BYRD II)
DONALD
BYRD
American jazz trumpeter and vocalist

1932-2013

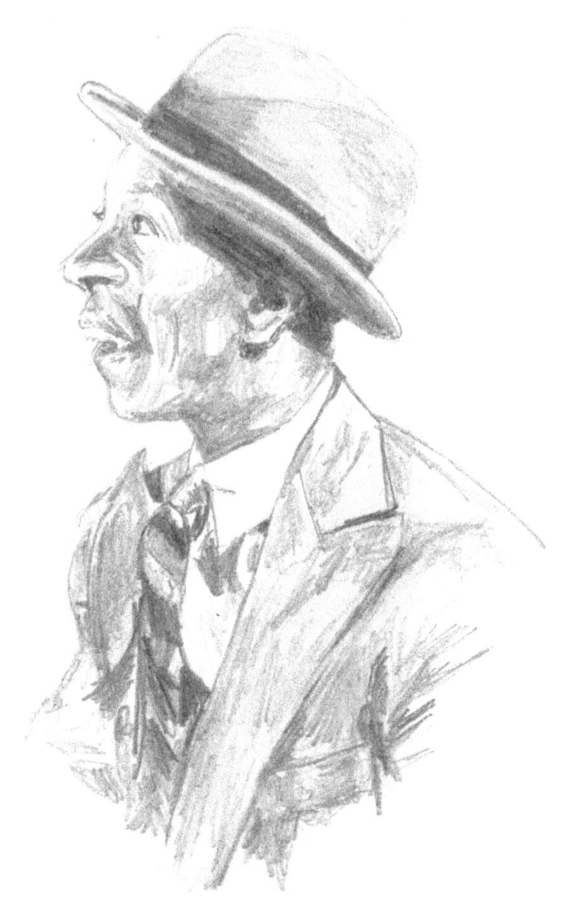

(JOHN WILLIAM SUBLETT)
JOHN W.
BUBBLES
American dancer, singer, entertainer and actor

1902-1986

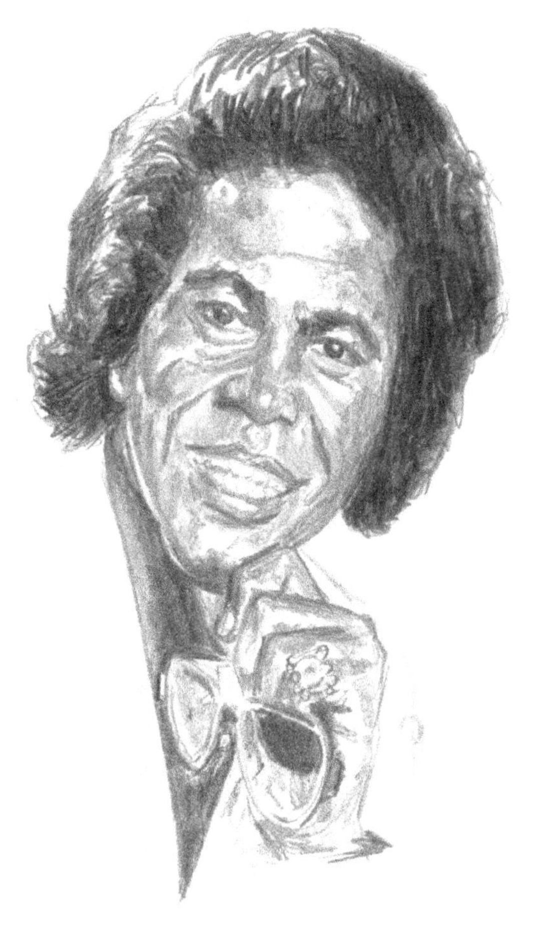

JAMES JOSEPH

BROWN

American singer, songwriter, musician and recording artist

1933 - 2006

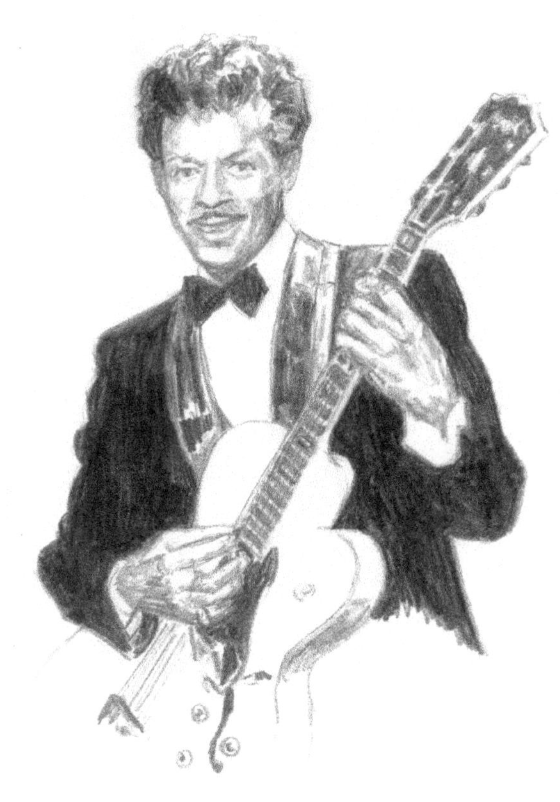

"CHUCK" CHARLES EDWARD ANDERSON
BERRY
American guitarist, singer and songwriter

1926 - 2017

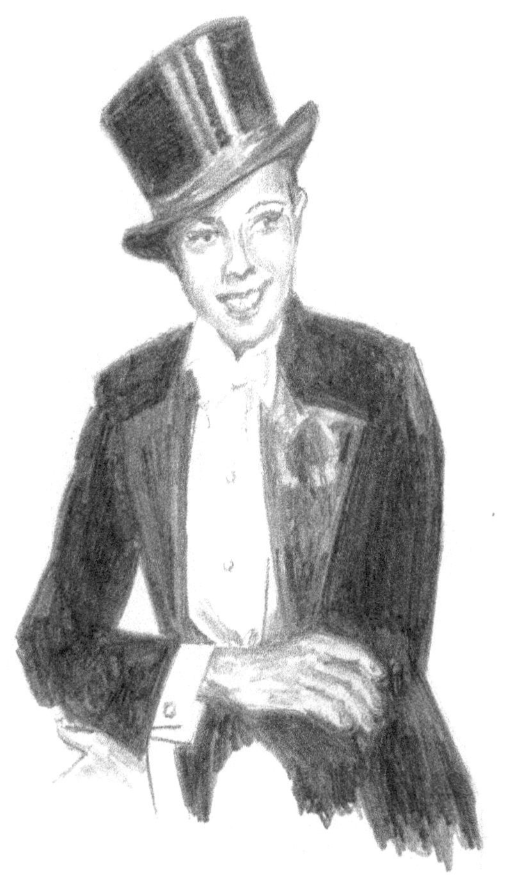

(JREDA JOSEPHINE McDONALD)
JOSEPHINE
BAKER
American-French entertainer, dancer,
singer, motion picture actress and free French
resistance fighter during World War II
1906 - 1975

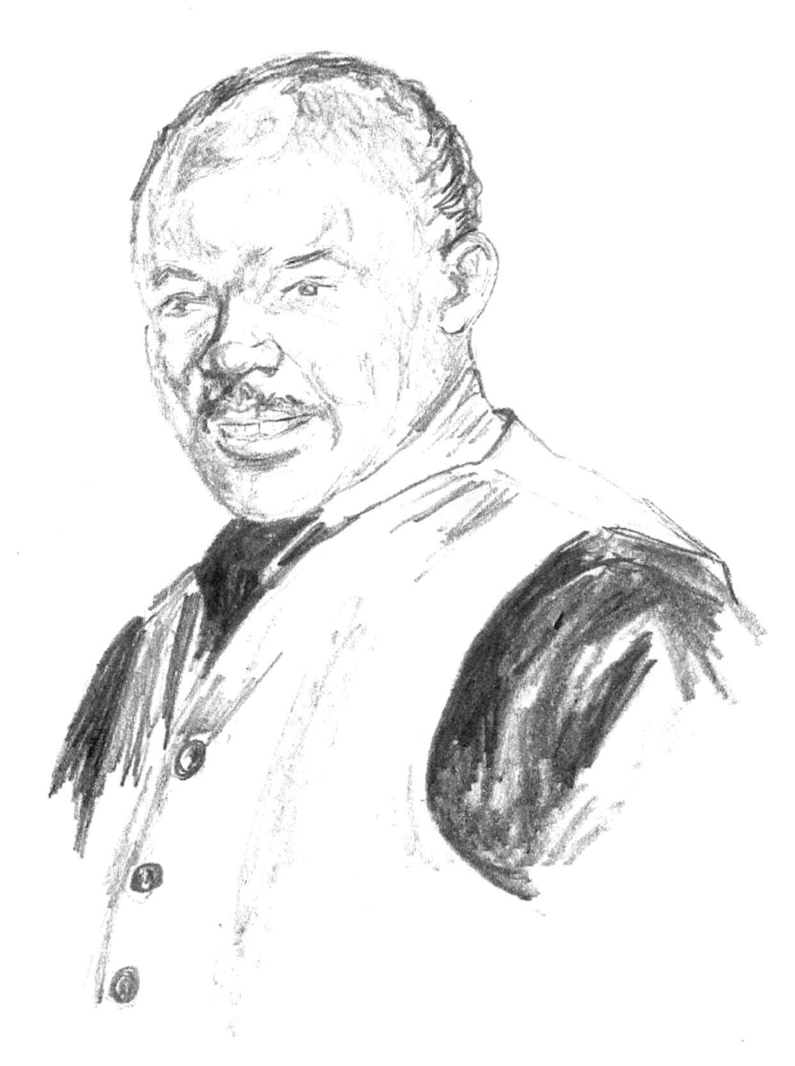

"Q" QUINCY DELIGHT
JONES Jr.

American record producer, conductor, composer,
arranger, musician, actor, television and film producer
entertainment executive and humanitarian

1933-2024

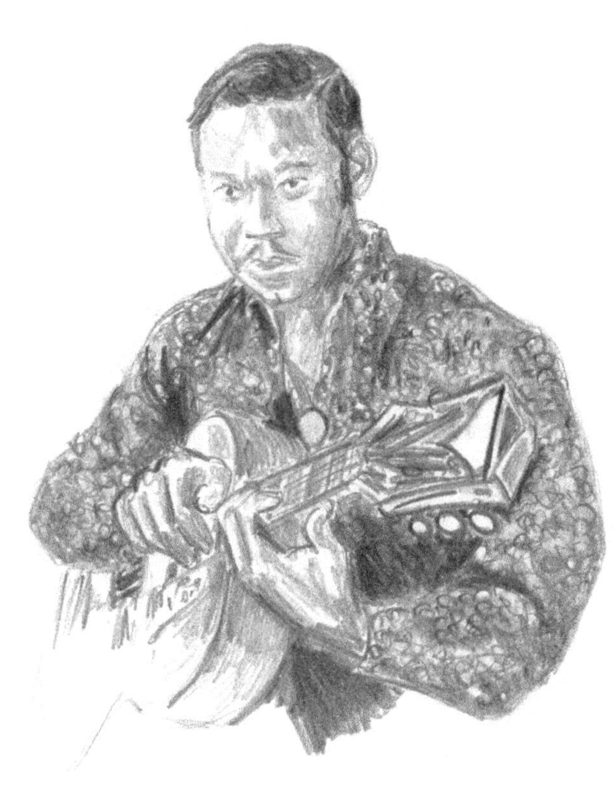

(MCKINLEY MORGANFIELD)
MUDDY
WATERS
American blues guitarist and singer

1915 - 1983

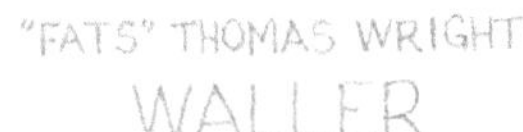

"FATS" THOMAS WRIGHT
WALLER
American jazz pianist, organist, composer, singer and entertainer

1904 - 1943

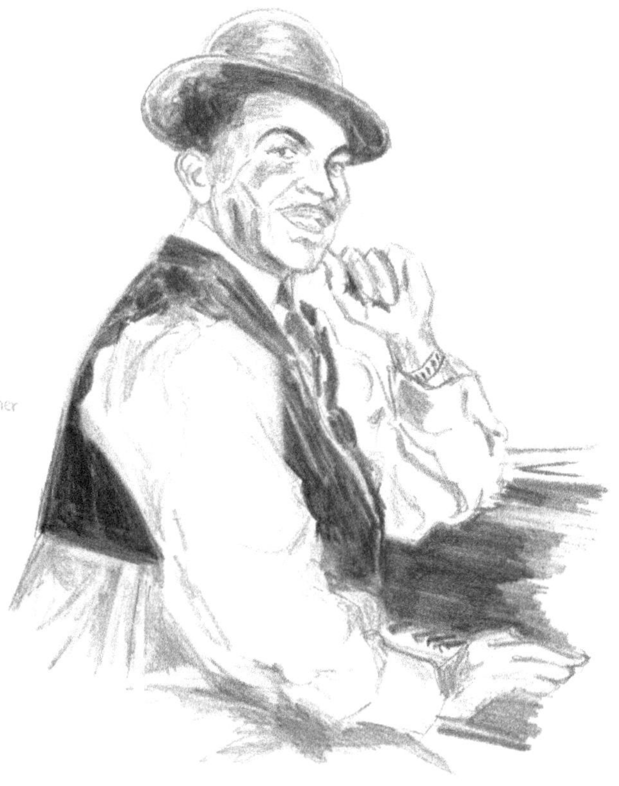

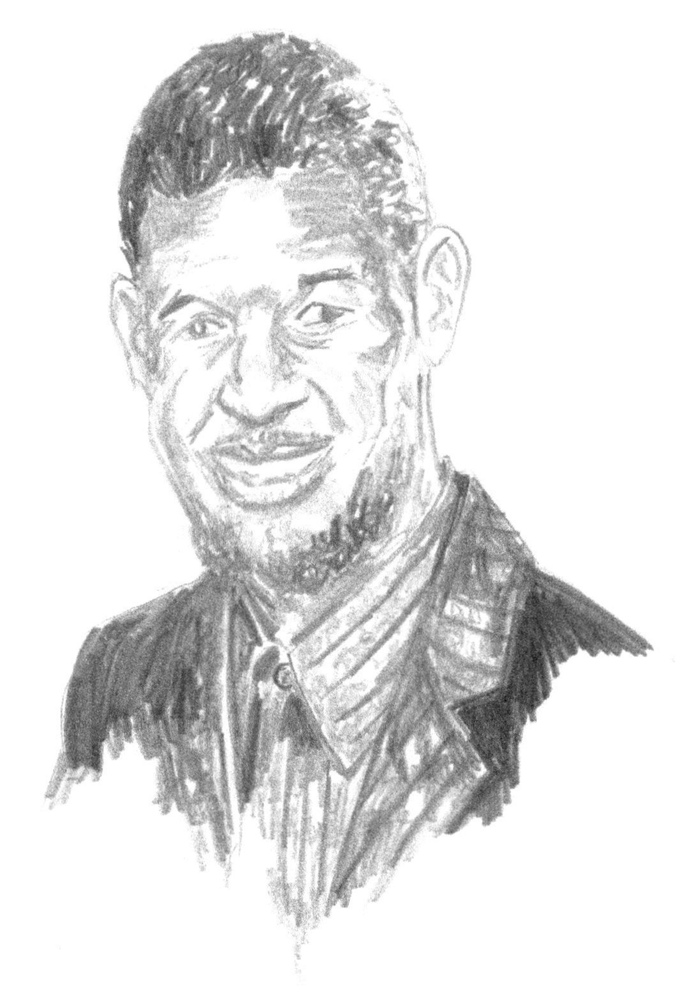

(USHER RAYMOND IV)

USHER

American singer, songwriter and dancer

1978-

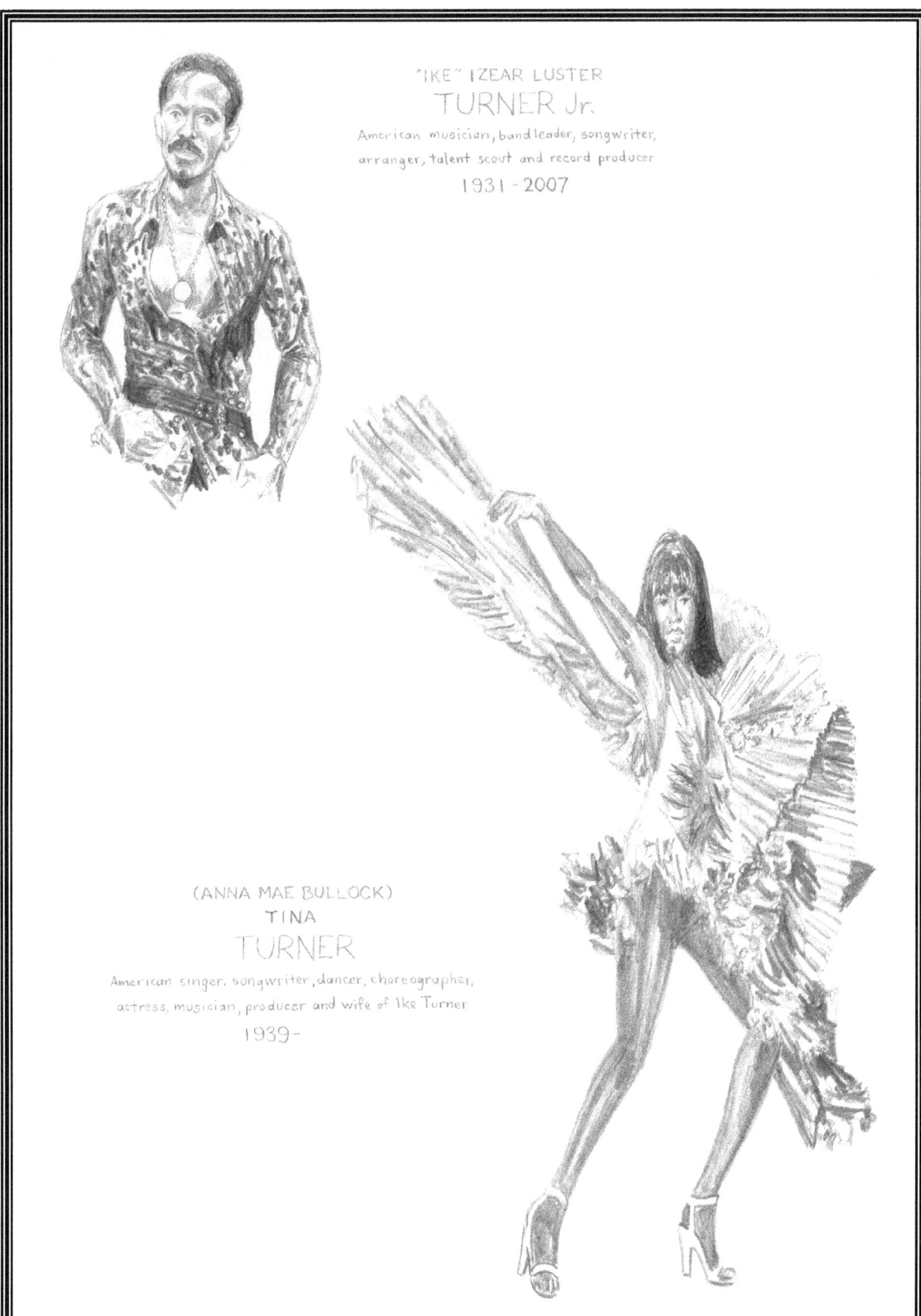

"IKE" IZEAR LUSTER
TURNER Jr.
American musician, band leader, songwriter,
arranger, talent scout and record producer
1931 - 2007
(ANNA MAE BULLOCK)
TINA
TURNER
American singer, songwriter, dancer, choreographer,
actress, musician, producer and wife of Ike Turner
1939 -

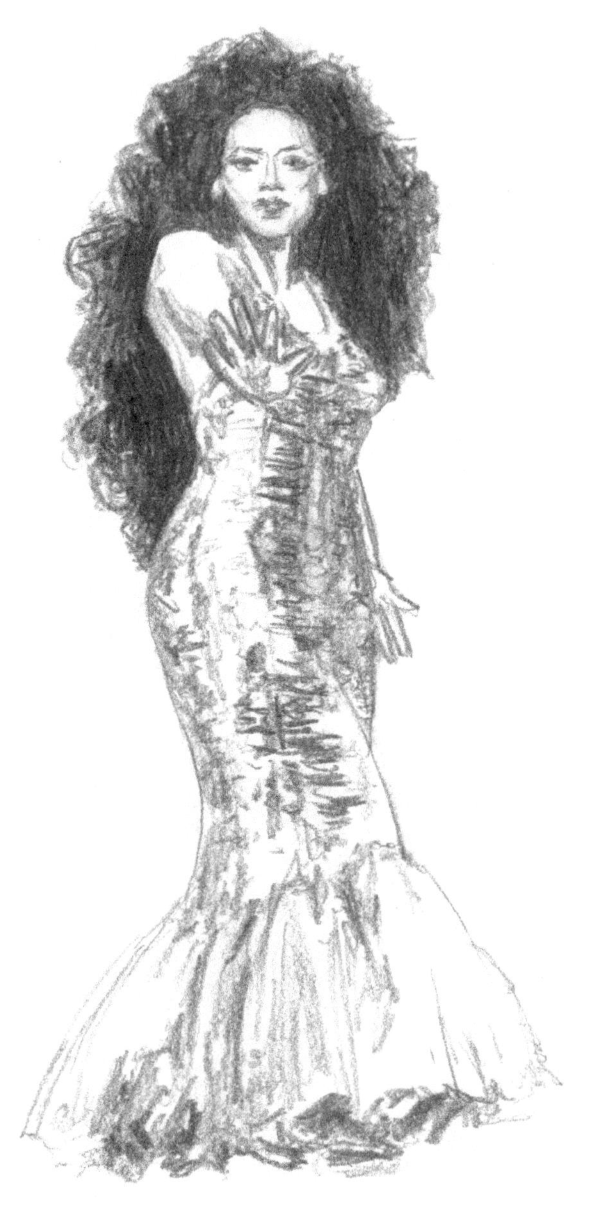

DIANA ERNESTINE EARLE
ROSS

American singer, actress and record producer

1944 –

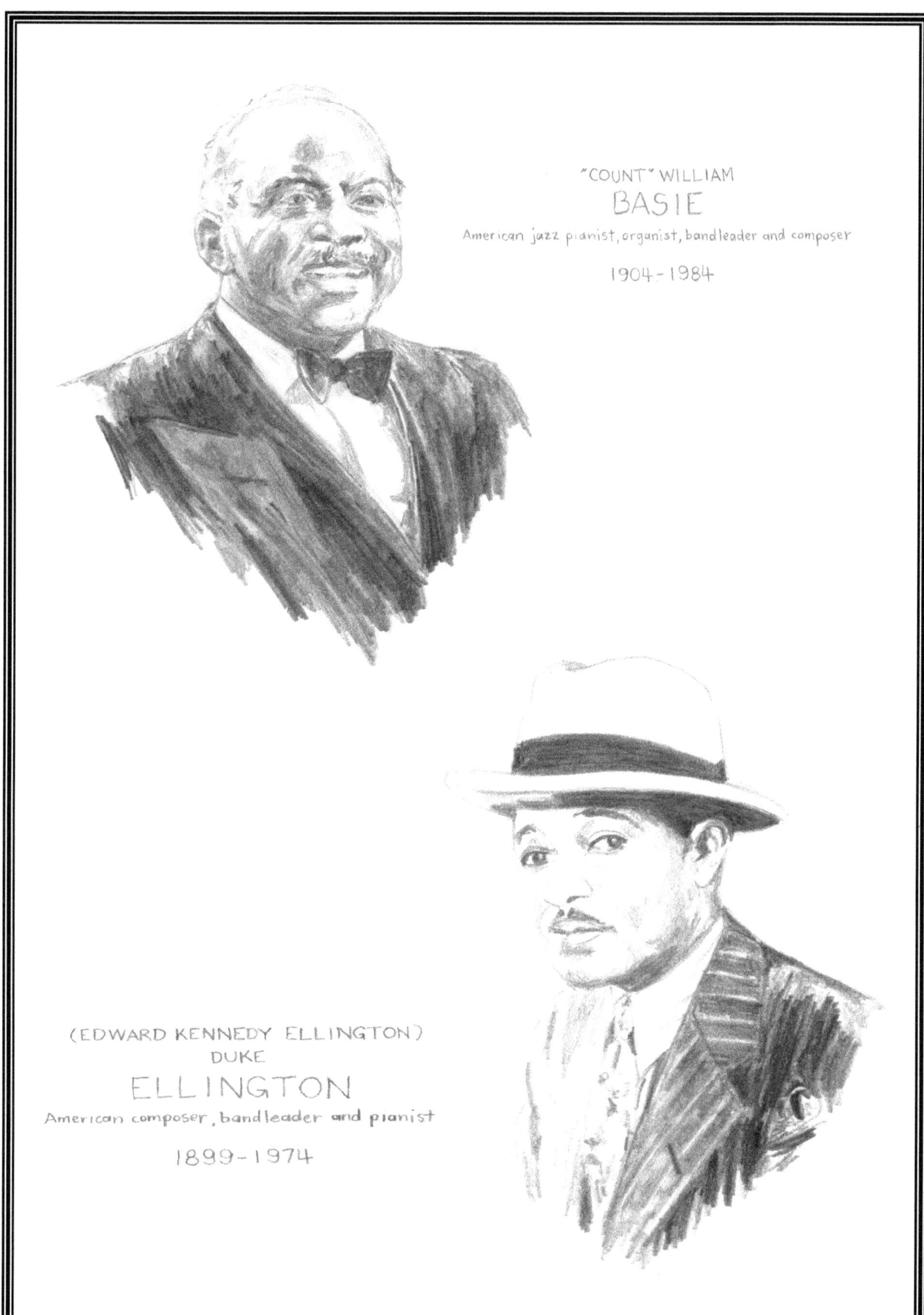

"COUNT" WILLIAM
BASIE
American jazz pianist, organist, bandleader and composer

1904-1984

(EDWARD KENNEDY ELLINGTON)
DUKE
ELLINGTON
American composer, bandleader and pianist

1899-1974

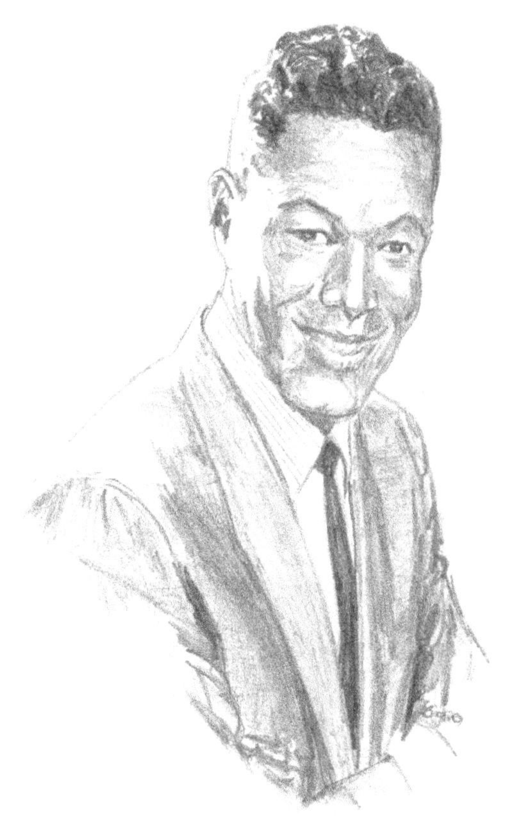

(NATHANIEL ADAMS COLES)
NAT KING
COLE
American jazz pianist, vocalist and television personality

1919-1965

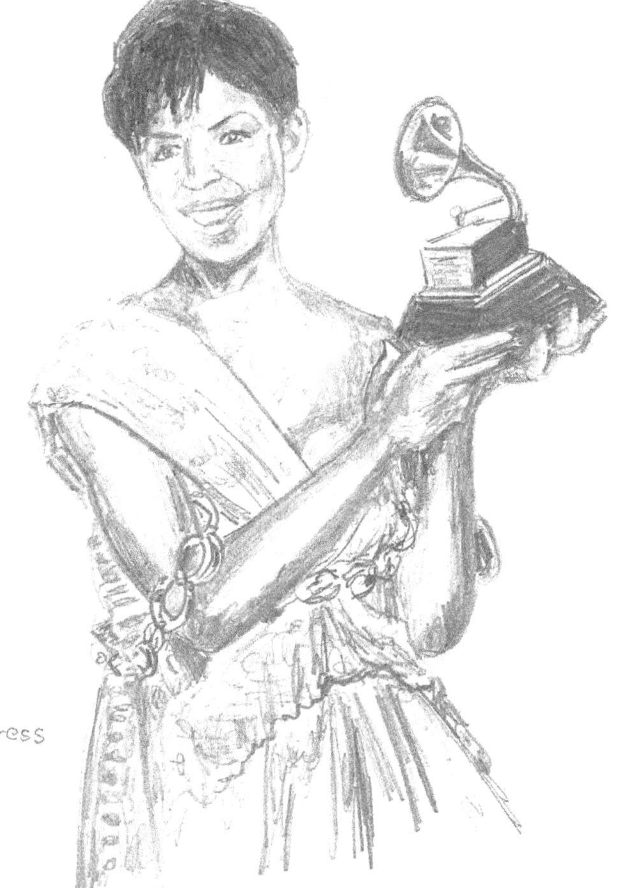

NATALIE MARIA
COLE
American singer, songwriter and actress
daughter of Nat King Cole
1950-2015

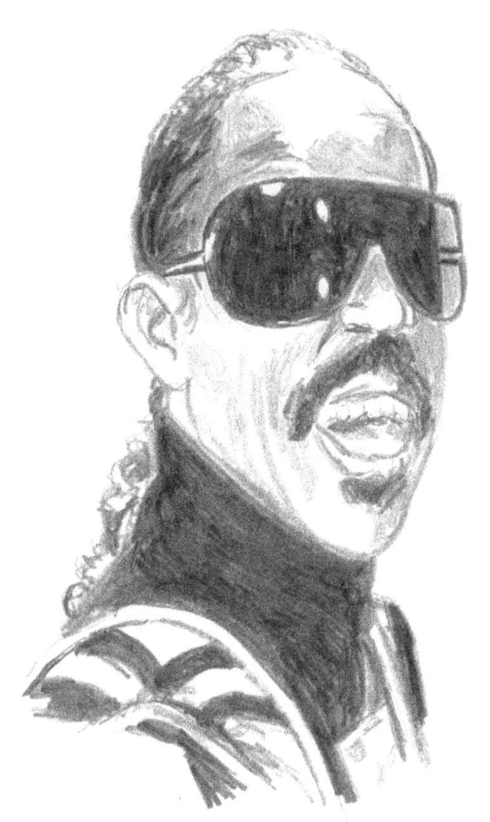

(STEVLAND HARDAWAY MORRIS)
STEVIE
WONDER

American singer, songwriter, musician,
record producer and multi instrumentalist

1950 –

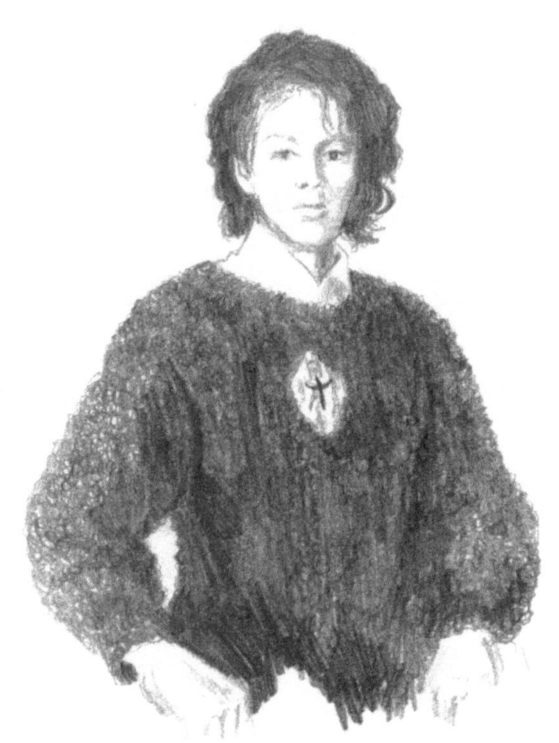

MICHAEL JOSEPH
JACKSON
American recording artist, entertainer and philanthropist

1958-2009

JANET DAMITA JO
JACKSON
American singer, songwriter, dancer, motion picture
actress and younger sister of Michael Jackson

1966-

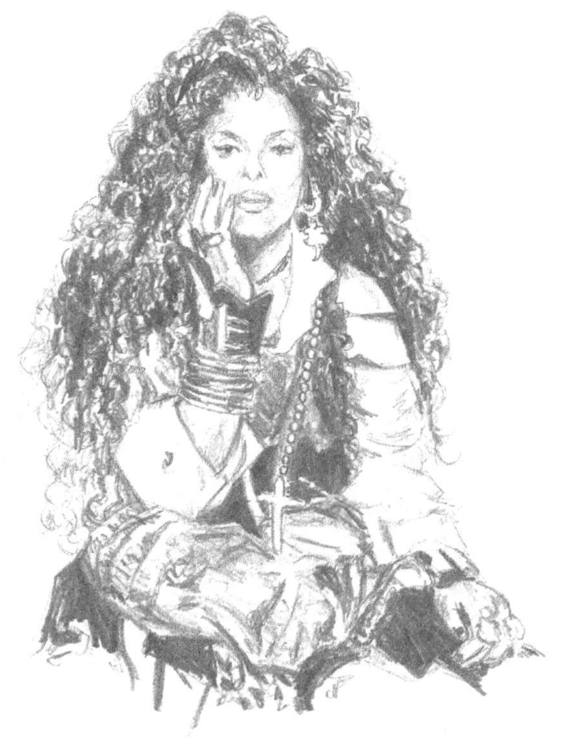

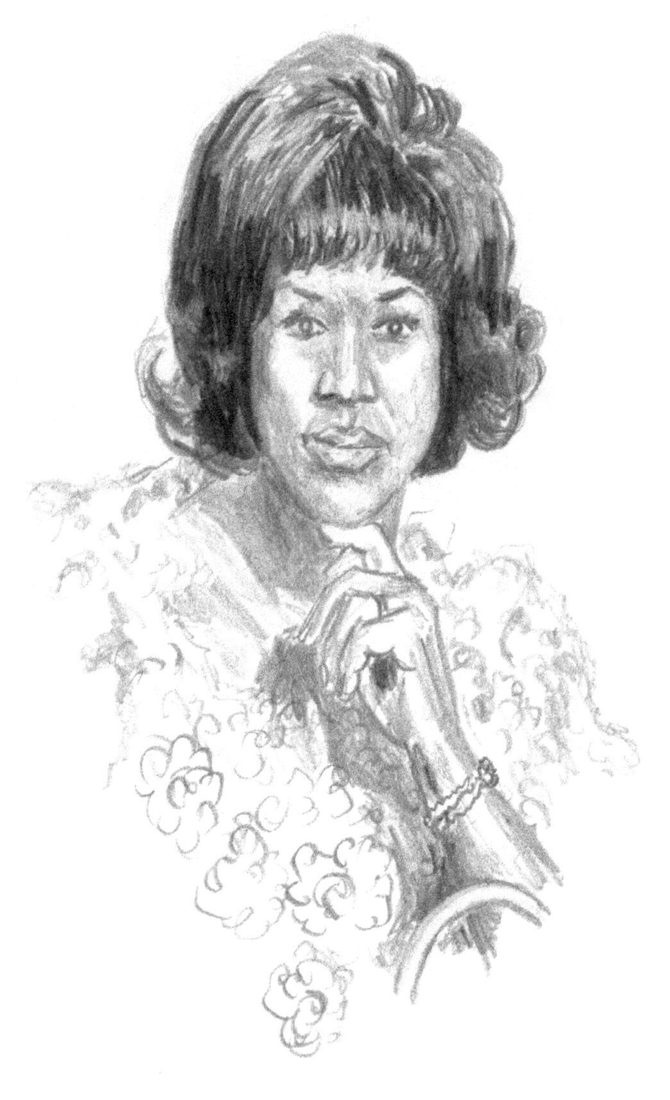

ARETHA LOUISE
FRANKLIN
American singer-Songwriter

1942-2018

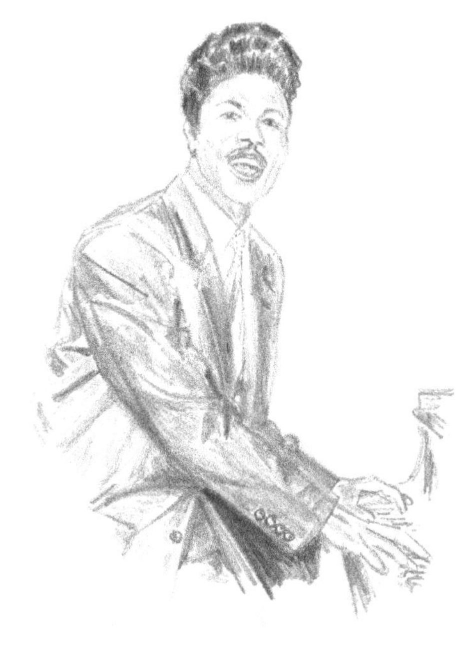

(RICHARD WAYNE PENNIMAN)
LITTLE RICHARD
American singer, songwriter and musician

1932-2020

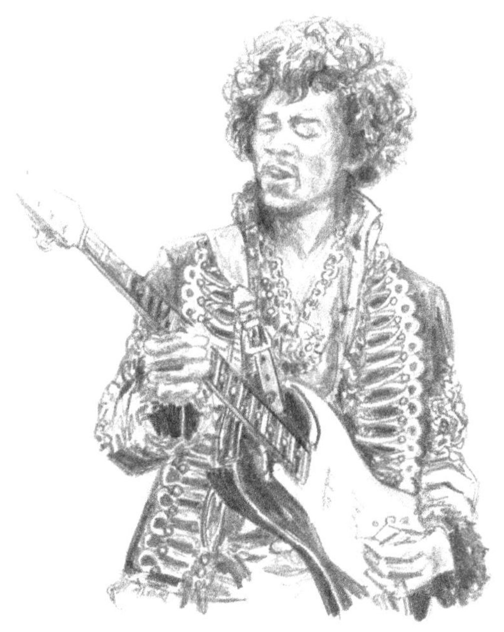

(JOHNNY ALLEN HENDRIX)
"JIMI" JAMES MARSHALL
HENDRIX
American guitarist and singer-songwriter

1942-1970

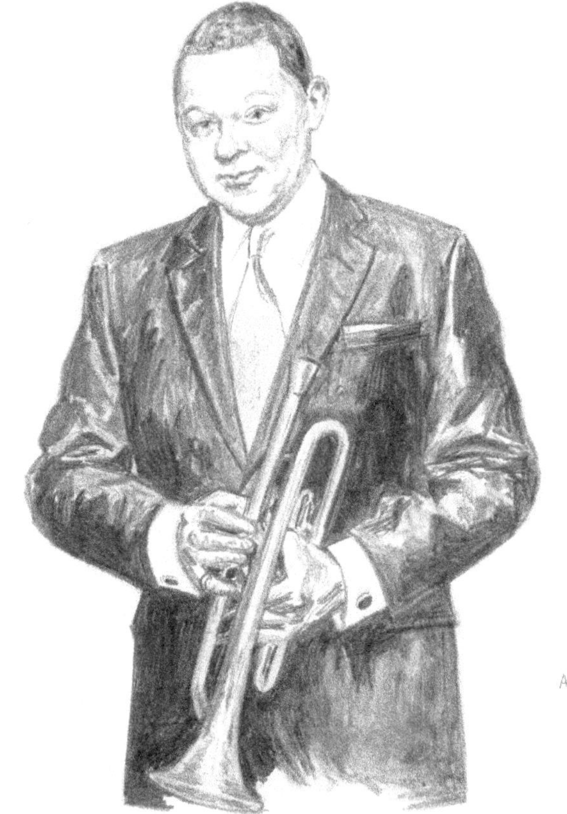

WYNTON LEARSON
MARSALIS
American trumpeter, composer, teacher and artistic director

1961-

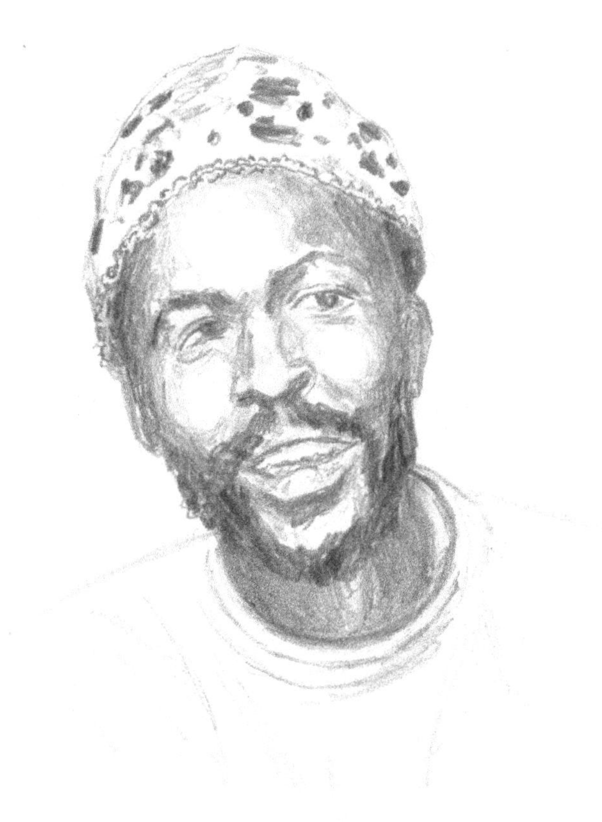

(MARVIN PENTZ GAY Jr.)
MARVIN
GAYE
American singer-songwriter and musician

1939 - 1984

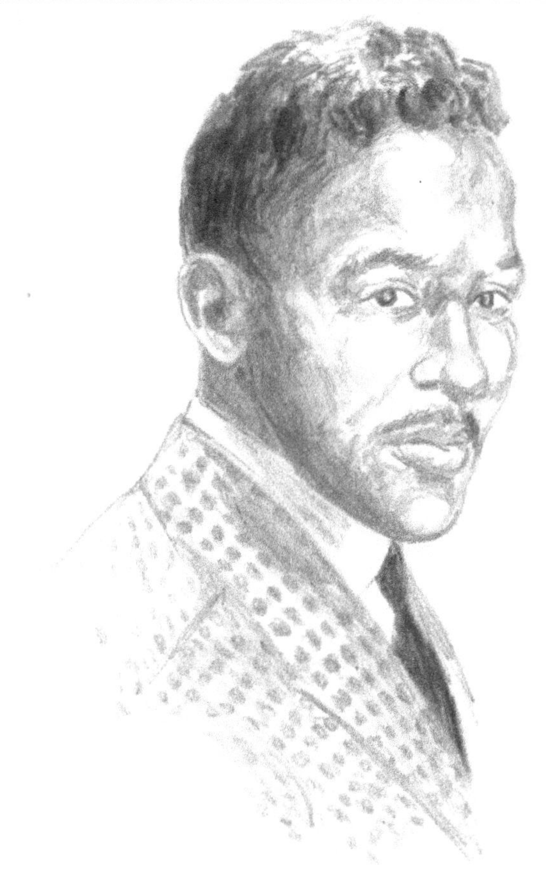

"BB" RILEY B.
KING
American electric guitarist, blues singer,
songwriter and record producer
1925-2015

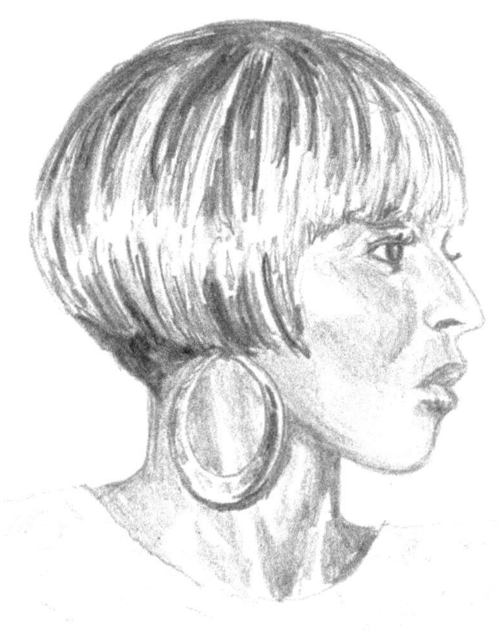

MARY JANE
BLIGE
American singer, songwriter, record producer and actress

1971-

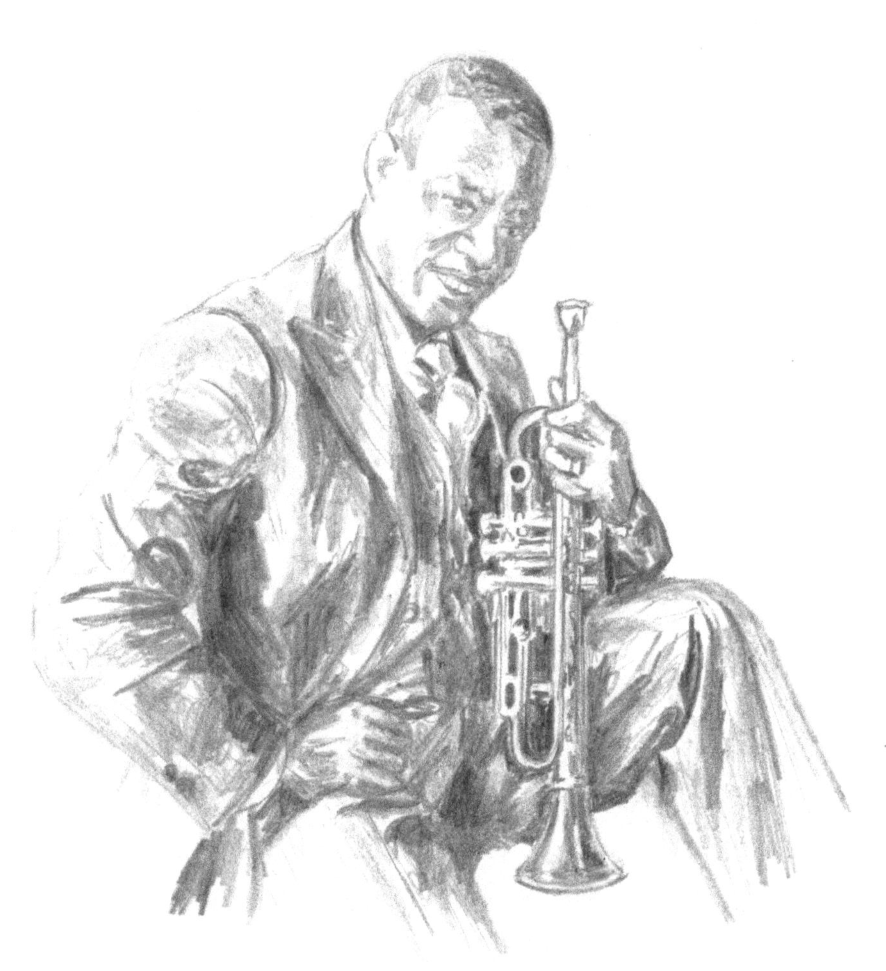

"SATCHMO" LOUIS DANIEL
ARMSTRONG
American jazz trumpeter, bandleader and singer

1901 – 1971

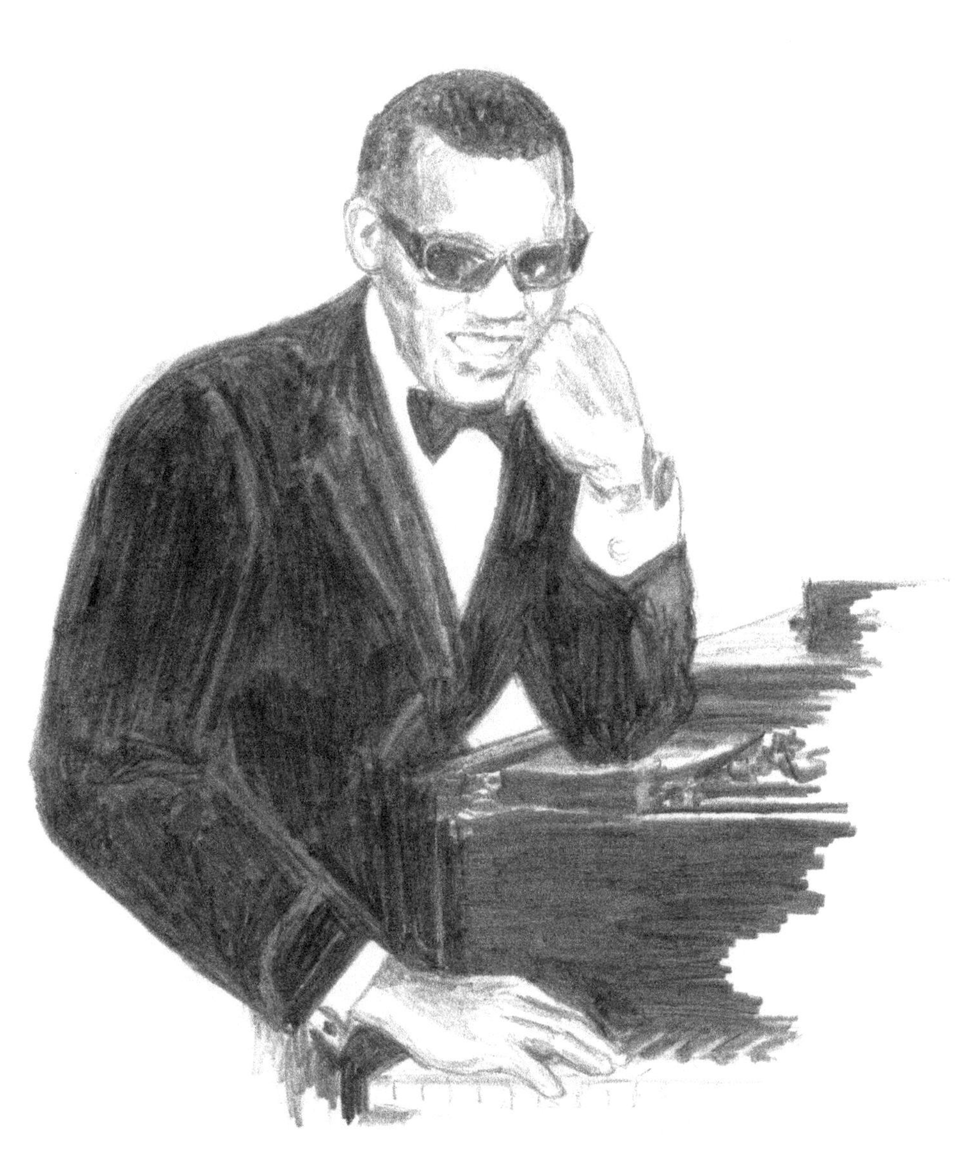

(RAY CHARLES ROBINSON)
RAY
CHARLES
American singer and musician

1930-2004

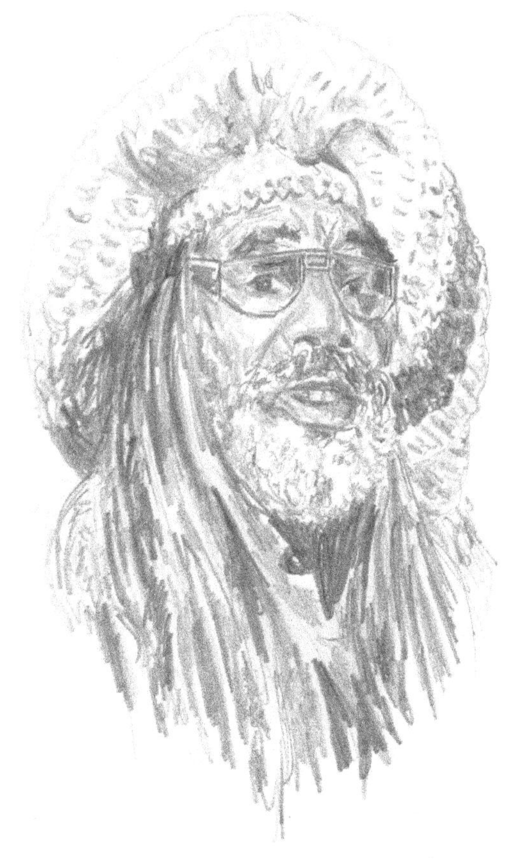

CLINTON

American singer, songwriter, bandleader and music producer

1941 -

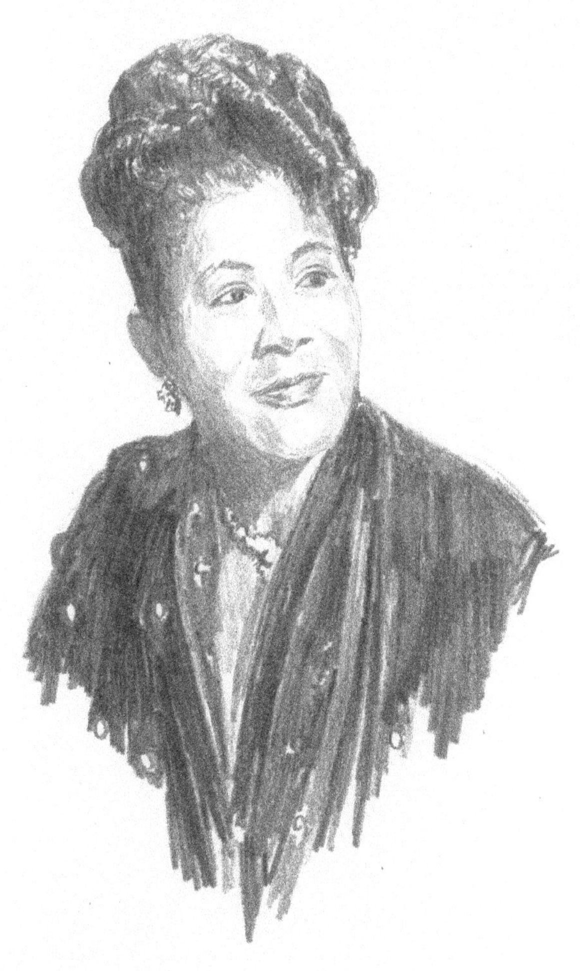

MAHALIA

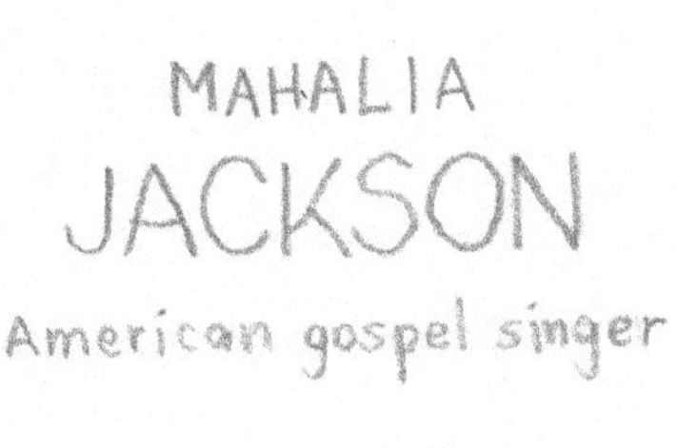

JACKSON

American gospel singer

1911 - 1972

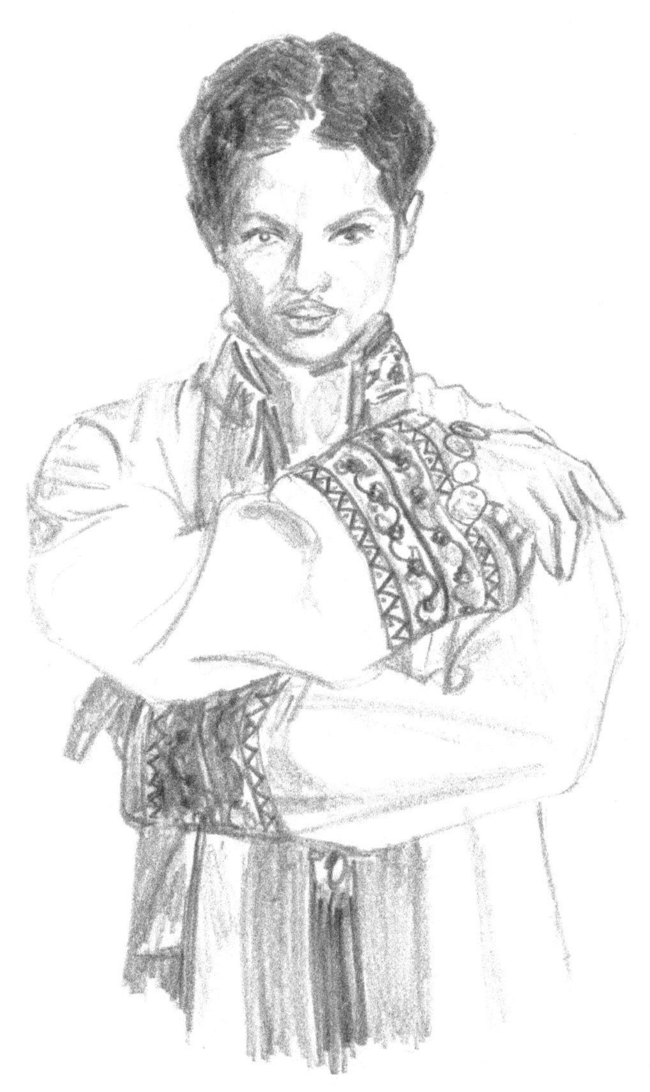

(PRINCE ROGERS NELSON)
PRINCE

American singer, songwriter, musician, record producer and filmmaker

1958 - 2016

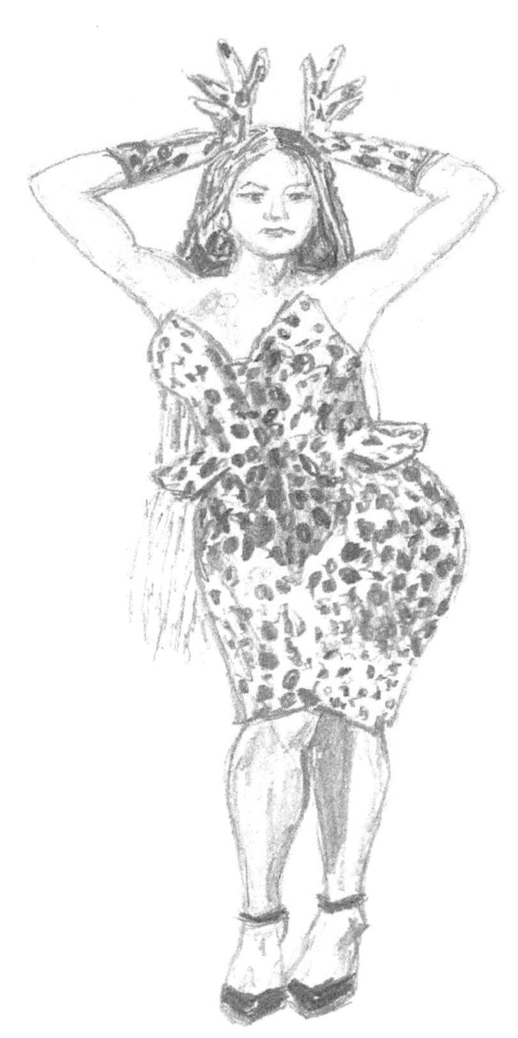

(BEYONCE GISELLE KNOWLES-CARTER)
BEYONCE
American singer, songwriter, actress, producer, director
businesswoman, philanthropist and wife of Jay-Z

1981 -

Actors, Actresses, Film Directors

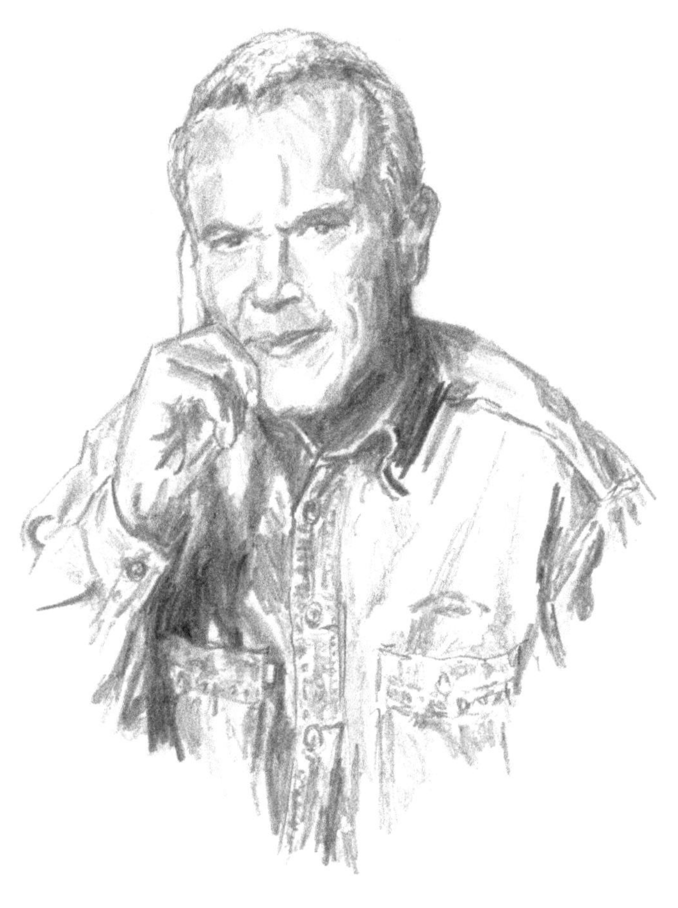

"HARRY" HAROLD GEORGE
BELAFONTE
American singer, actor and social activist

1927- 2023

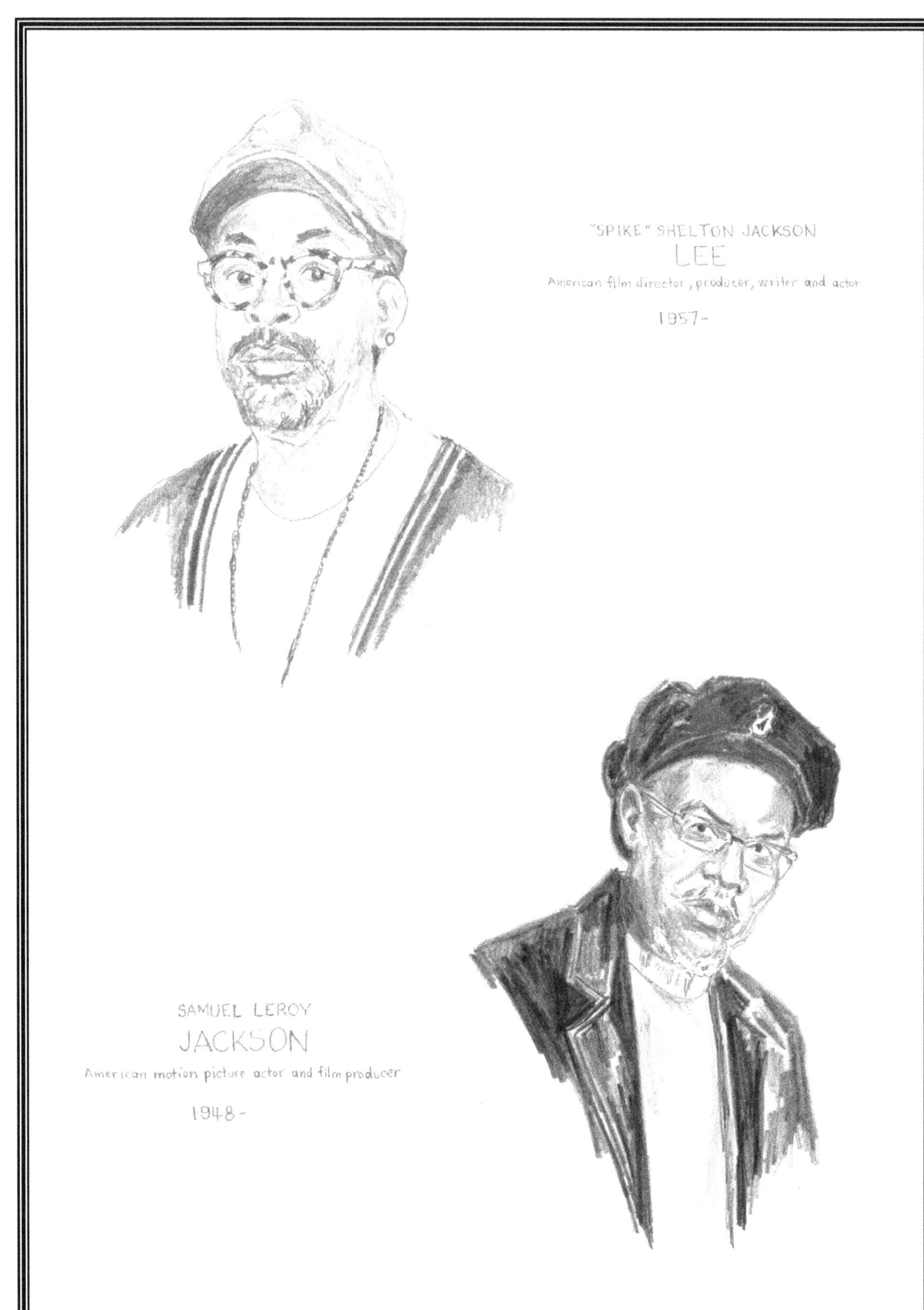

"SPIKE" SHELTON JACKSON
LEE
American film director, producer, writer and actor

1957-

SAMUEL LEROY
JACKSON
American motion picture actor and film producer

1948-

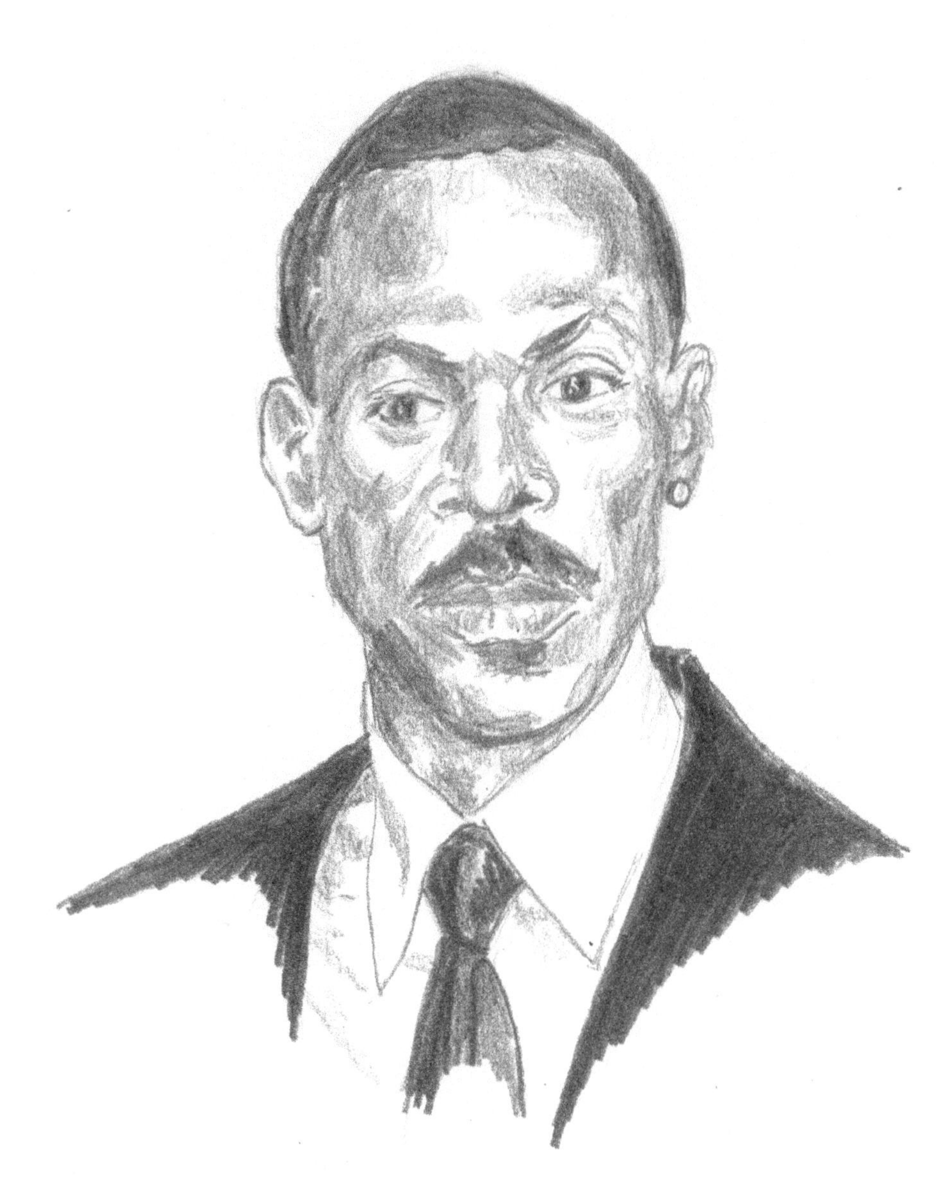

"EDDIE" EDWARD REGAN
MURPHY

American stand-up comedian, motion picture
actor, writer, singer, director and musician

1961 –

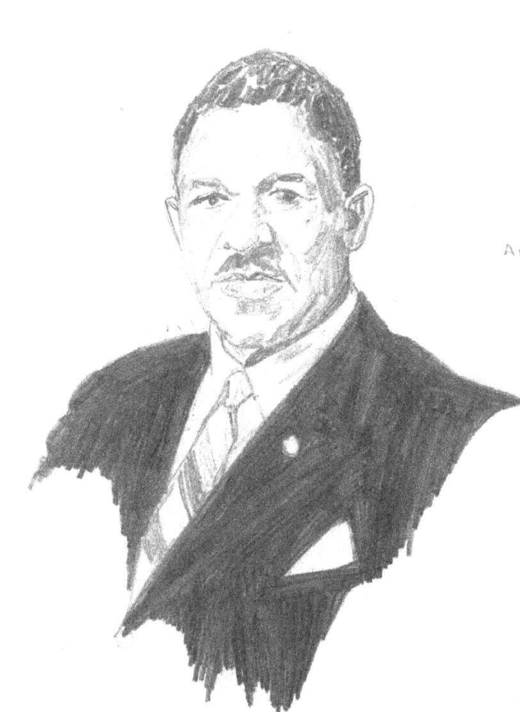

FREDERICK DOUGLAS
O'NEAL
American actor, theater producer and television director

1905-1992

HATTIE
McDANIEL
American stage and motion picture actress
singer-songwriter and comedian

1895-1952

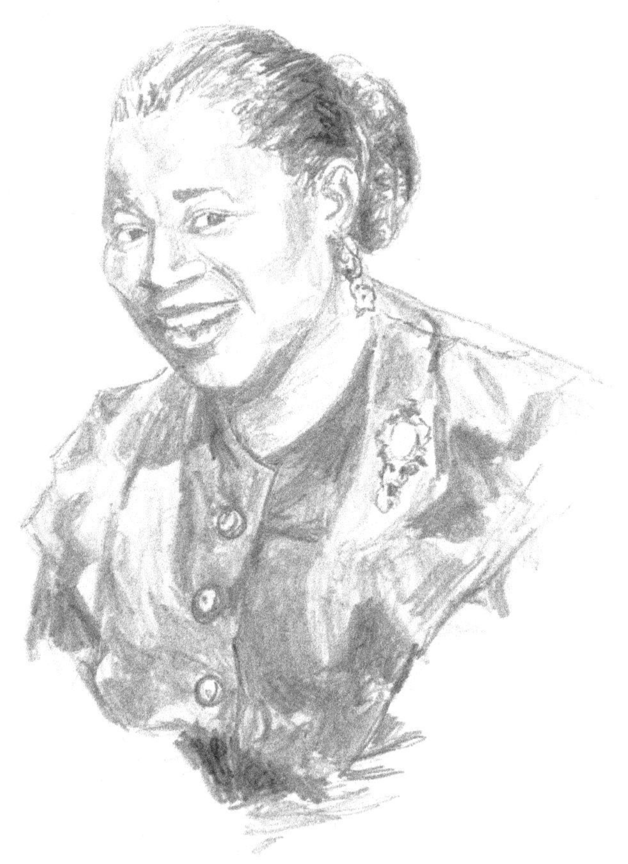

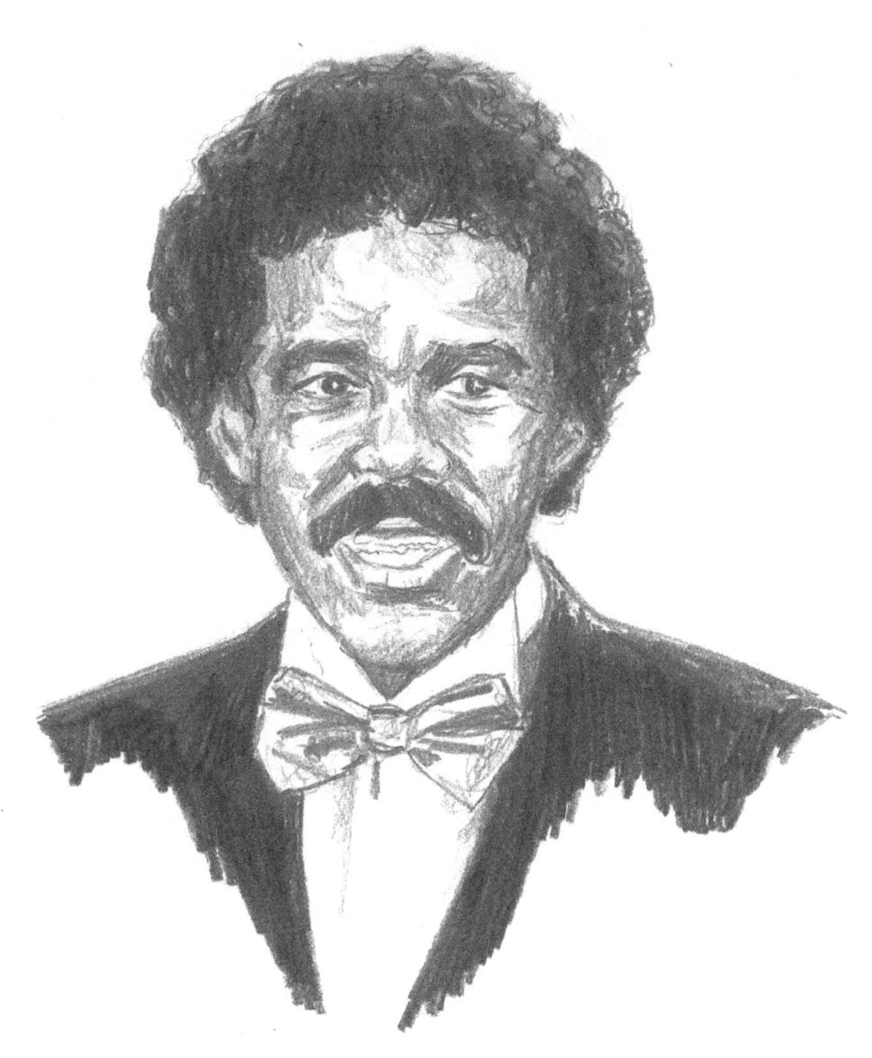

RICHARD FRANKLIN LENNOX THOMAS
PRYOR
American stand-up comedian, actor and social critic

1940-2005

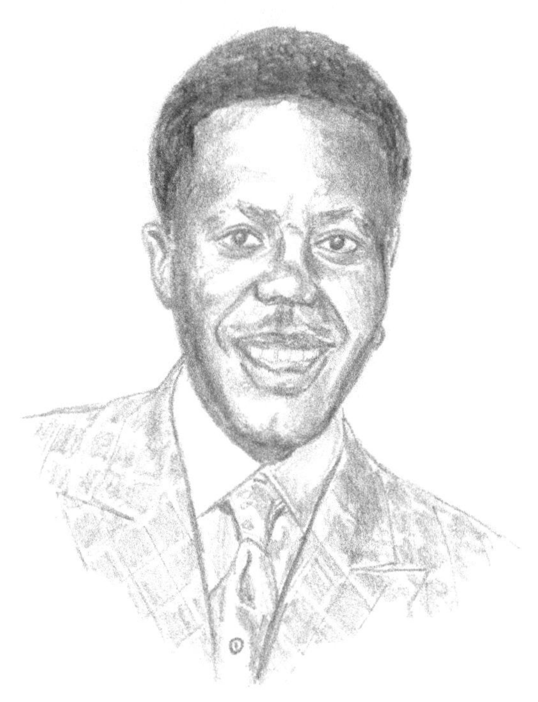

(BERNARD JEFFREY McCULLOUGH)
BERNIE
MAC

American stand-up comedian and actor

1957-2008

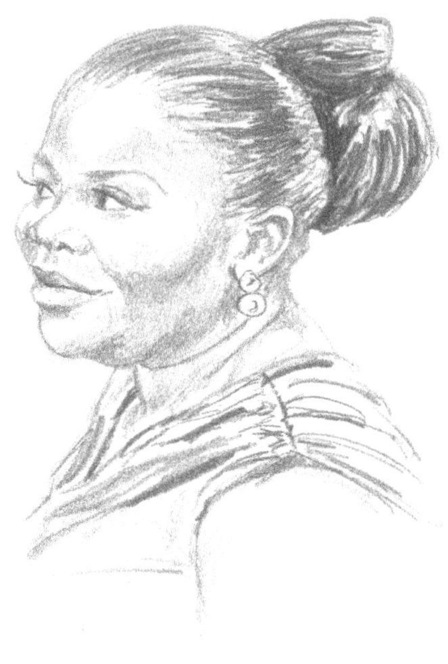

(MONIQUE ANGELA HICKS)
MO´NIQUE

American comedian and motion picture actress

1967-

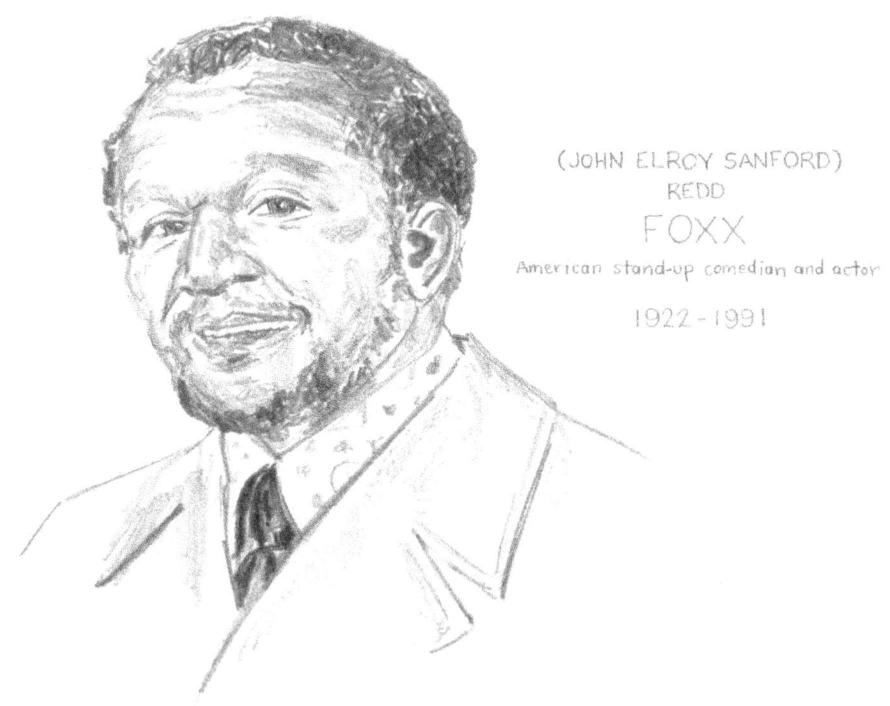

(JOHN ELROY SANFORD)
REDD
FOXX

American stand-up comedian and actor

1922-1991

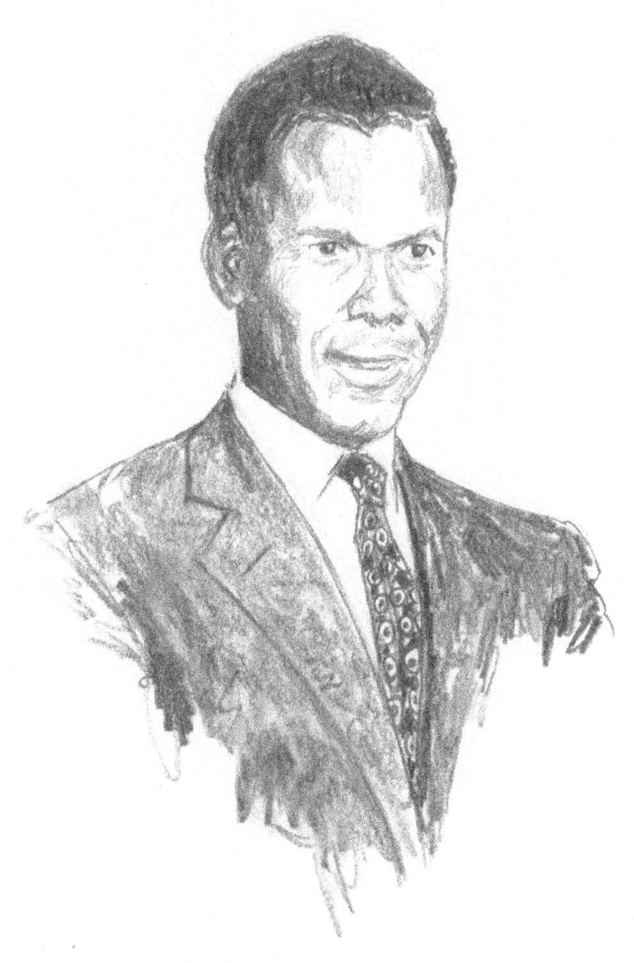

Bahamian-American motion picture actor, film director, author and diplomat, Ambassador to Japan for the Bahamas 1997-2007

1927-2022

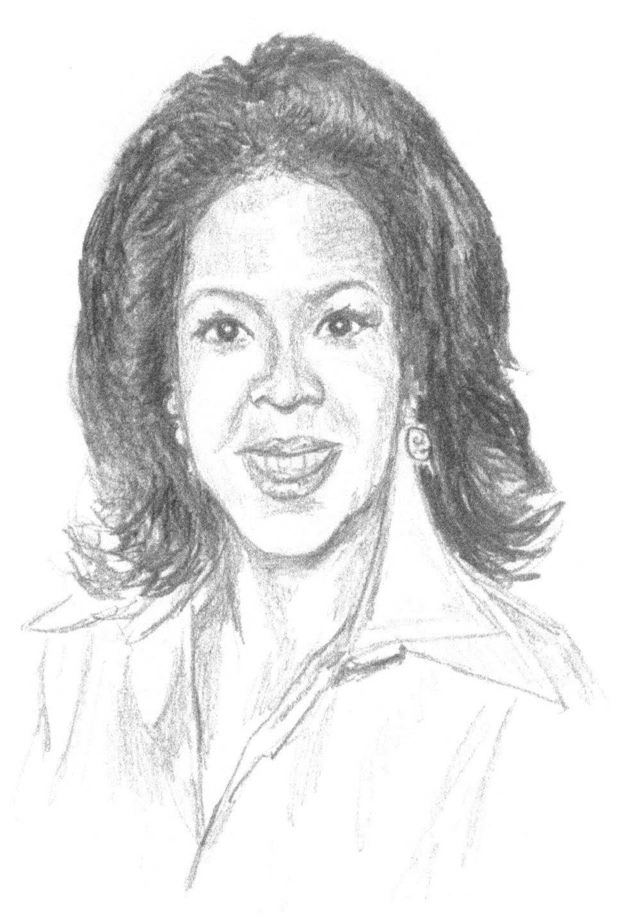

OPRAH GAIL
WINFREY
American media executive, motion picture actress,
talk show host, television producer and philanthropist

1954–

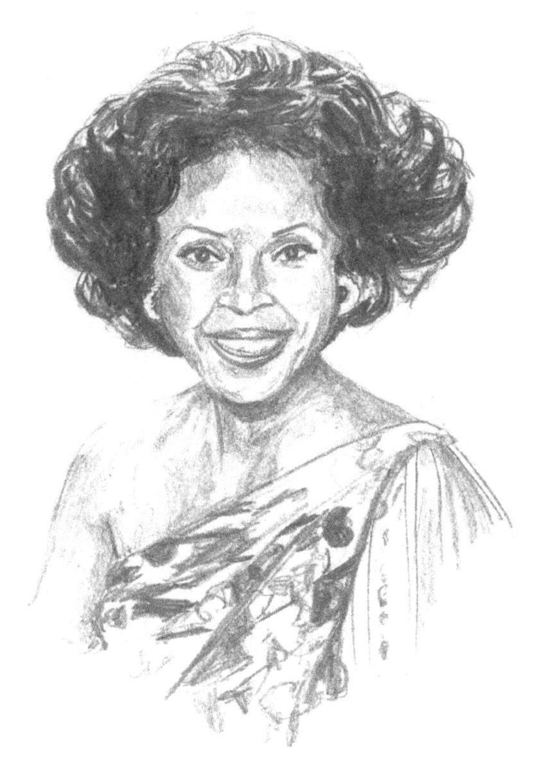

(CAROL DIAHANN JOHNSON)
DIAHANN
CARROLL
American motien picture actress and singer

1935-2019

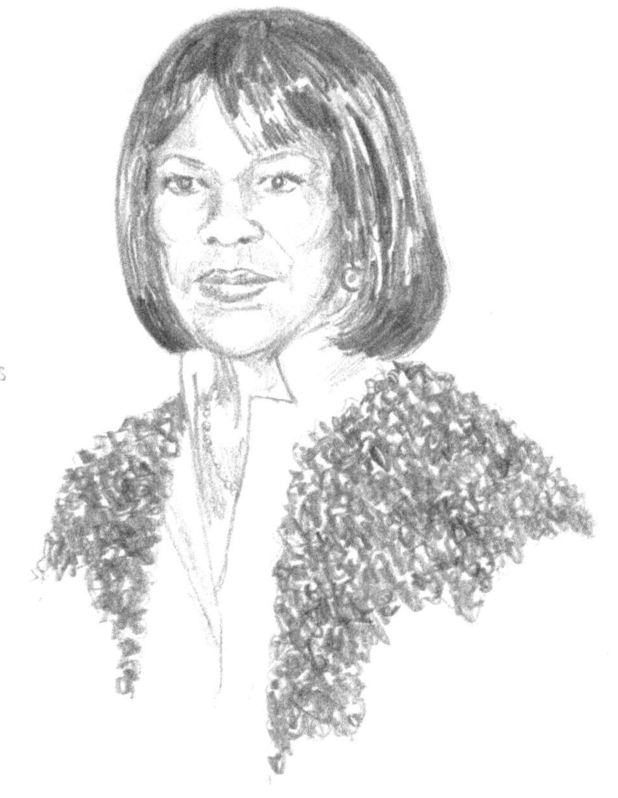

CICELY
TYSON
American actress, fashion model and wife of Miles Davis

1924-2021

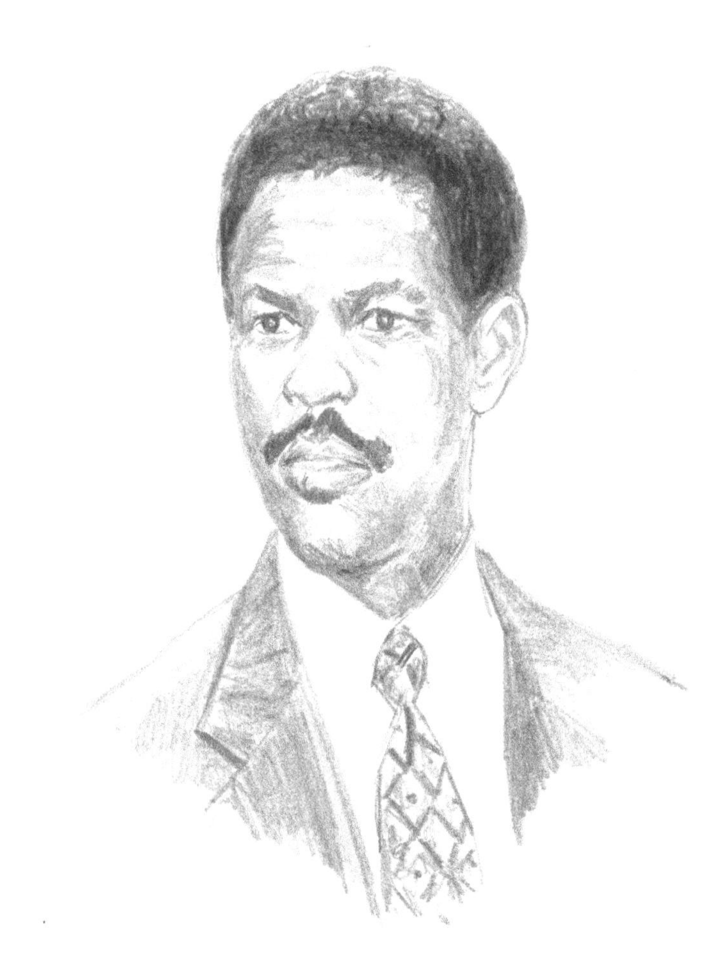

DENZEL HAYES
WASHINGTON Jr.

American motion picture actor, director and producer

1954 –

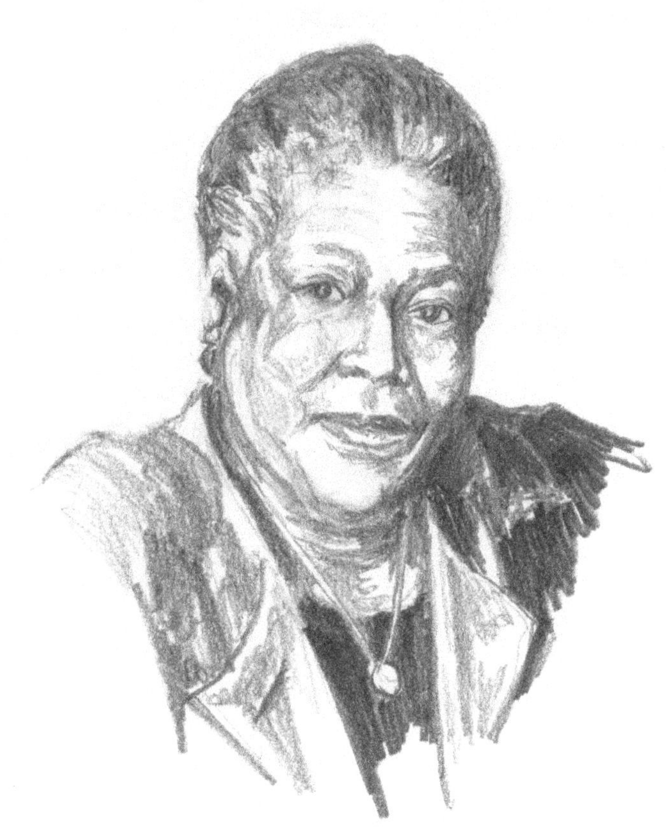

ESTHER
ROLLE
American actress

1920-1998

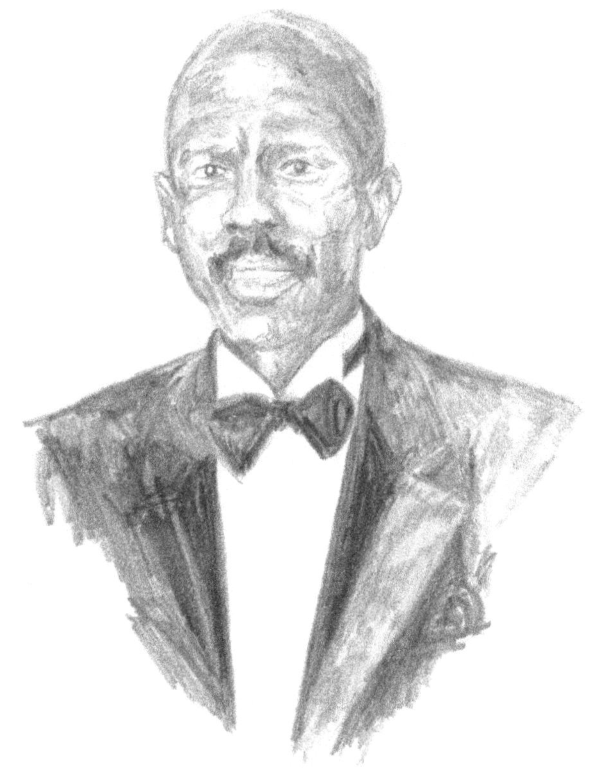

LOUIS CANERON
GOSSETT Jr.
American motion picture actor

1936-2024

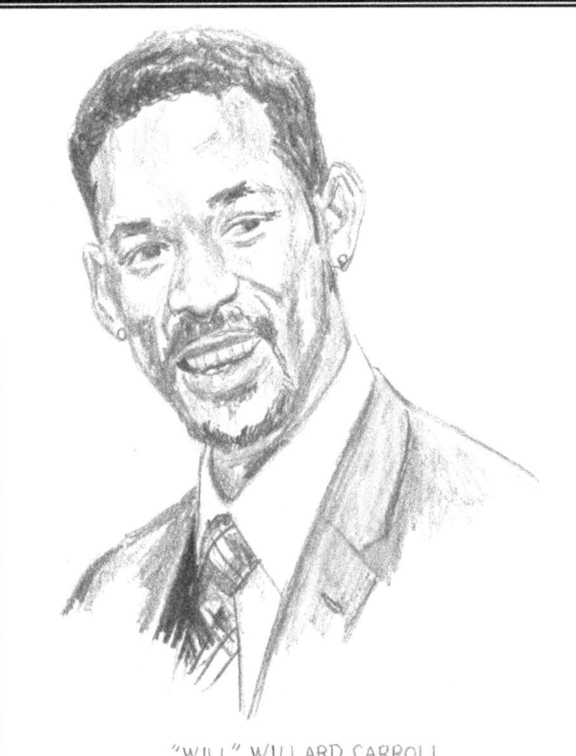

"WILL" WILLARD CARROLL
SMITH
American rapper, actor, songwriter, comedian and record producer

1968-

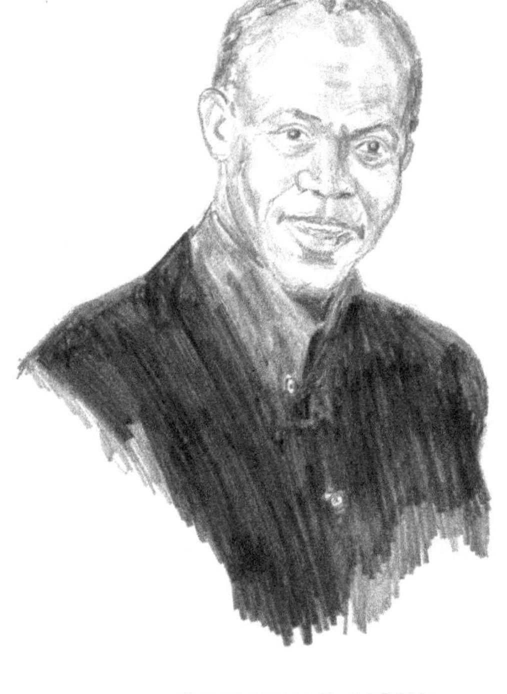

"DANNY" DANIEL LEBERN
GLOVER
American motion picture actor,
film director and political activist

1946 -

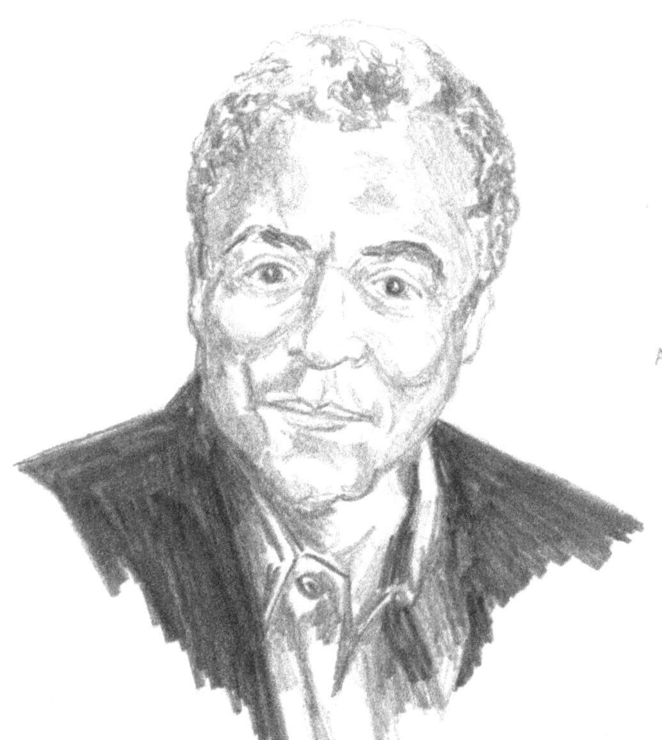

JAMES EARL
JONES
American motion picture actor

1931 - 2024

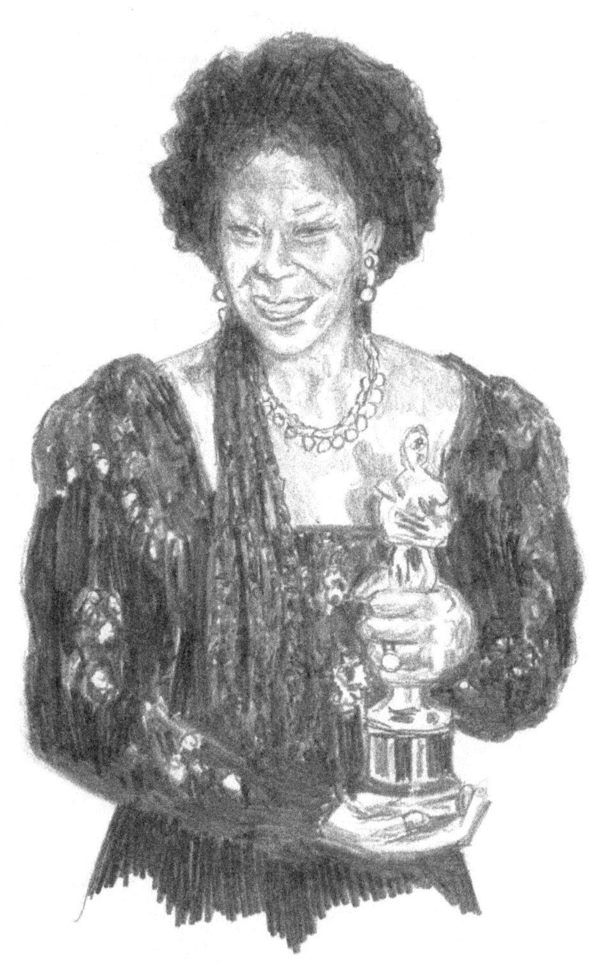

(CARYN ELAINE JOHNSON)
WHOOPI
GOLDBERG
American motion picture actress,
comedian, author and television host

1955-

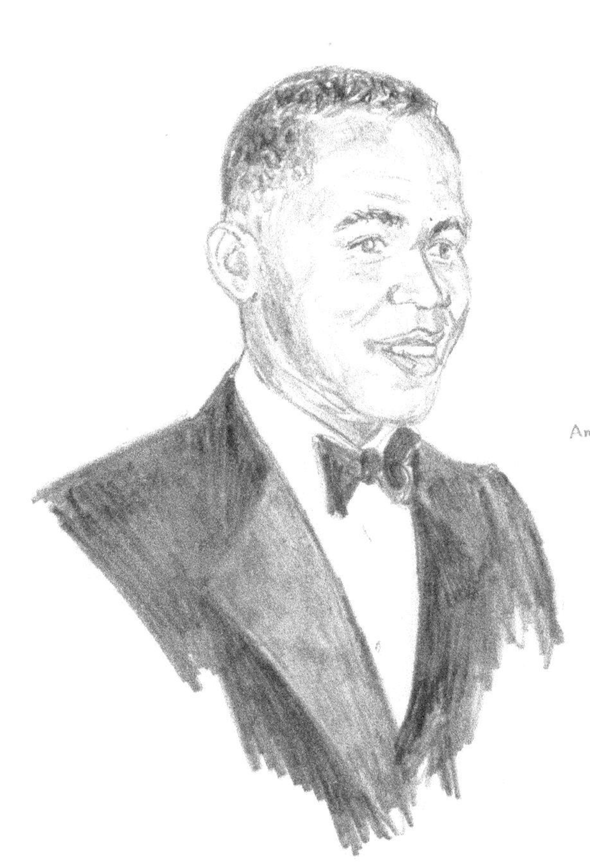

CUBA
GOODING Jr.
American motion picture actor, comedian and voice artist

1968-

(RAIFORD CHATMAN DAVIS)
OSSIE
DAVIS
American motion picture actor, director, poet
playwright, writer and social activist

1917-2005

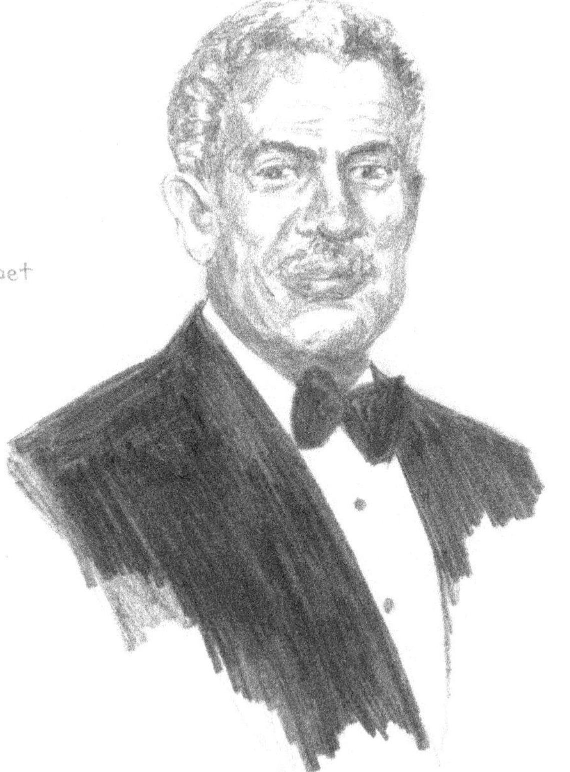

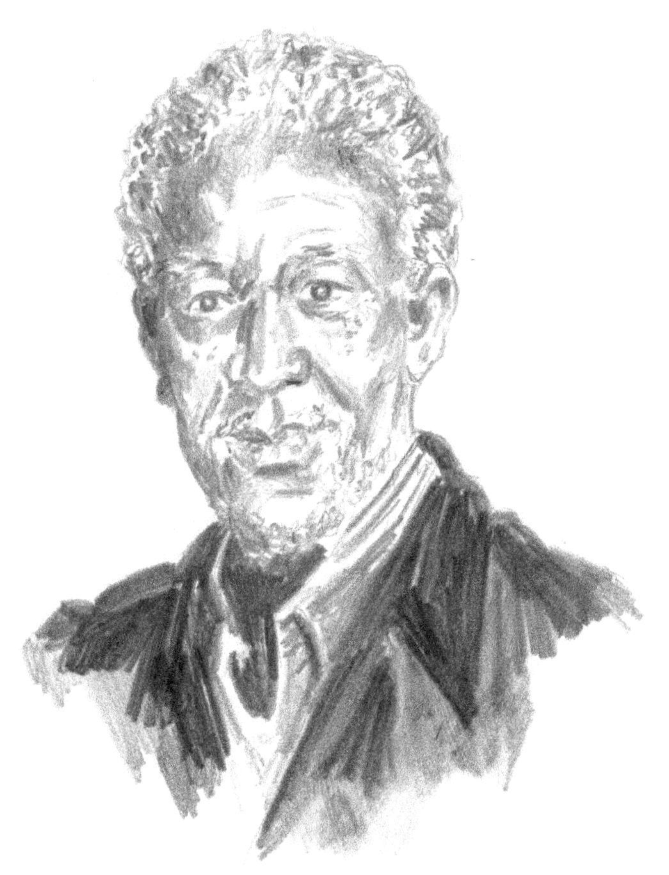

MORGAN
FREEMAN
American motion picture actor, producer and narrator

1937-

Athletes

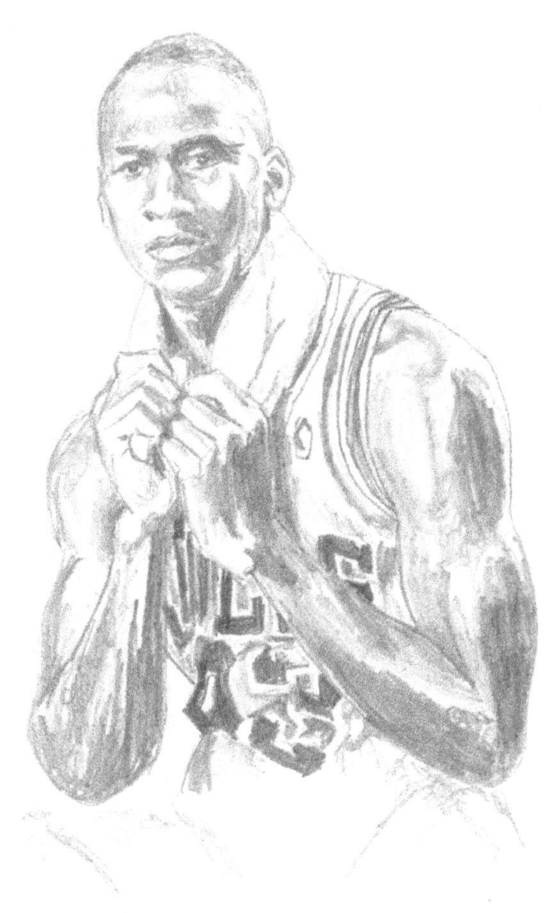

MICHAEL JEFFREY
JORDAN
American professional basketball player and businessman

1963-

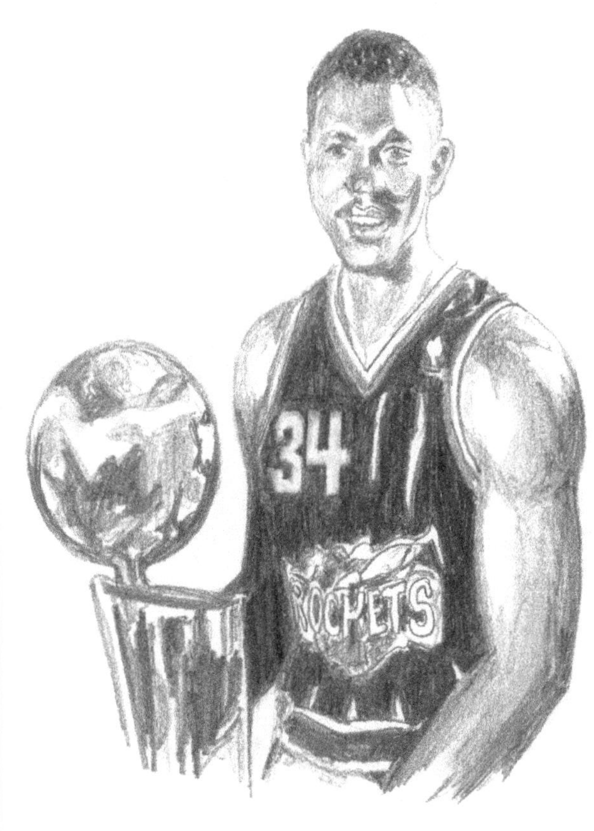

(AKEEM OLAJUWON)
HAKEEM ABDUL
OLAJUWON
Nigerian-American professional basketball player

1963-

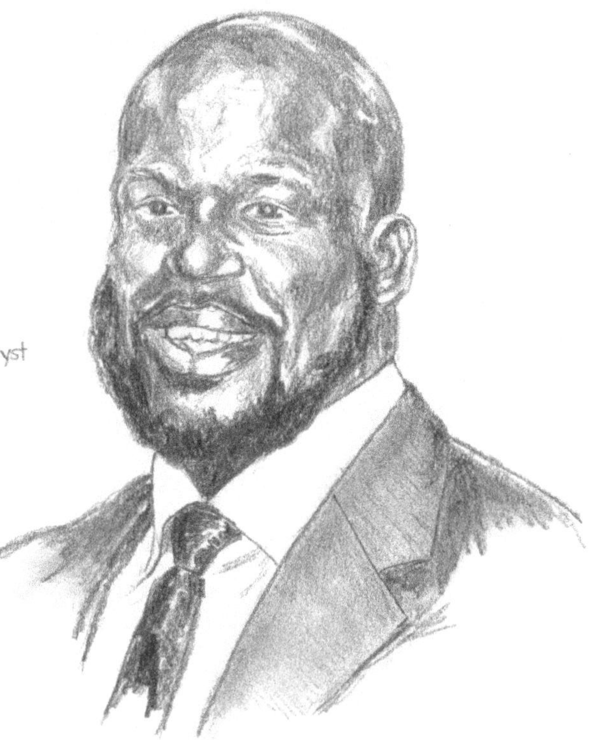

"SHAQ" SHAQUILLE RASHAUN
O'NEAL
American professional basketball player and sports analyst

1972-

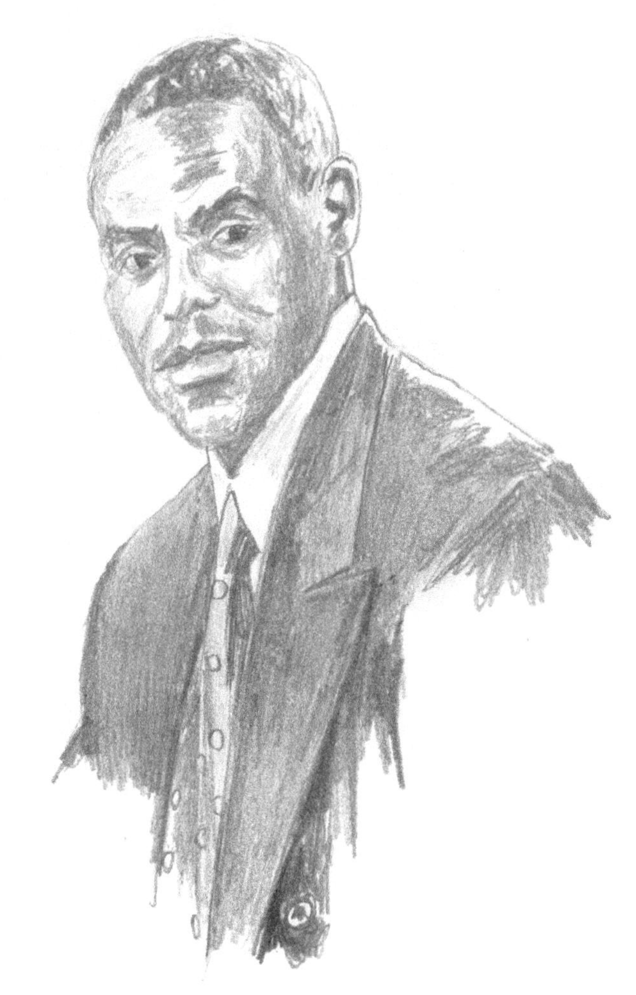

"CARL" FREDERICK CARLTON
LEWIS
American track and field athlete

1961 -

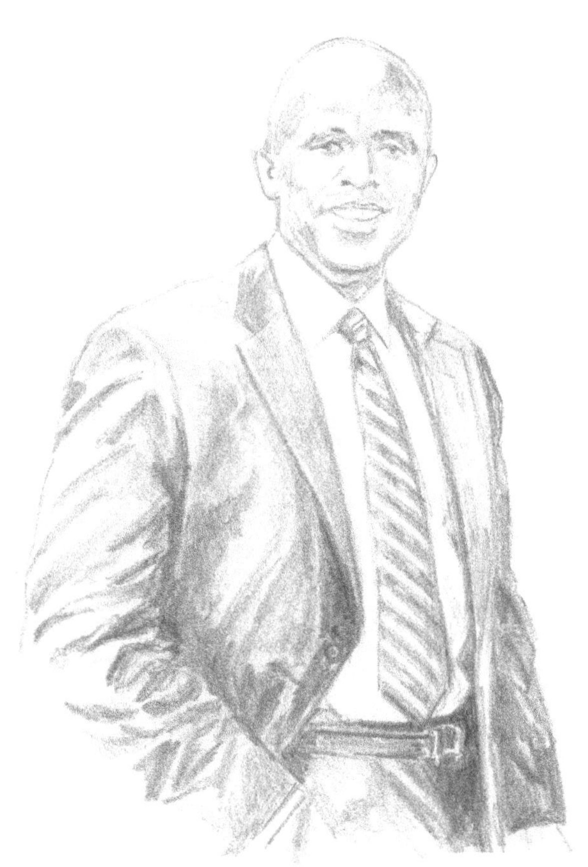

BARRY LAMAR
BONDS
American baseball player

1964 –

"HANK" HENRY LOUIS
AARON
American baseball player

1934 – 2021

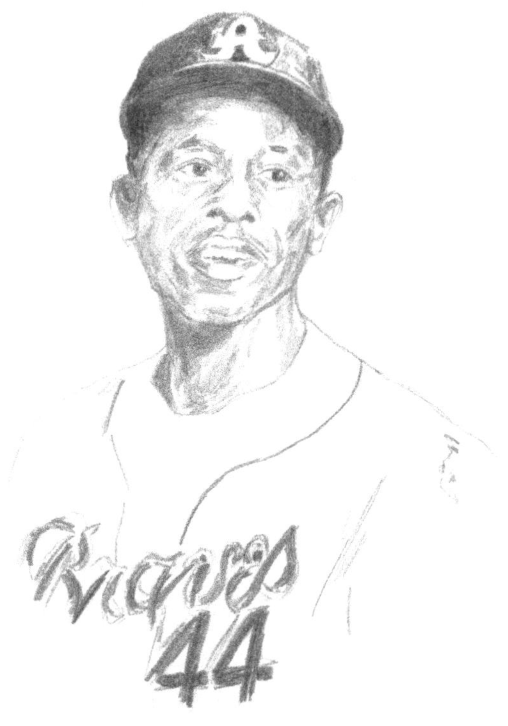

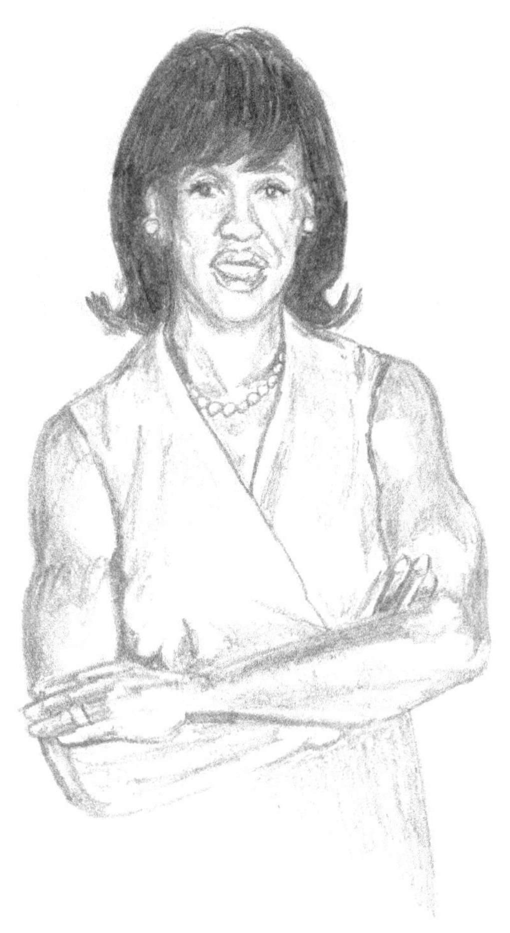

"JACKIE" JACQUELINE
JOYNER-KERSEE
American track and field athlete

1962–

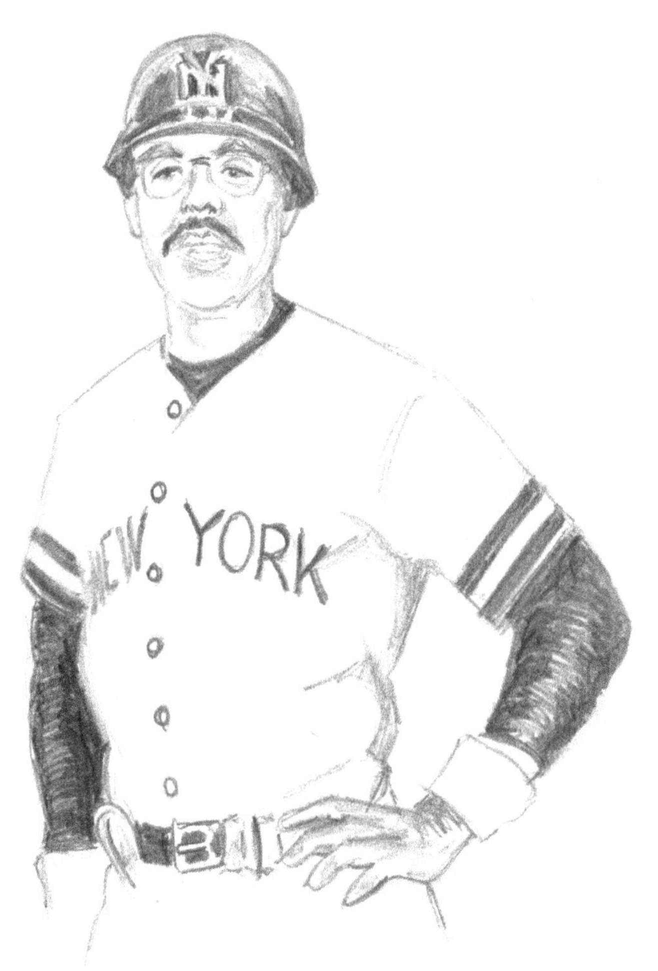

"REGGIE" REGINALD MARTINEZ

JACKSON

American major league baseball player

1946-

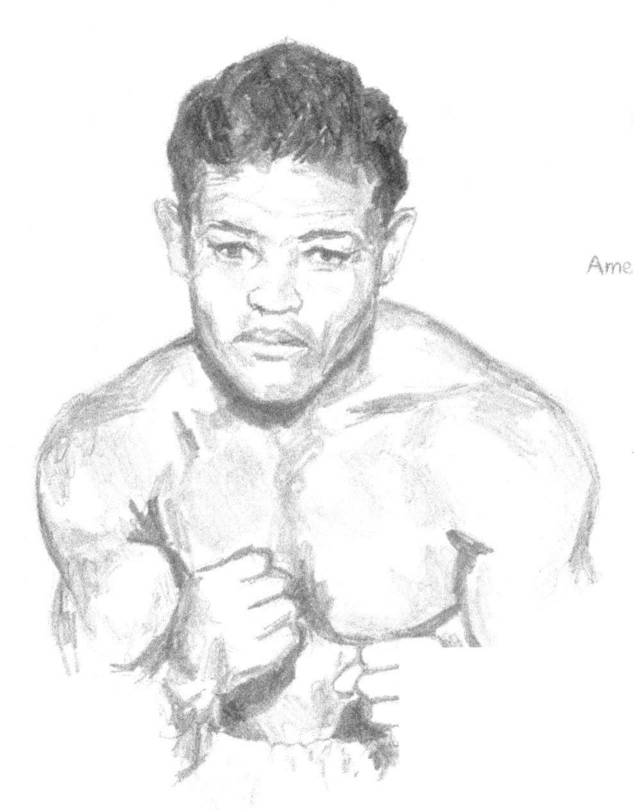

(JOSEPH LOUIS BARROW)
"BROWN BOMBER" JOE
LOUIS
American athlete and world heavyweight
boxing champion 1937-1949
1914 - 1981

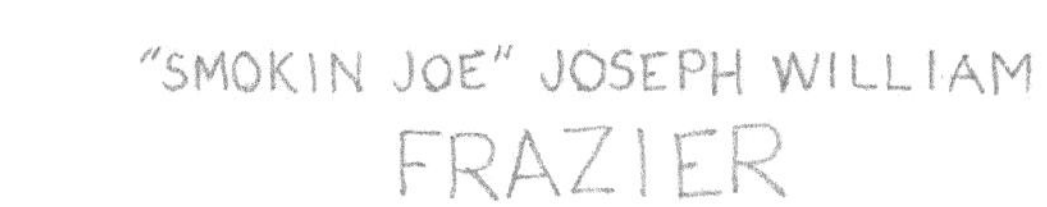

"SMOKIN JOE" JOSEPH WILLIAM
FRAZIER
American world heavyweight boxing champion 1970-1973

1944 - 2011

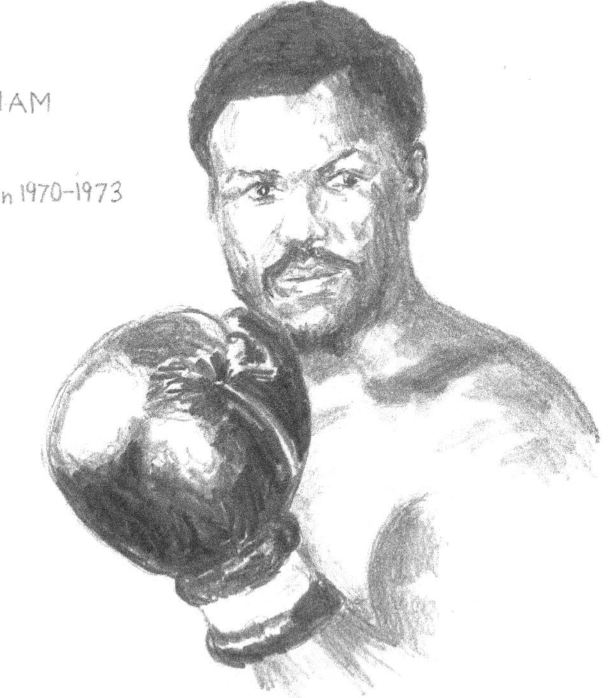

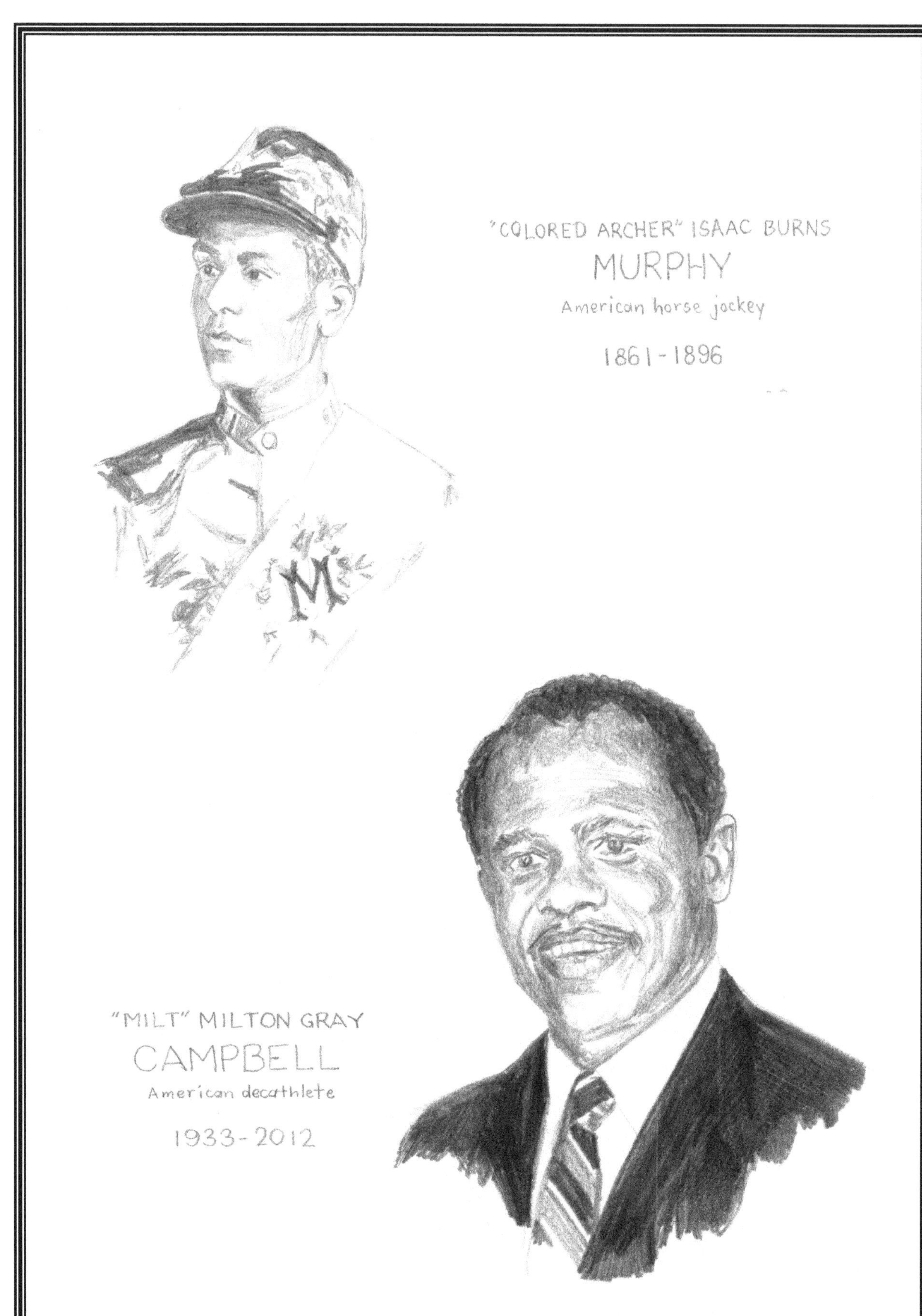

"COLORED ARCHER" ISAAC BURNS
MURPHY
American horse jockey

1861 - 1896

"MILT" MILTON GRAY
CAMPBELL
American decathlete

1933 - 2012

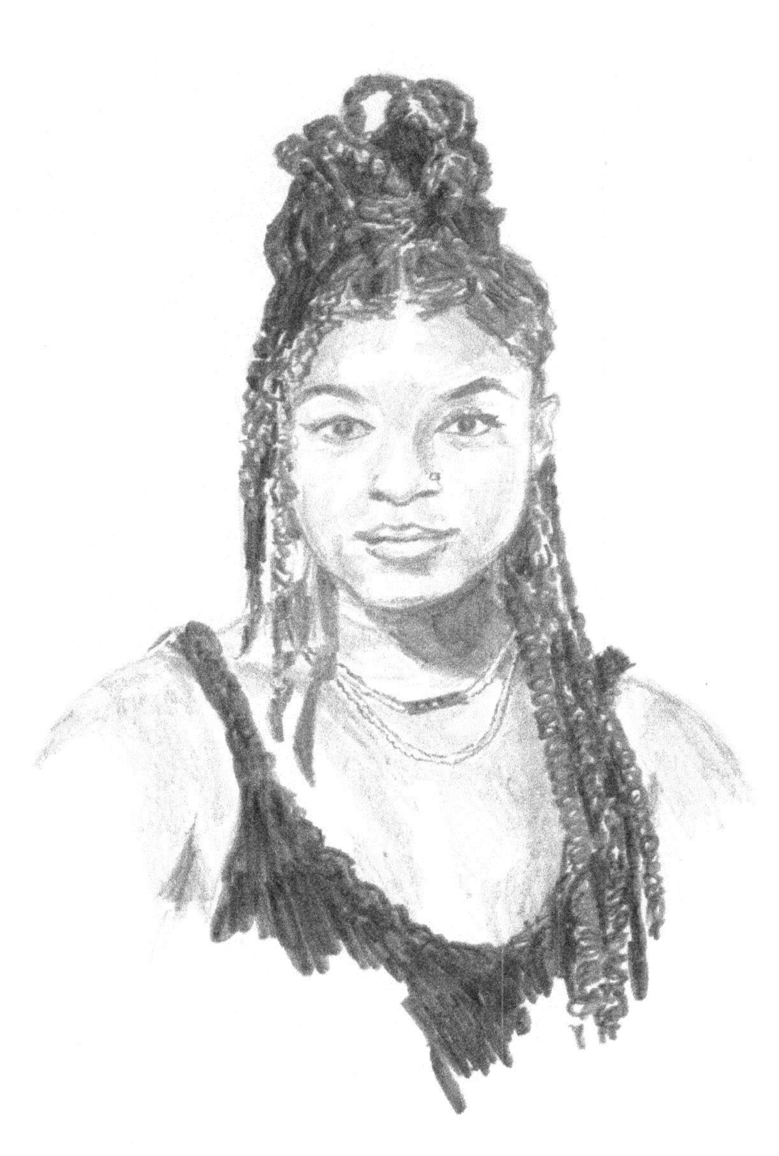

SIMONE ARIANNE
BILES
American artistic gymnast

1997-

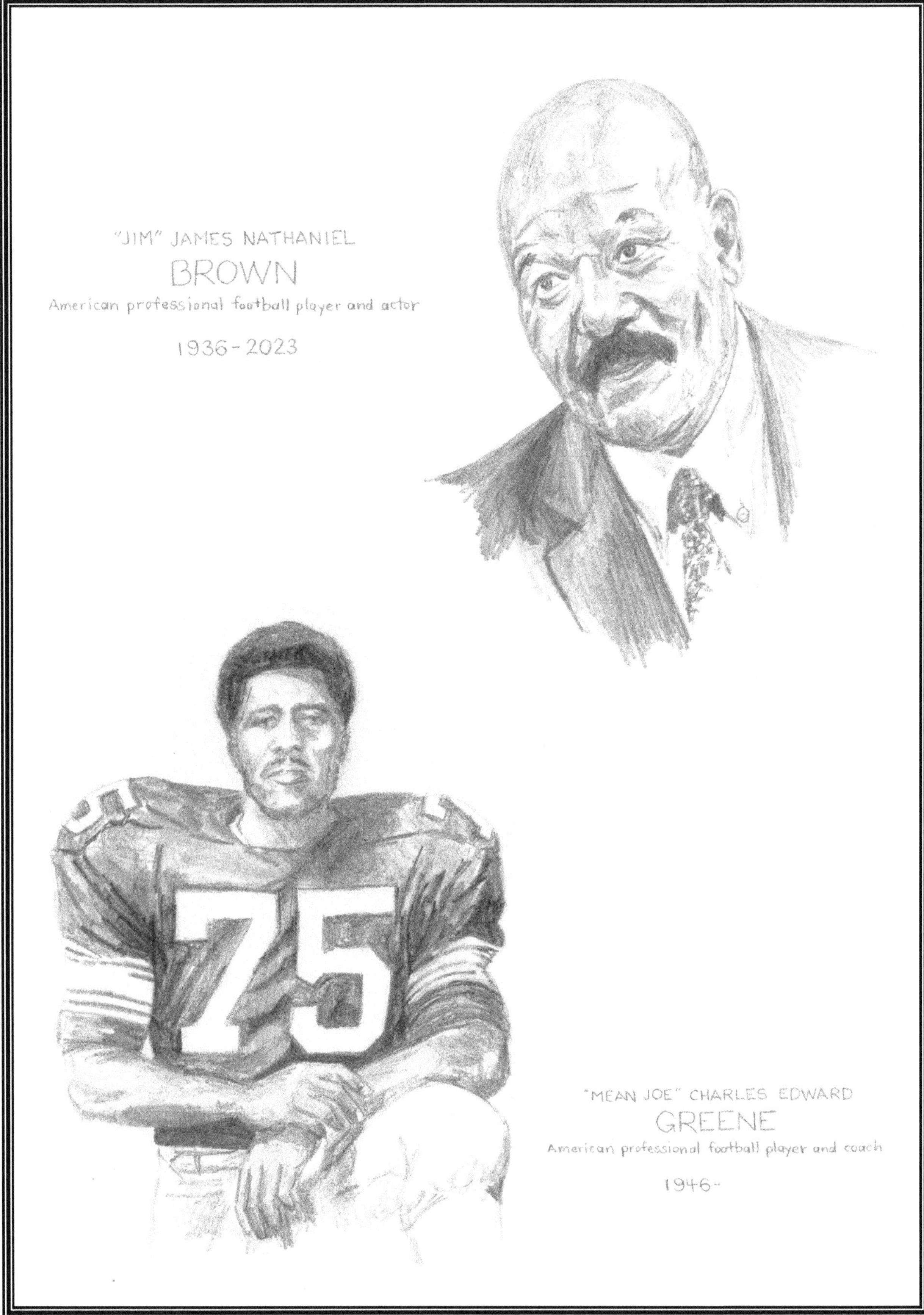

"JIM" JAMES NATHANIEL
BROWN
American professional football player and actor

1936-2023

"MEAN JOE" CHARLES EDWARD
GREENE
American professional football player and coach

1946-

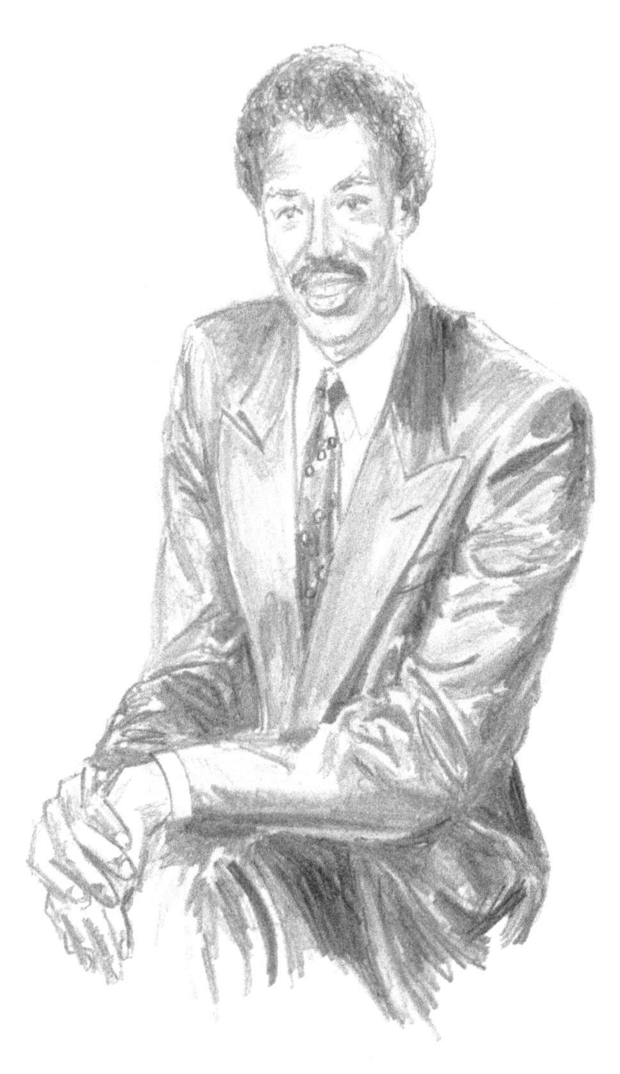

"Dr. J" JULIUS WINFIELD
ERVING
American basketball player and businessman

1950 -

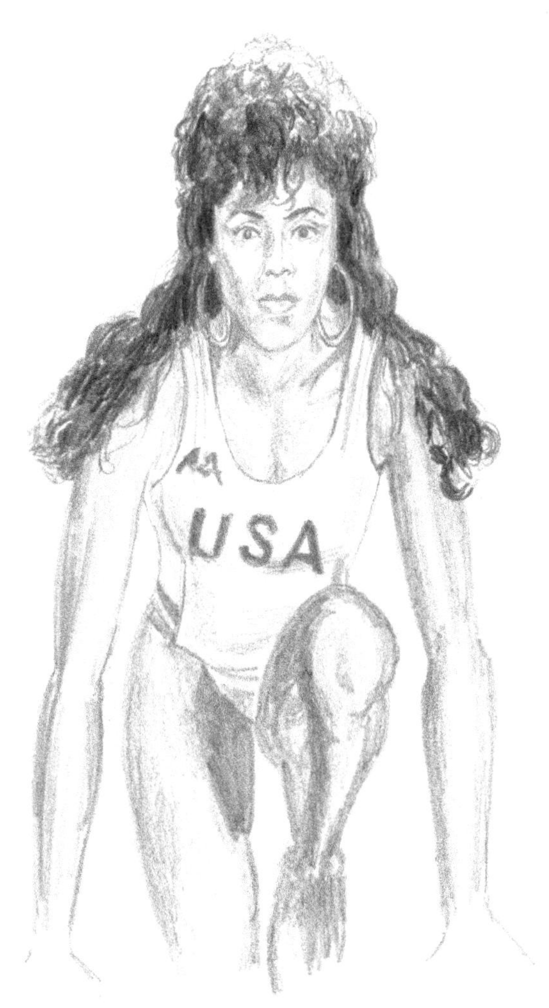

"FLO JO" FLORENCE DELOREZ

GRIFFITH JOYNER

American track and field athlete

1959 - 1998

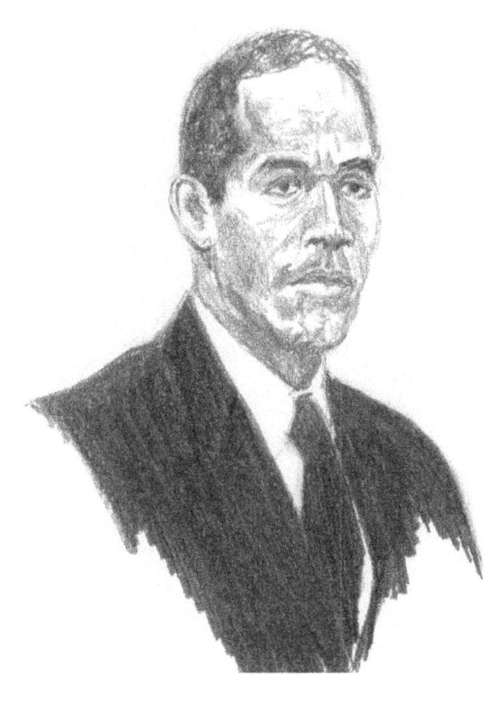

"THE JUICE" ORENTHAL JAMES
SIMPSON
American professional football player, broadcaster,
motion picture actor and advertising spokesman
1947-2024

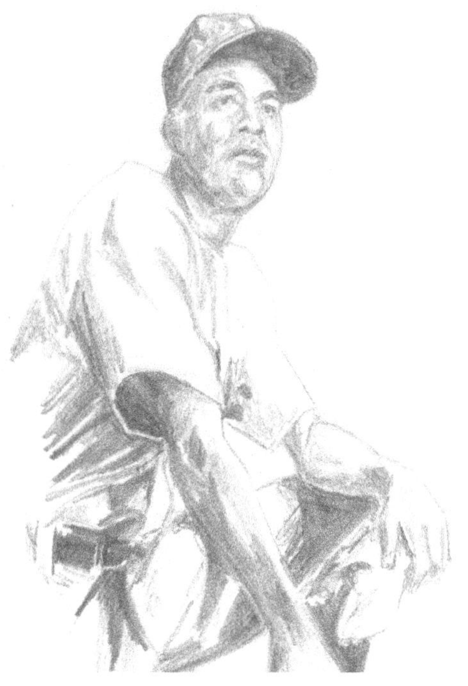

"LARRY" LAWRENCE EUGENE
DOBY
American professional baseball player

1923-2003

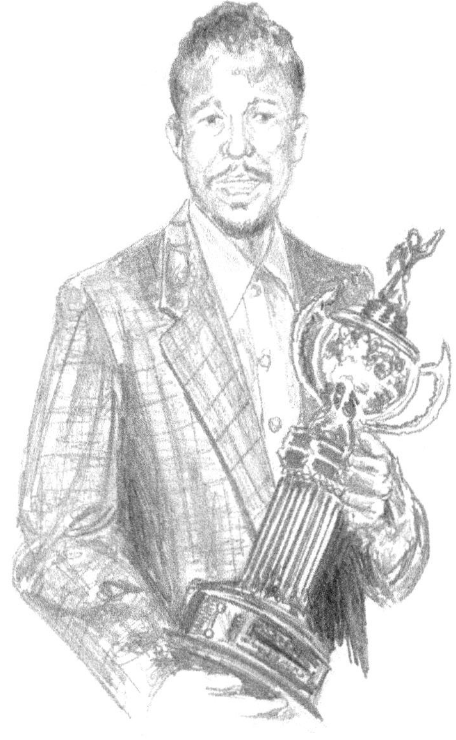

(WALKER SMITH Jr.)
SUGAR RAY
ROBINSON
American professional boxer

1921-1989

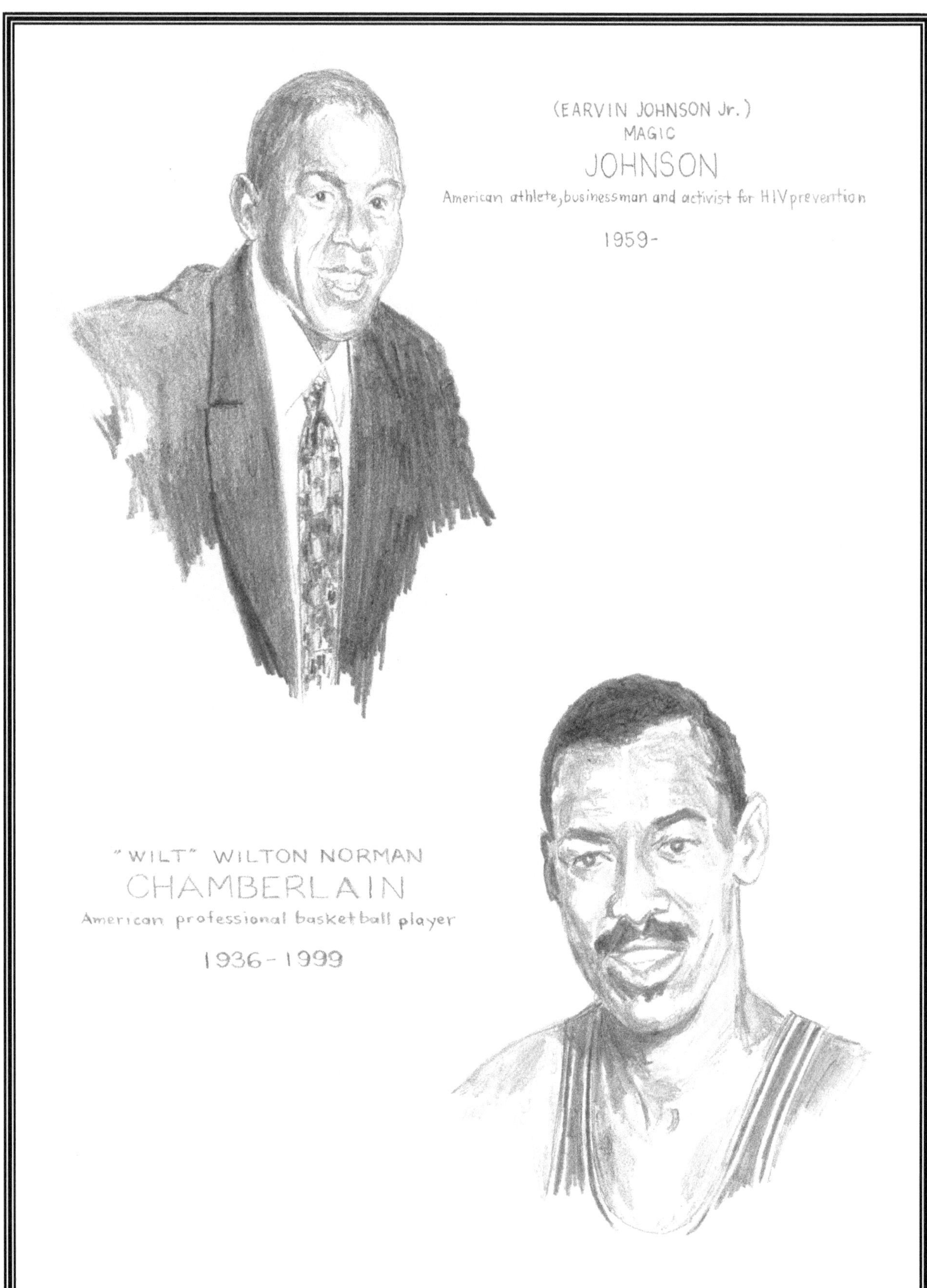

(EARVIN JOHNSON Jr.)
MAGIC
JOHNSON
American athlete, businessman and activist for HIV prevention
1959-

"WILT" WILTON NORMAN
CHAMBERLAIN
American professional basketball player
1936-1999

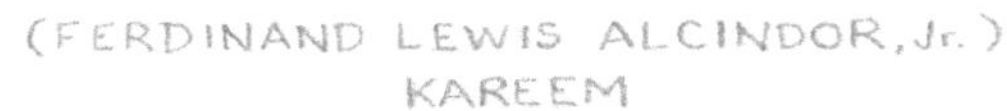

(FERDINAND LEWIS ALCINDOR, Jr.)
KAREEM

ABDUL-JABBAR

American basketball player, coach, actor and author

1947-

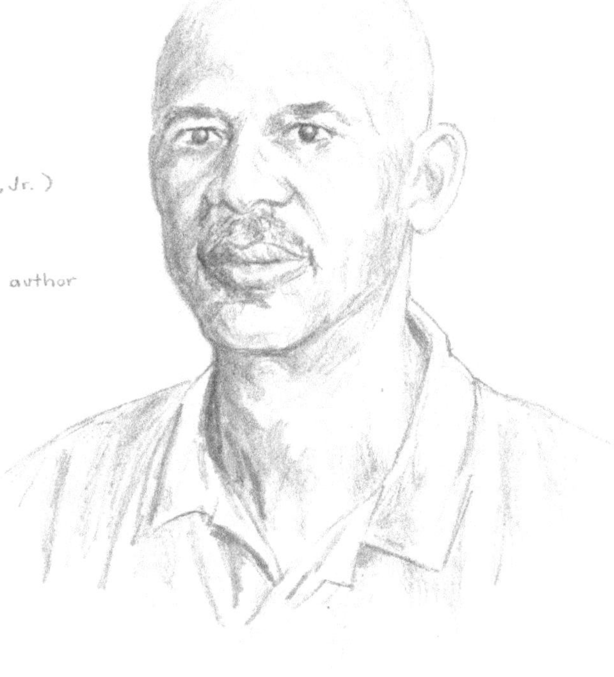

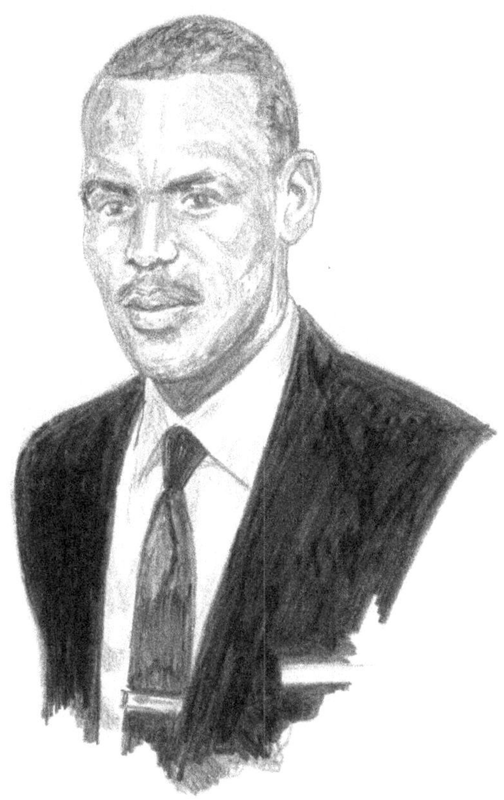

LeBRON RAYMONE

JAMES

American professional basketball player

1984-

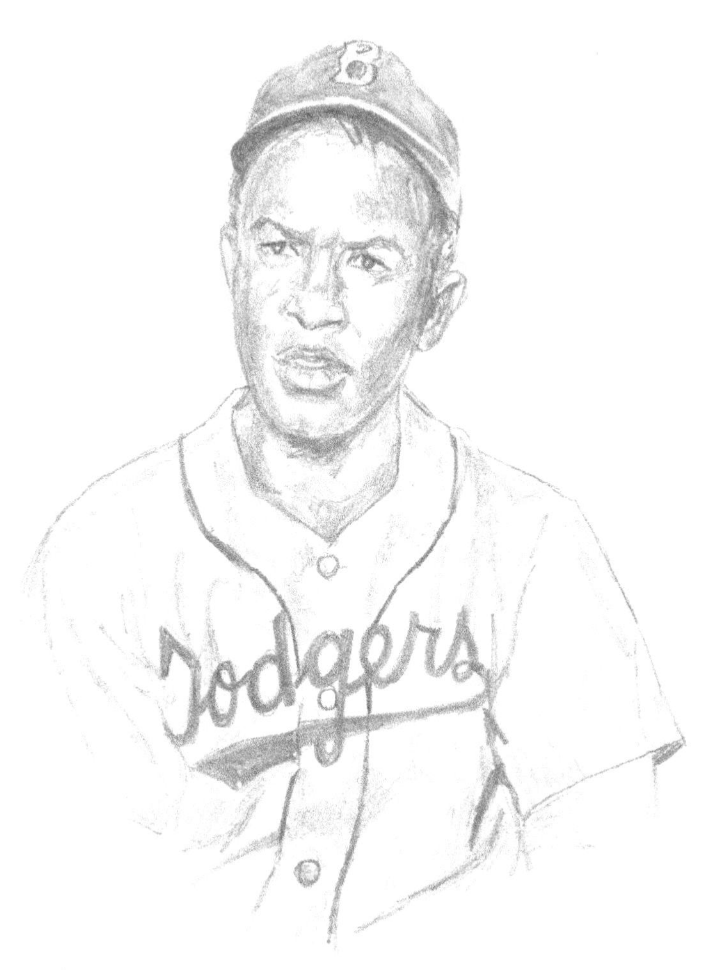

"JACKIE" JACK ROOSEVELT
ROBINSON

American major league baseball player

1919-1972

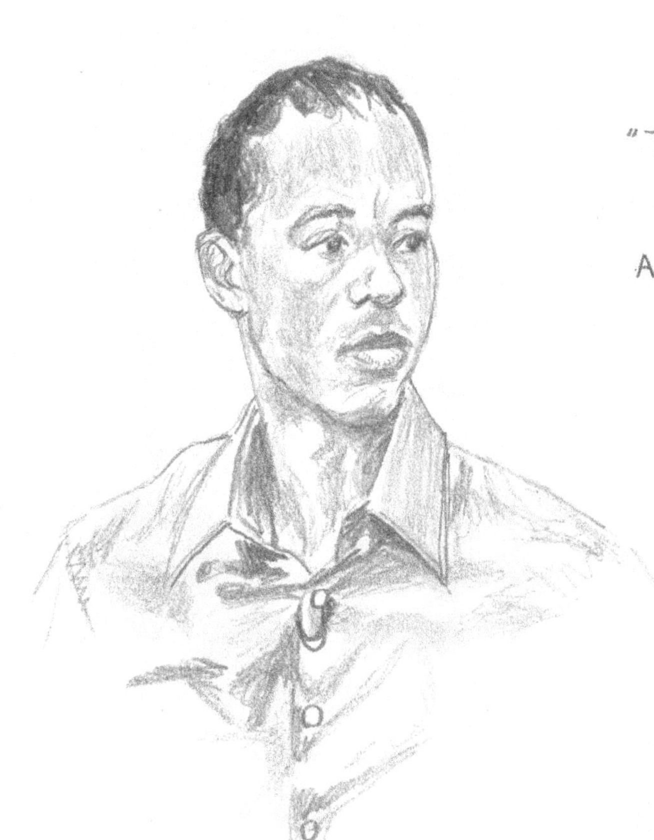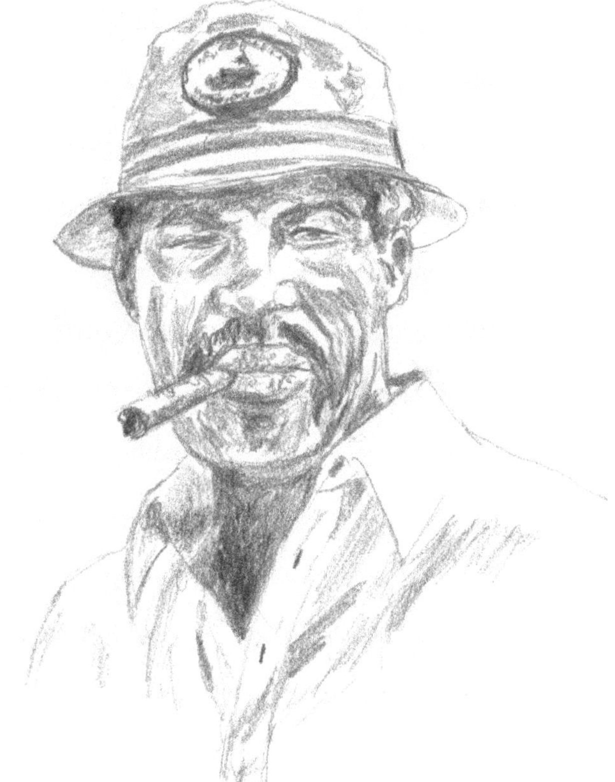

"TIGER" ELDRICK TONT
WOODS
American professional golfer

1975–

CHARLES LUTHER
SIFFORD
American professional golfer

1922–2015

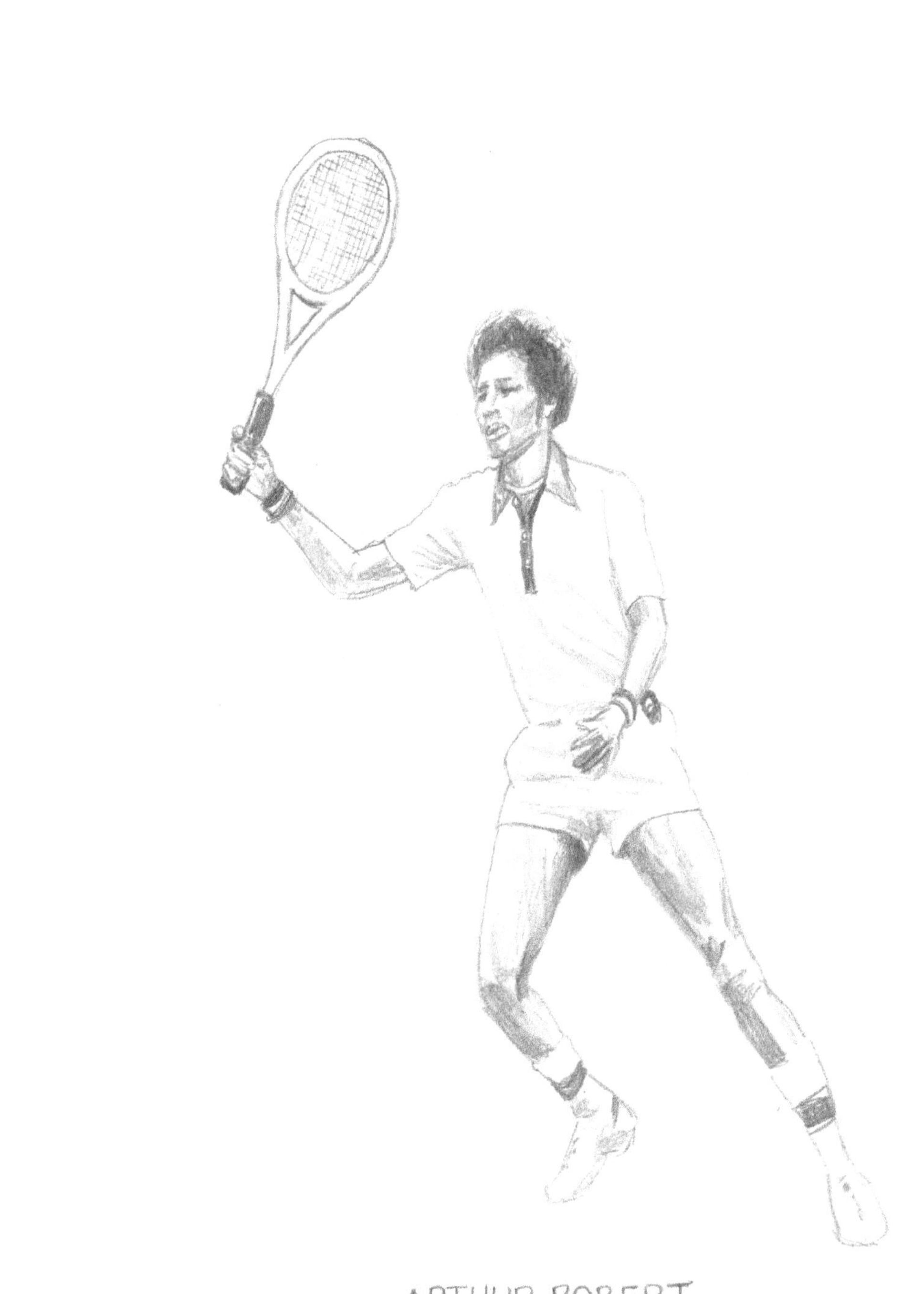

ARTHUR ROBERT
ASHE
American tennis player

1943 – 1993

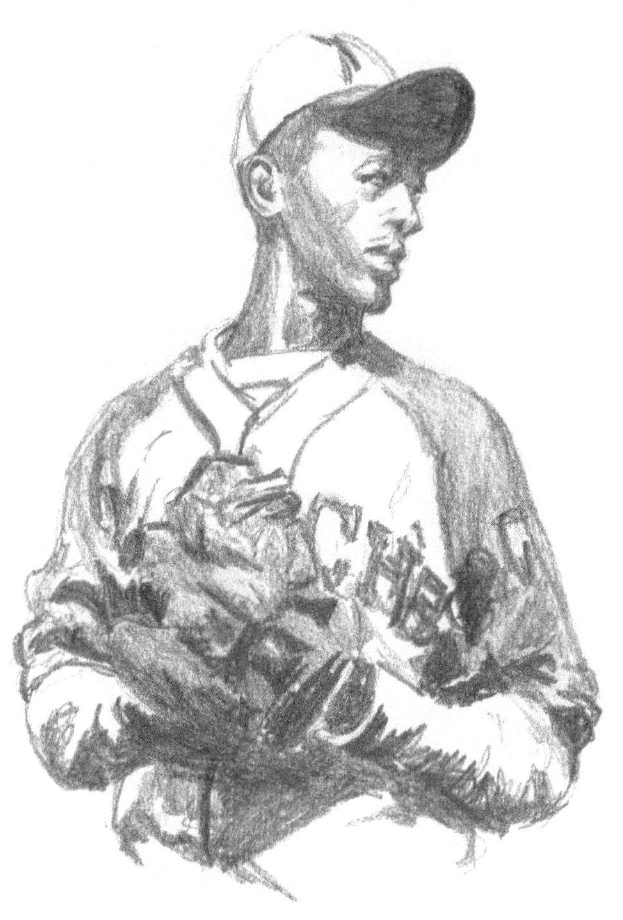

"SATCHEL" LEROY ROBERT
PAIGE
American professional baseball player

1906—1982

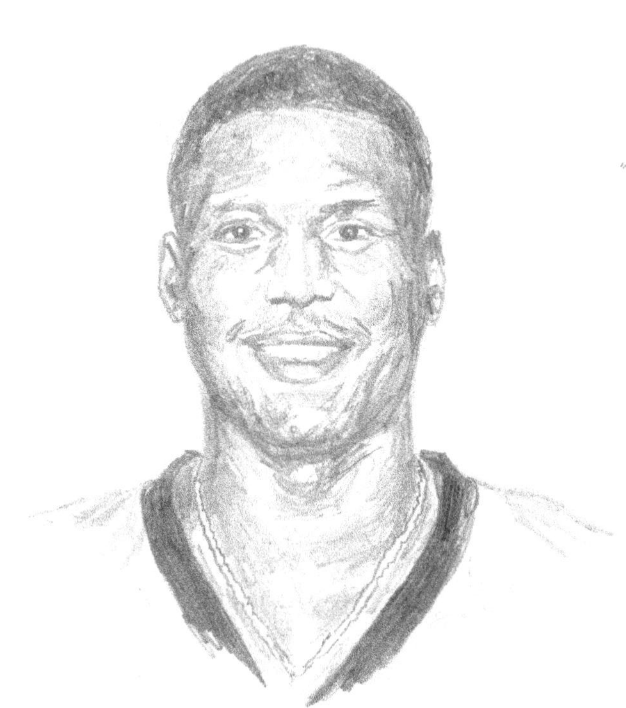

"AIR McNAIR" STEPHEN LaTREAL
McNAIR
American professional football player

1973-2009

PATRICK LAVON
MAHOMES
American professional football quarterback

1995-

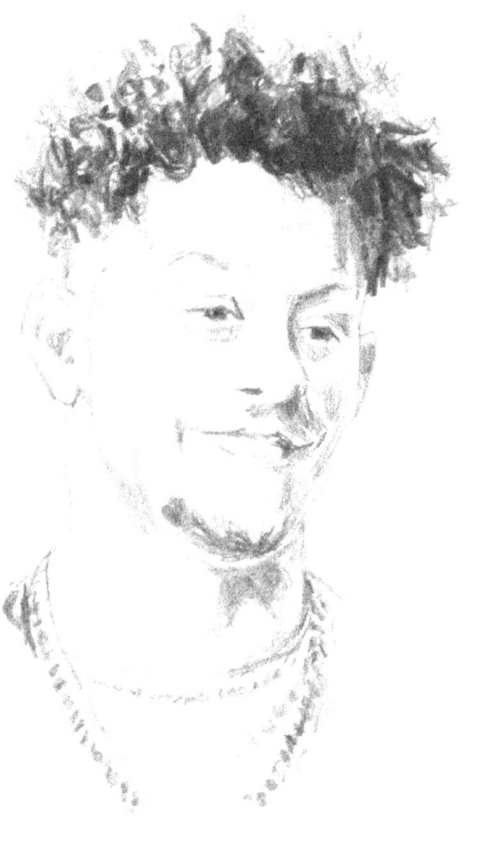

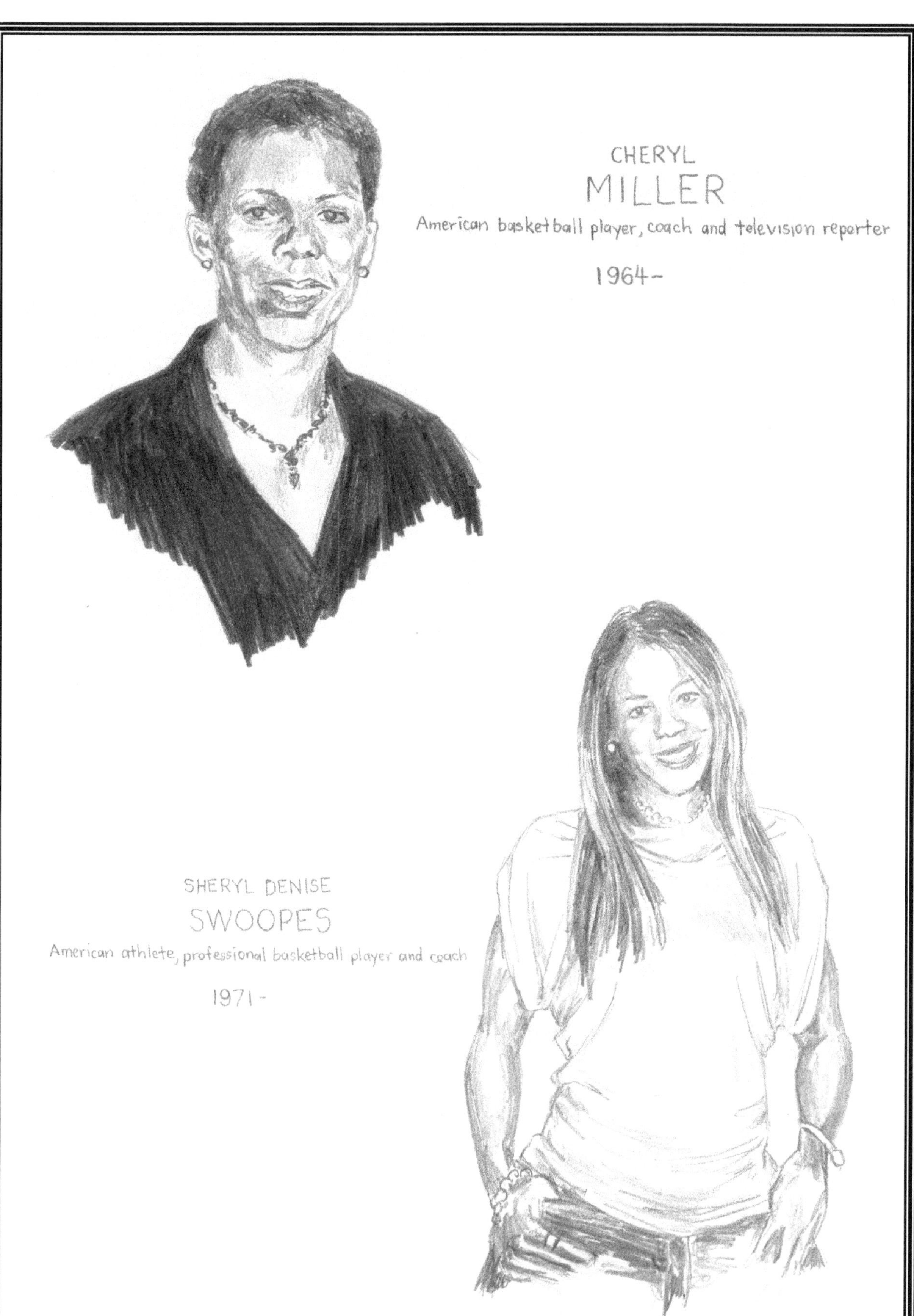

CHERYL
MILLER
American basketball player, coach and television reporter

1964–

SHERYL DENISE
SWOOPES
American athlete, professional basketball player and coach

1971–

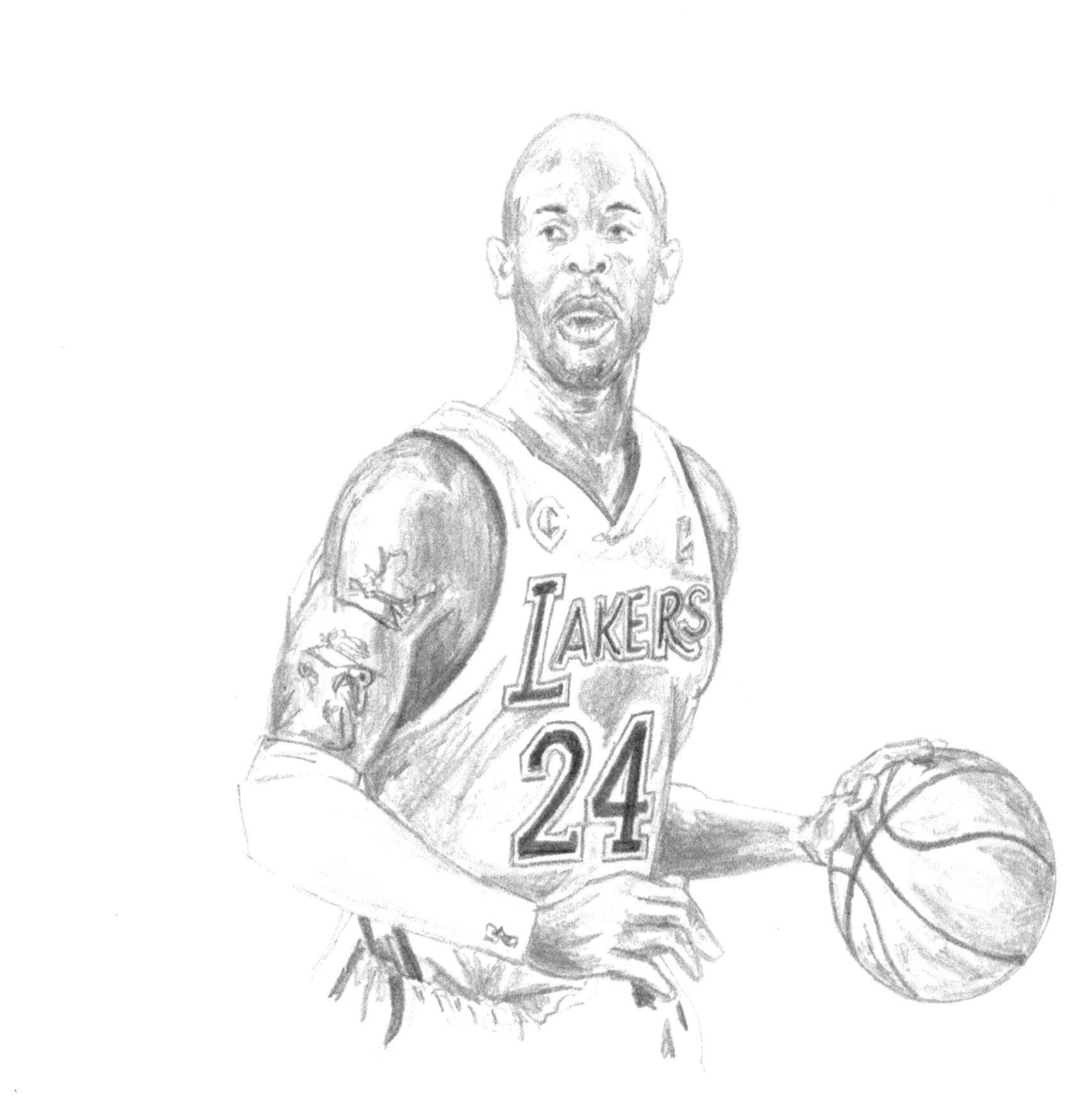

KOBE BEAN
BRYANT
American professional basketball player

1978-2020

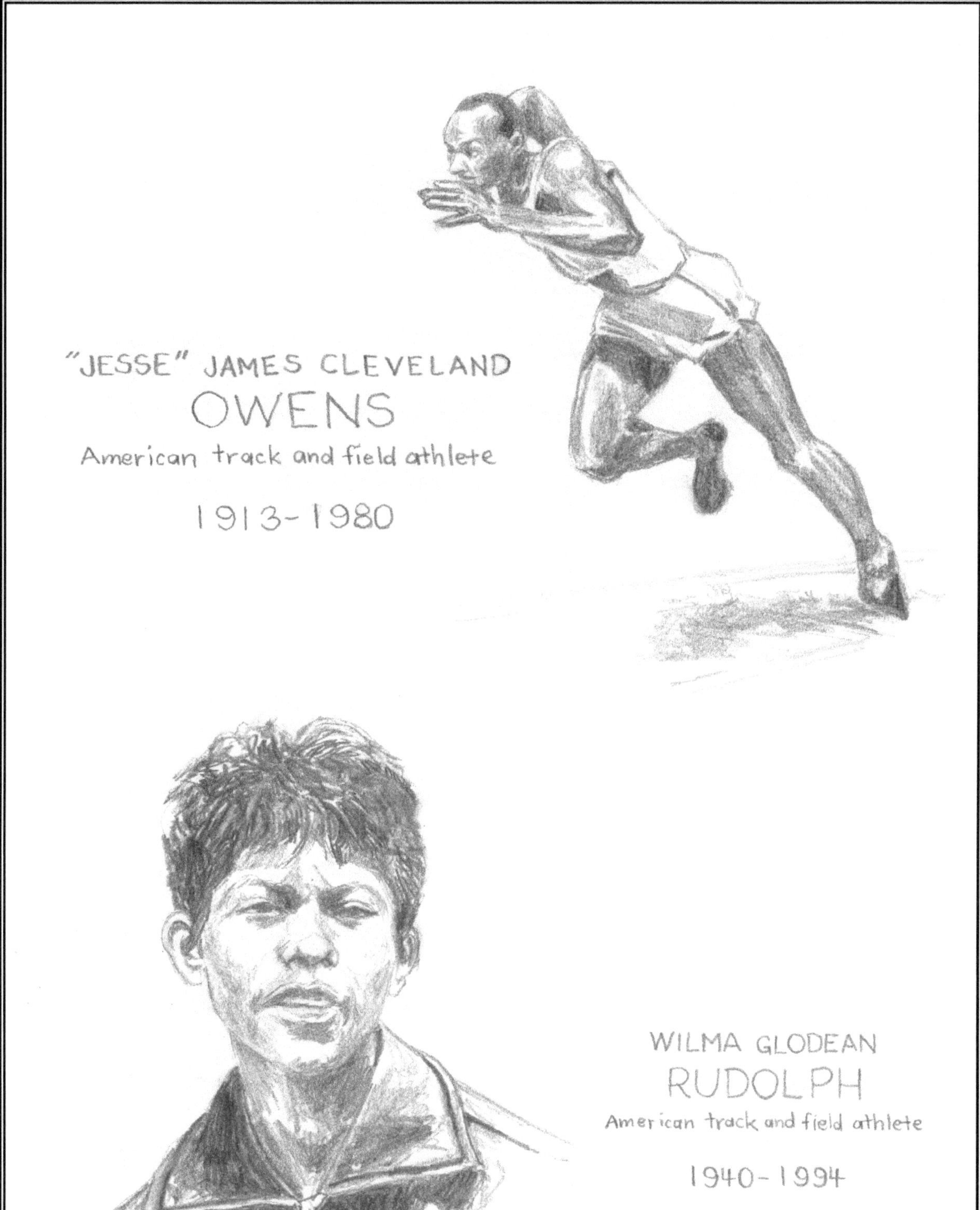
"JESSE" JAMES CLEVELAND
OWENS
American track and field athlete

1913-1980

WILMA GLODEAN
RUDOLPH
American track and field athlete

1940-1994

ALTHEA
GIBSON
American tennis player and professional golfer

1927-2003

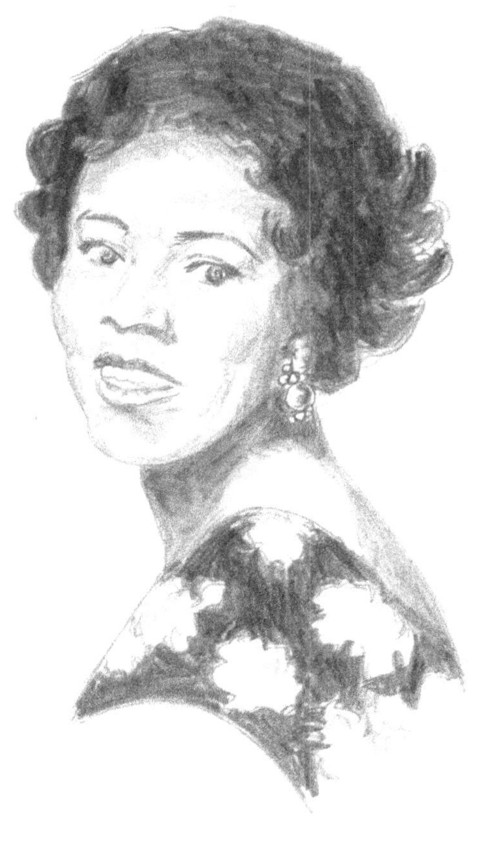

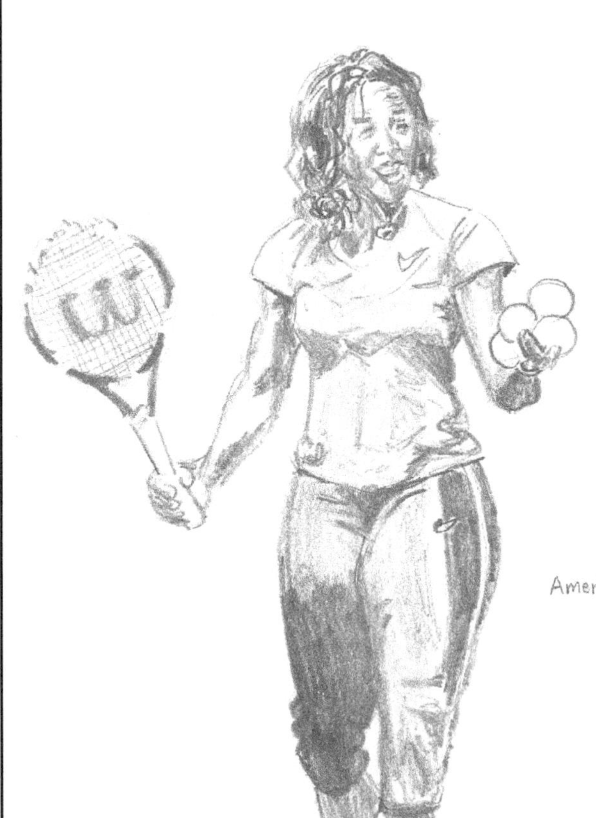

SERENA JAMEKA
WILLIAMS
American professional tennis player, sister of Venus Williams

1981-

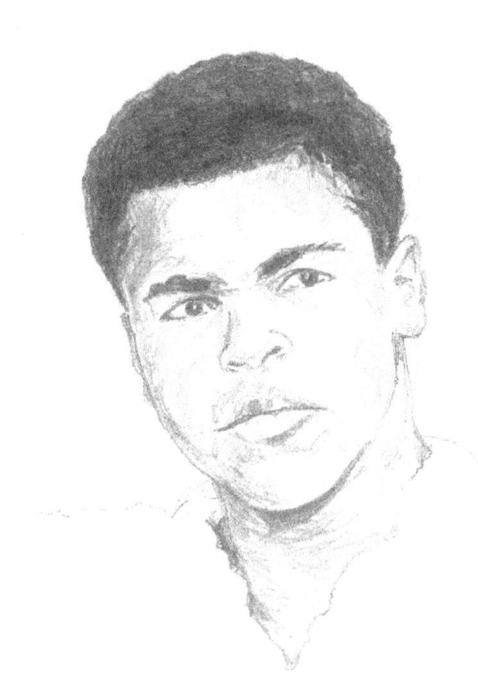

(CASSIUS MARCELLUS CLAY Jr.)
"THE GREATEST" MUHAMMAD
ALI
American professional boxer and world champion and activist

1942-2016

GEORGE EDWARD
FOREMAN
American world heavyweight boxing champion 1973,1974
baptist minister, author and entrepreneur

1949-2025

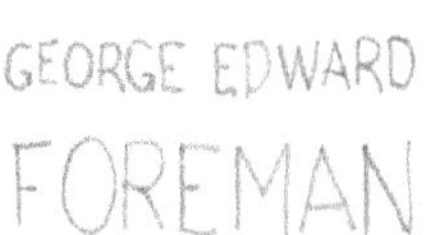

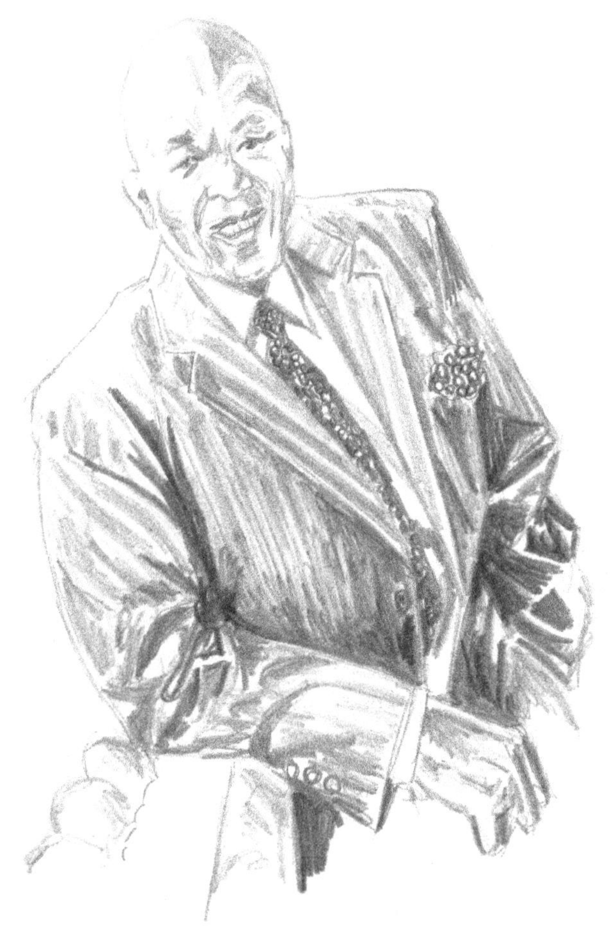

Business Leaders & Entrepreneurs

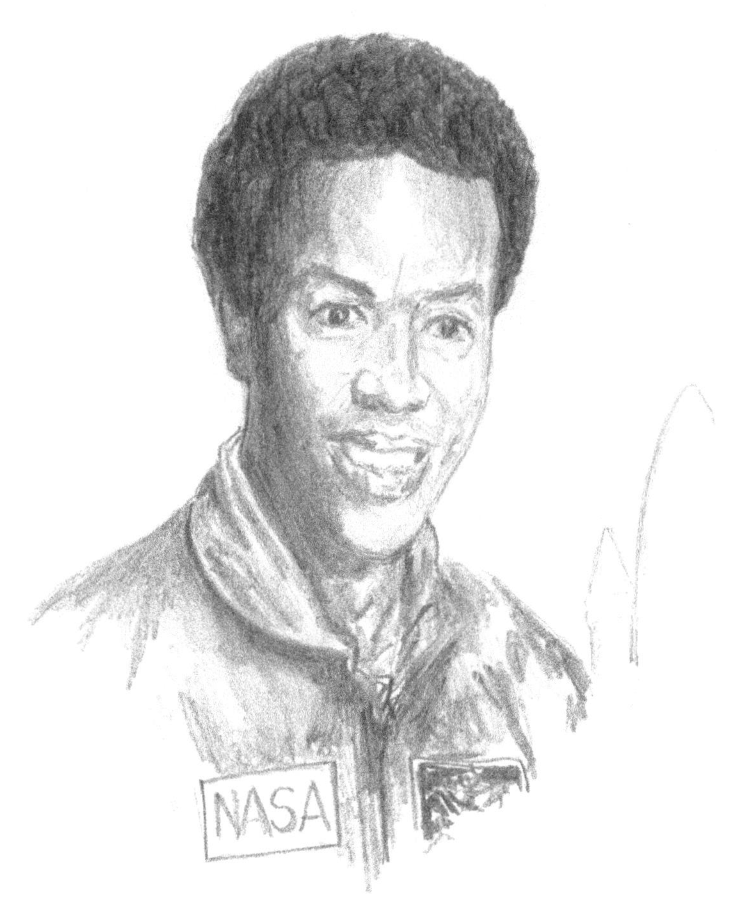

"GUY" GUION
BLUFORD
American air force pilot, engineer and astronaut

1942-

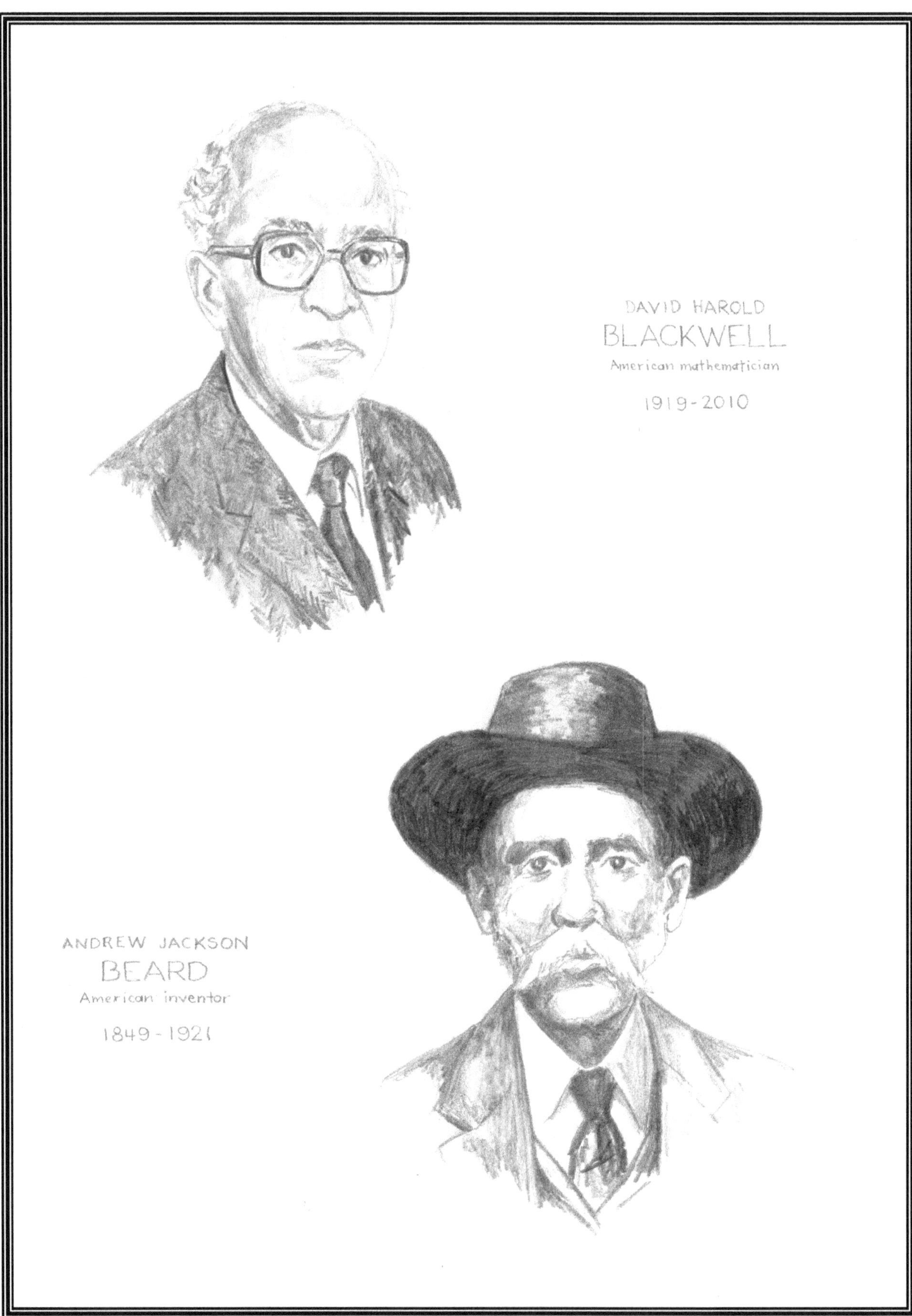

DAVID HAROLD
BLACKWELL
American mathematician

1919 - 2010

ANDREW JACKSON
BEARD
American inventor

1849 - 1921

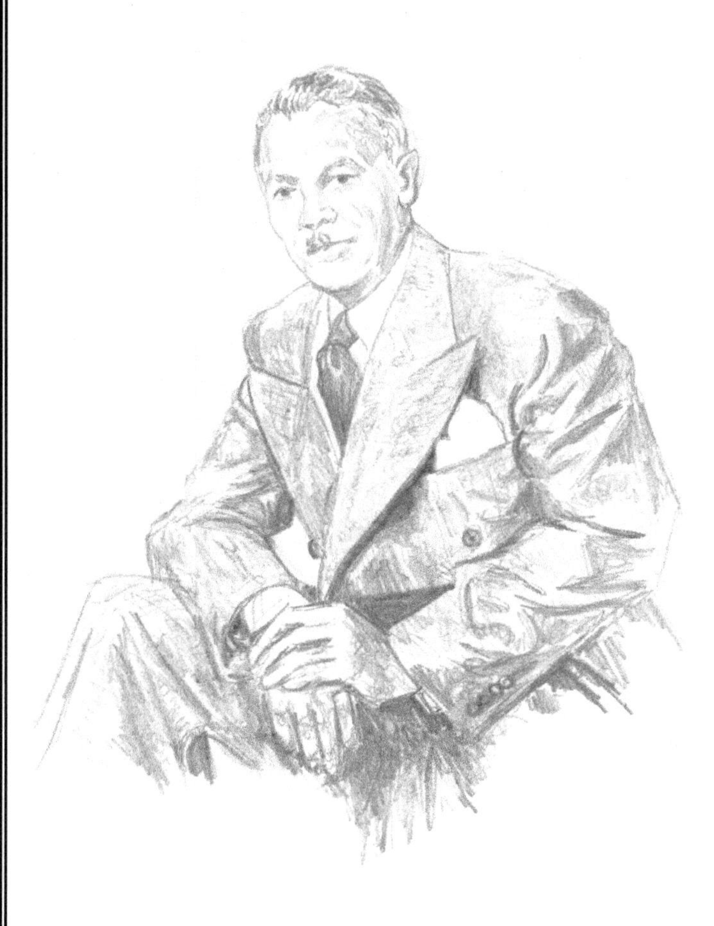

PAUL REVERE
WILLIAMS
American architect

1894-1980

"OZZIE" OSWALD
WILLIAMS
American aeronautical engineer and businessman

1921-2005

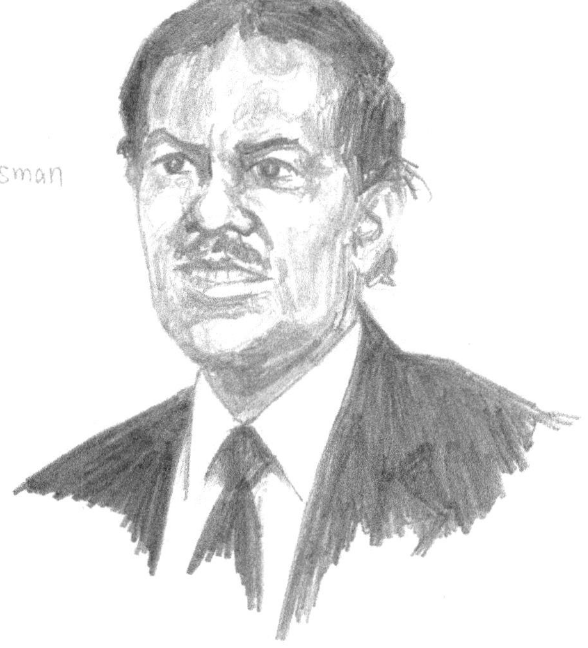

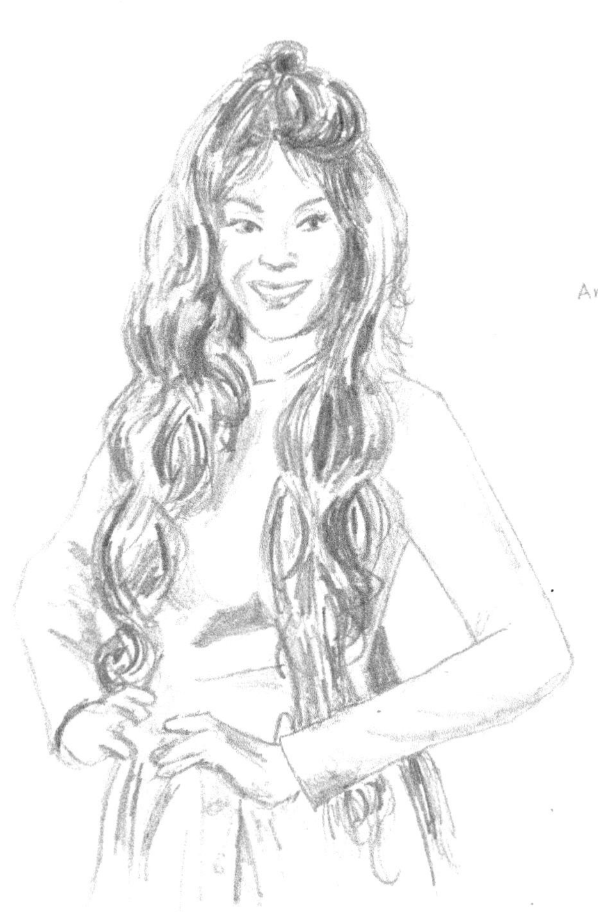

TYRA LYNNE
BANKS
American model, actress and businesswoman

1973-

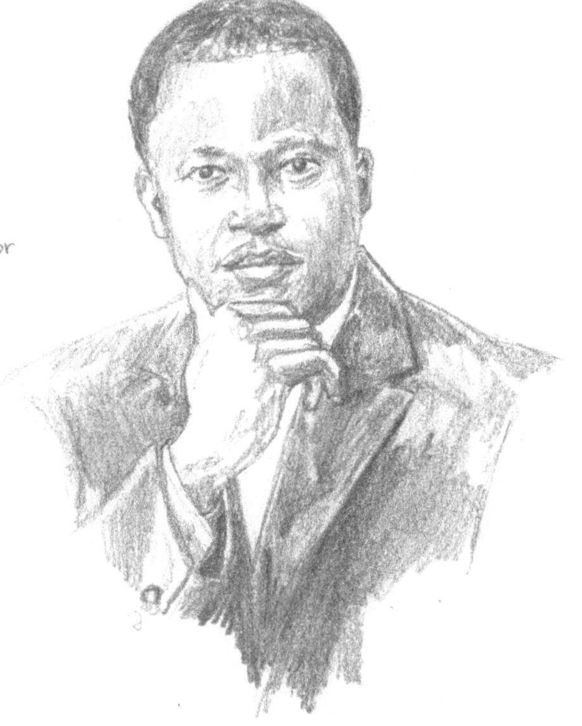

MAURICE
ASHLEY
Jamaican-American chess player and grandmaster,
author, commentator, app designer, puzzle inventor and orator
1966-

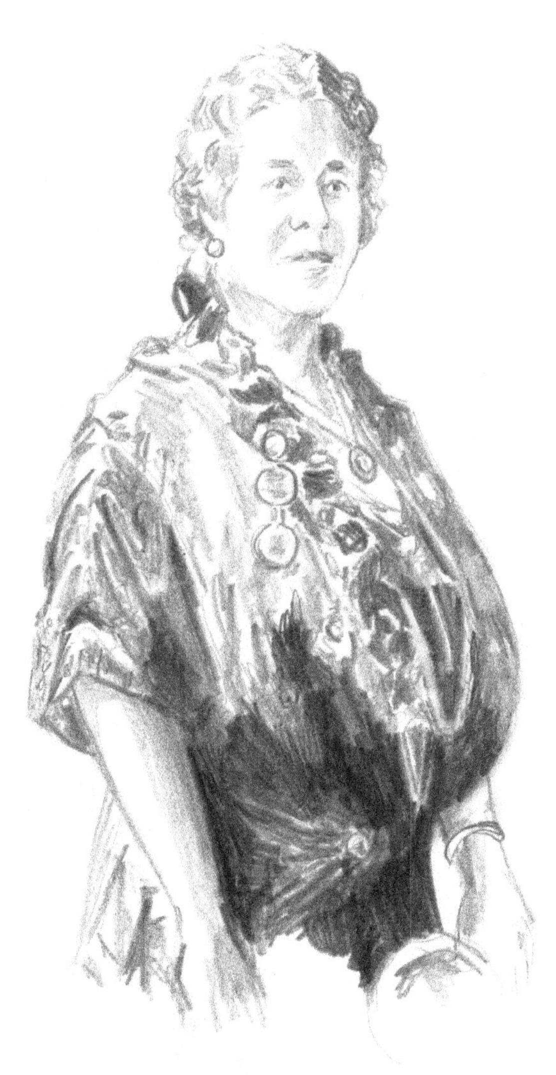

MAGGIE LENA
WALKER
American teacher and businesswoman

1864 - 1934

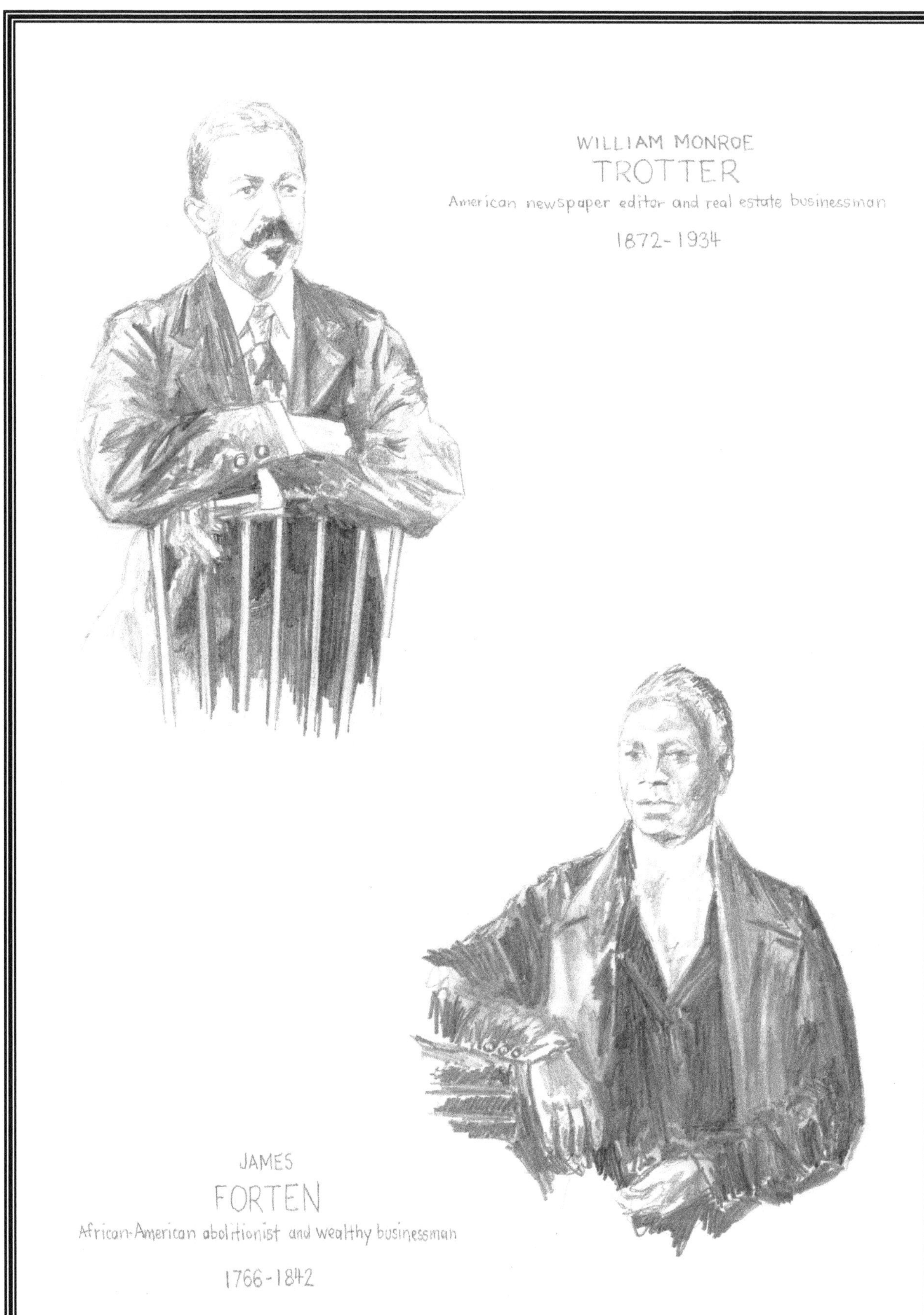

WILLIAM MONROE
TROTTER
American newspaper editor and real estate businessman
1872-1934

JAMES
FORTEN
African-American abolitionist and wealthy businessman
1766-1842

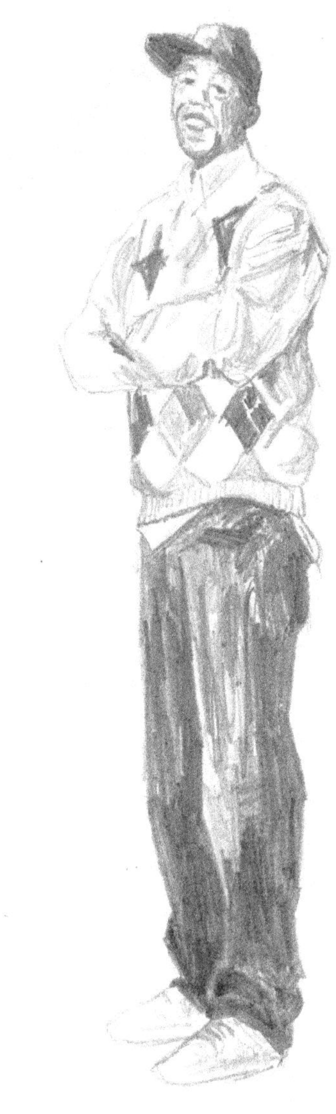

RUSSELL WENDELL
SIMMONS
American entrepreneur, record
executive, writer and film producer
1957–

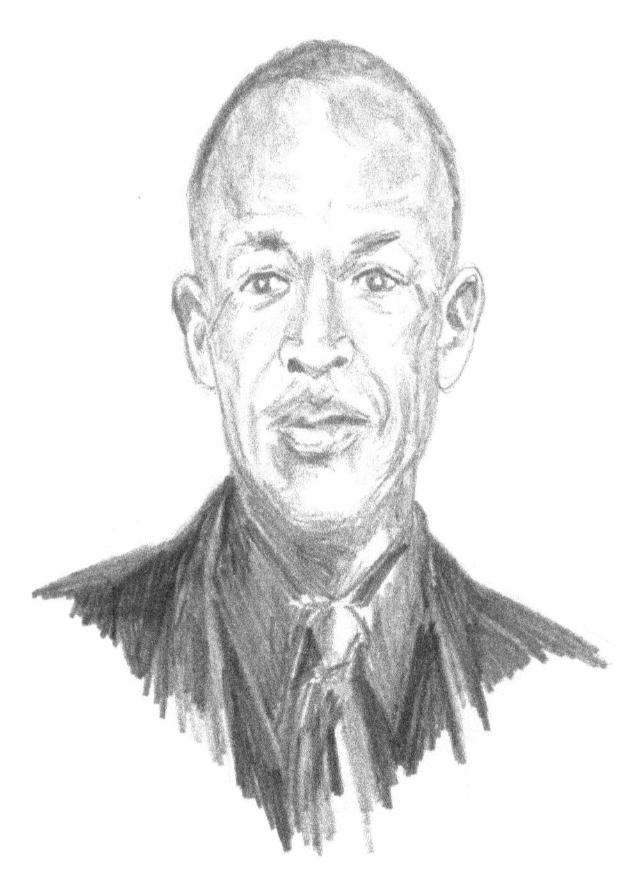

(ANDRE ROMELLE YOUNG)

Dr. DRE

American rapper, record producer and entrepreneur

1965-

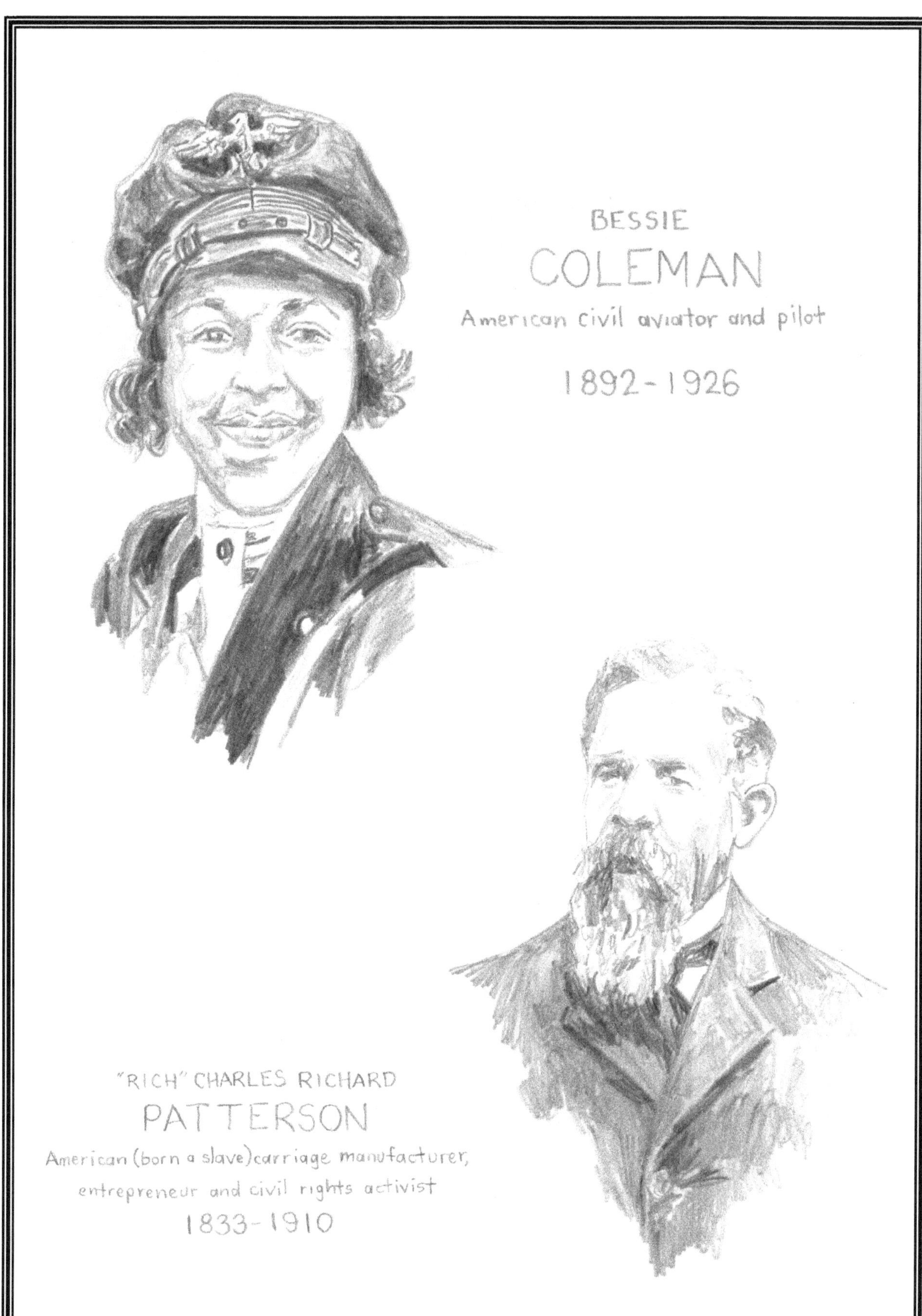

BESSIE
COLEMAN
American civil aviator and pilot

1892-1926

"RICH" CHARLES RICHARD
PATTERSON
American (born a slave) carriage manufacturer,
entrepreneur and civil rights activist
1833-1910

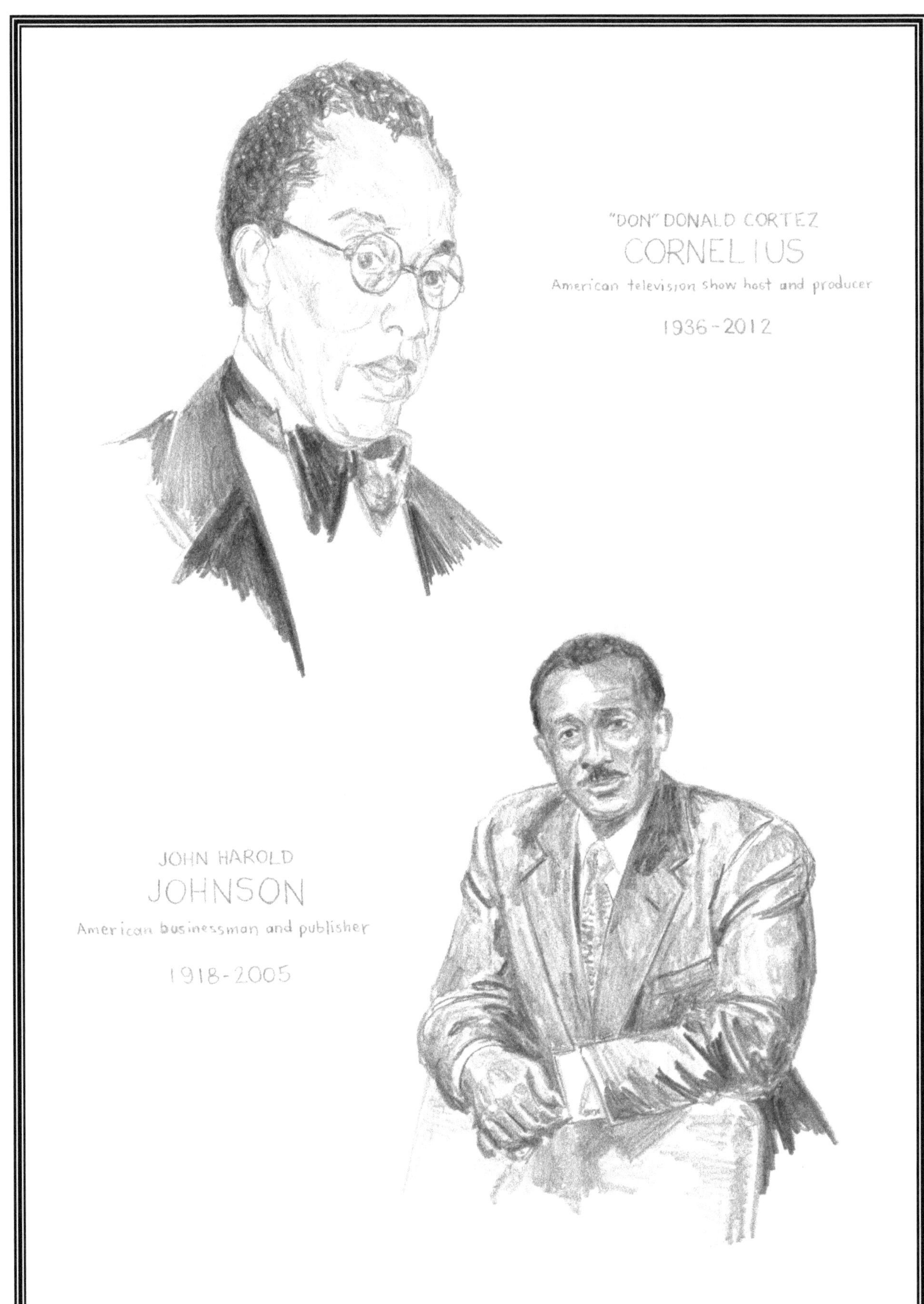

"DON" DONALD CORTEZ
CORNELIUS
American television show host and producer

1936-2012

JOHN HAROLD
JOHNSON
American businessman and publisher

1918-2005

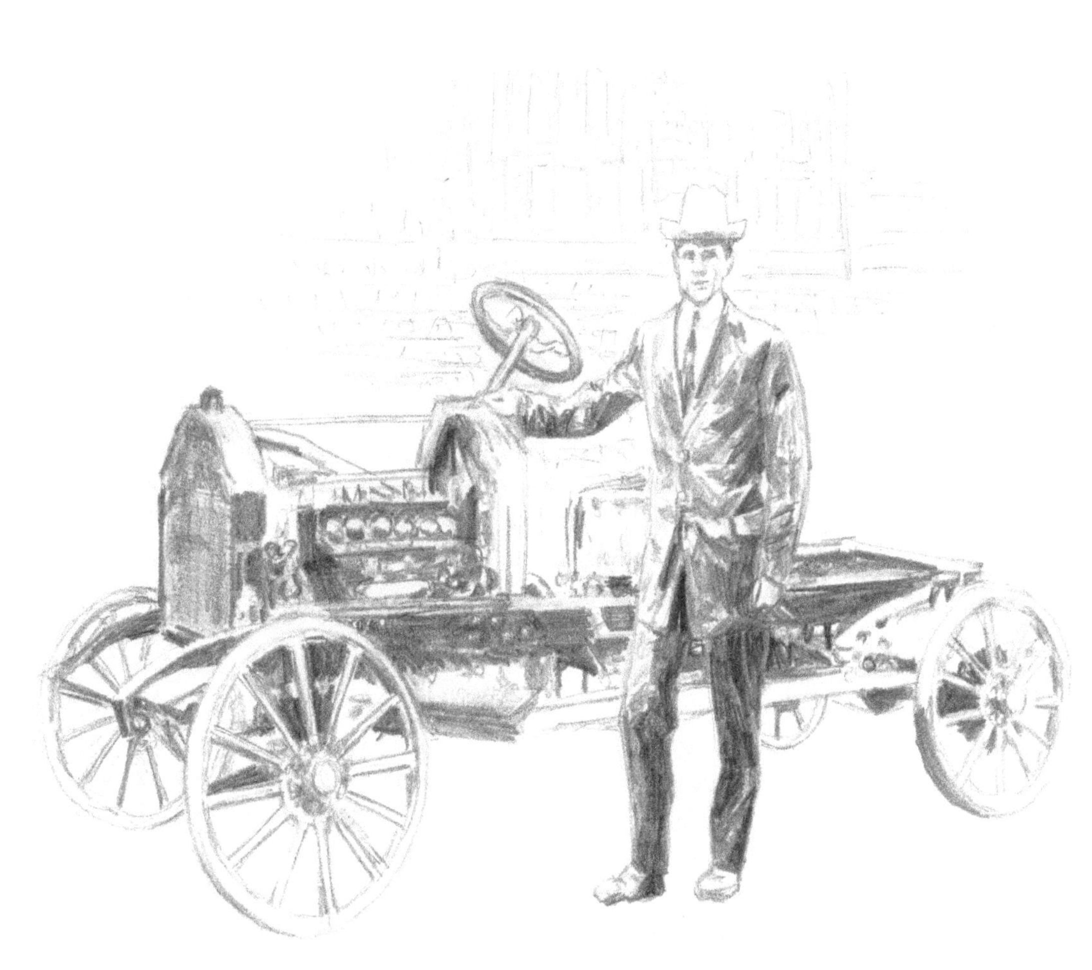

FREDERICK DOUGLAS
PATTERSON
American entrepreneur, businessman and automobile
manufacturer, son of Charles Richard Patterson
1871 - 1932

Artists

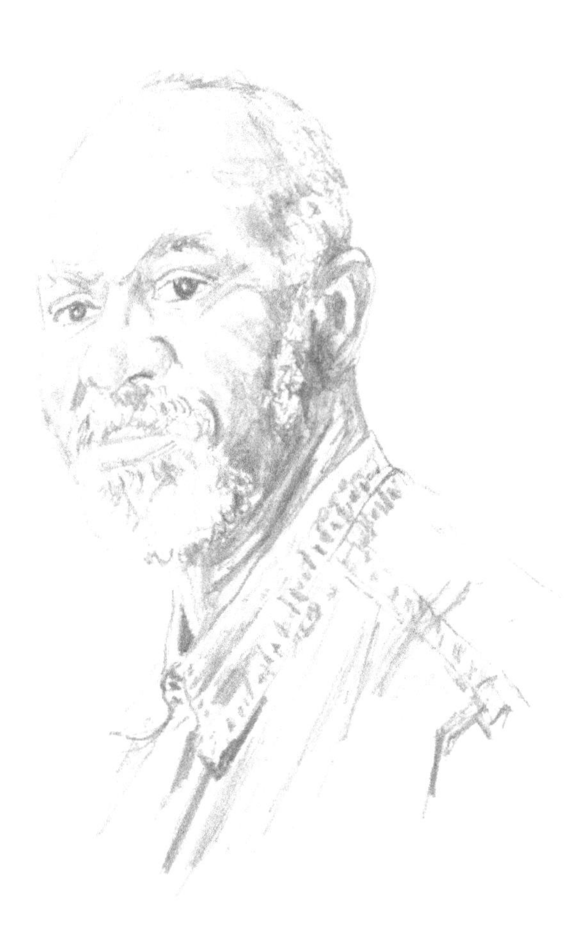

KERRY JAMES
MARSHALL
American artist

1955-

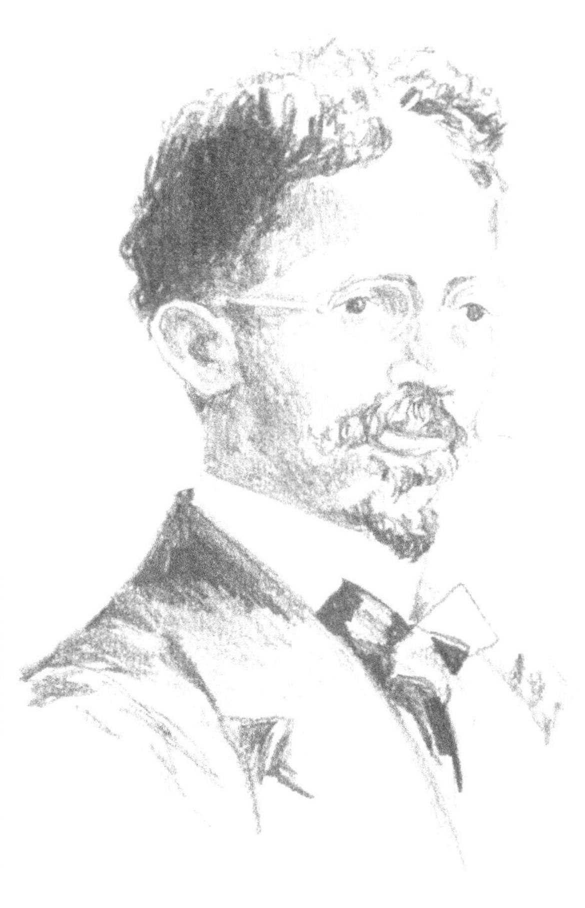

HENRY OSSAWA
TANNER
American artist and painter

1859-1937

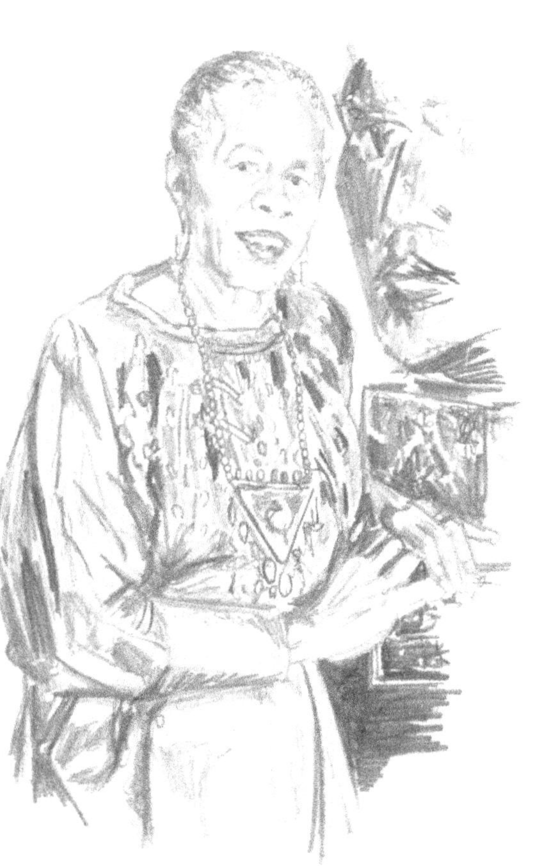

(MARGARET TAYLOR GOSS BURROUGHS)
MARGARET
TAYLOR-BURROUGHS
American visual artist, writer,
poet, educator and art organizer

1917-2010

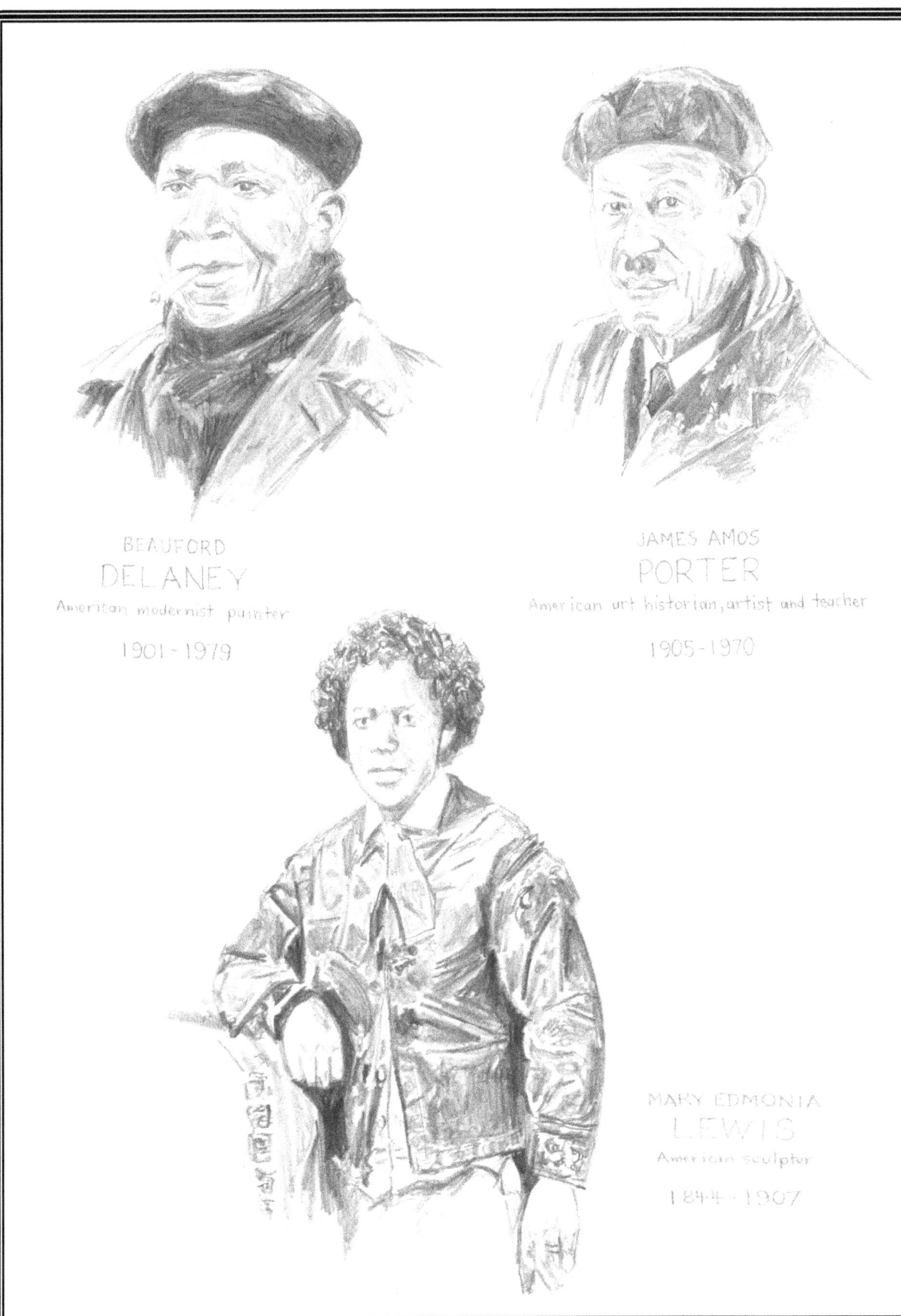

BEAUFORD
DELANEY
American modernist painter

1901 - 1979

JAMES AMOS
PORTER
American art historian, artist and teacher

1905 - 1970

MARY EDMONIA
LEWIS
American sculptor

1844 - 1907

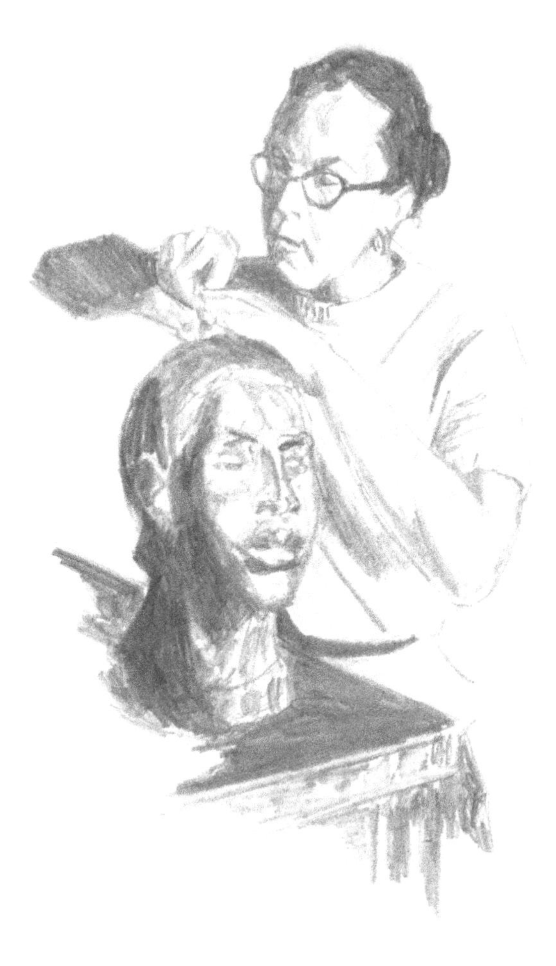

ELIZABETH
CATLETT
American sculptor and graphic artist

1915-2012

HORACE
PIPPIN
American painter

1888-1946

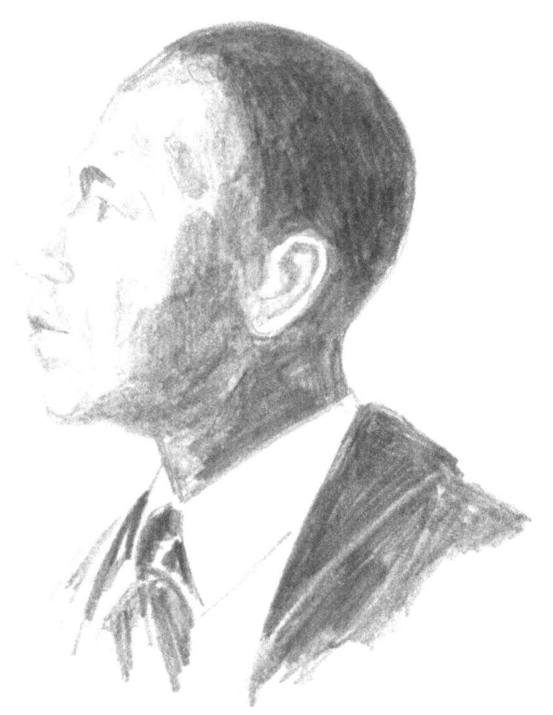

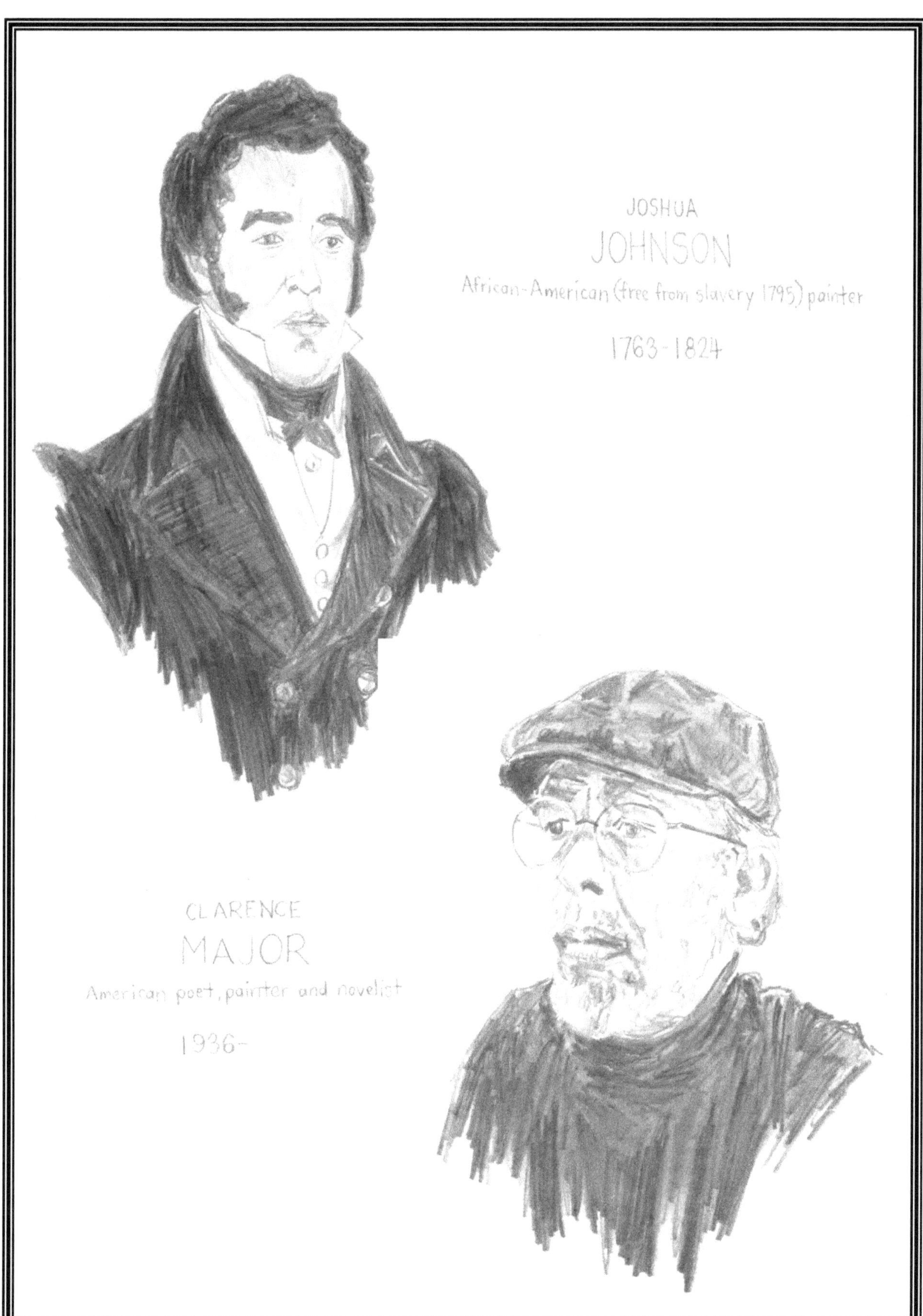
JOSHUA
JOHNSON
African-American (free from slavery 1795) painter
1763-1824
CLARENCE
MAJOR
American poet, painter and novelist
1936-

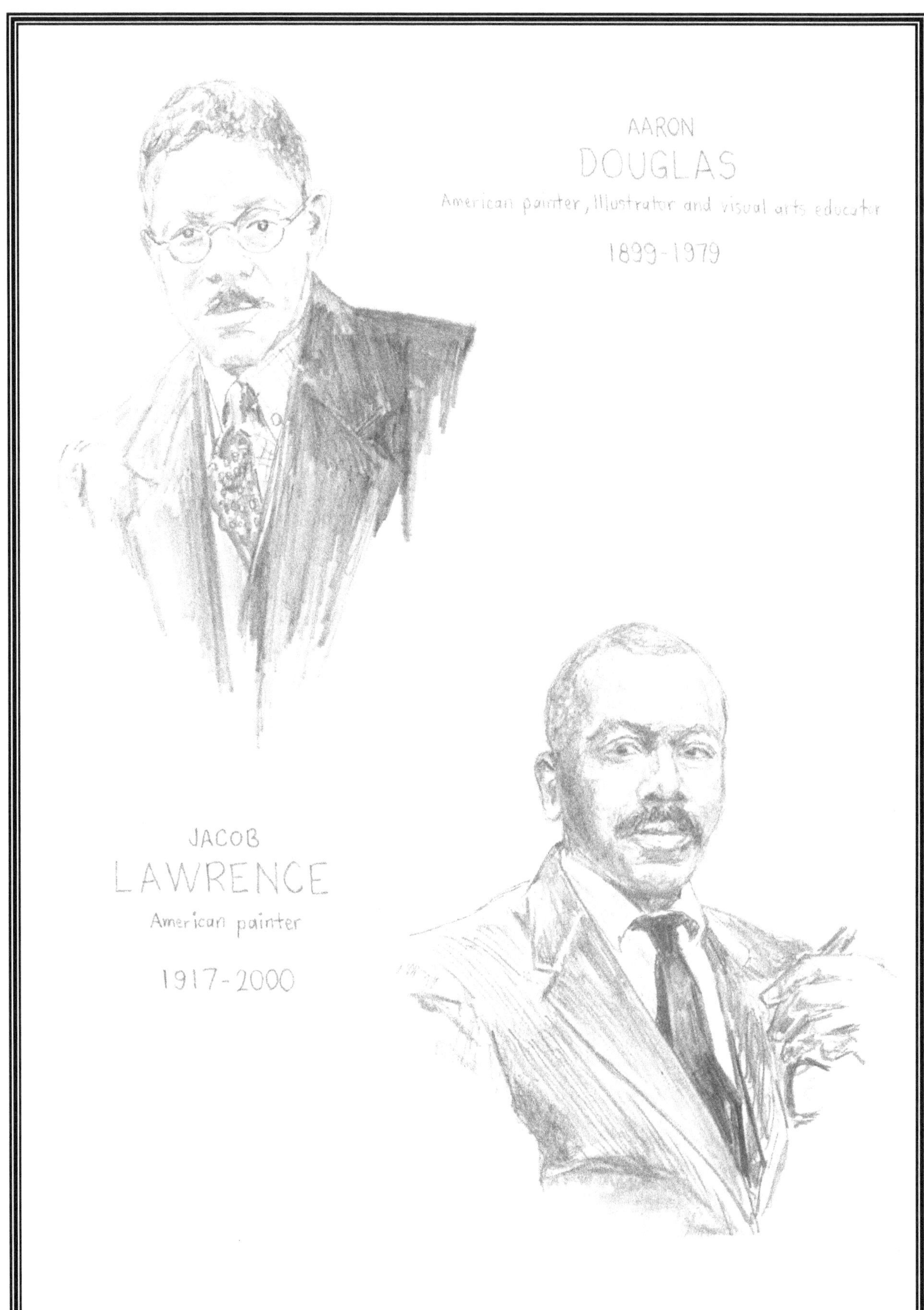

AARON
DOUGLAS
American painter, Illustrator and visual arts educator
1899-1979
JACOB
LAWRENCE
American painter
1917-2000

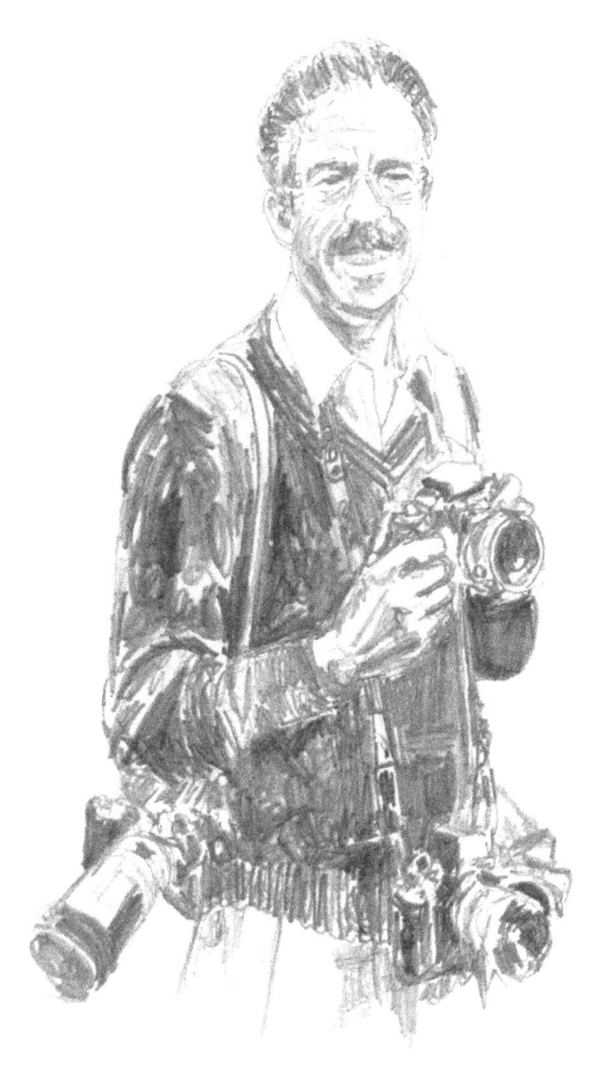

MONETA
SLEET Jr.
American press photographer

1926 - 1996

Activists and Advocates

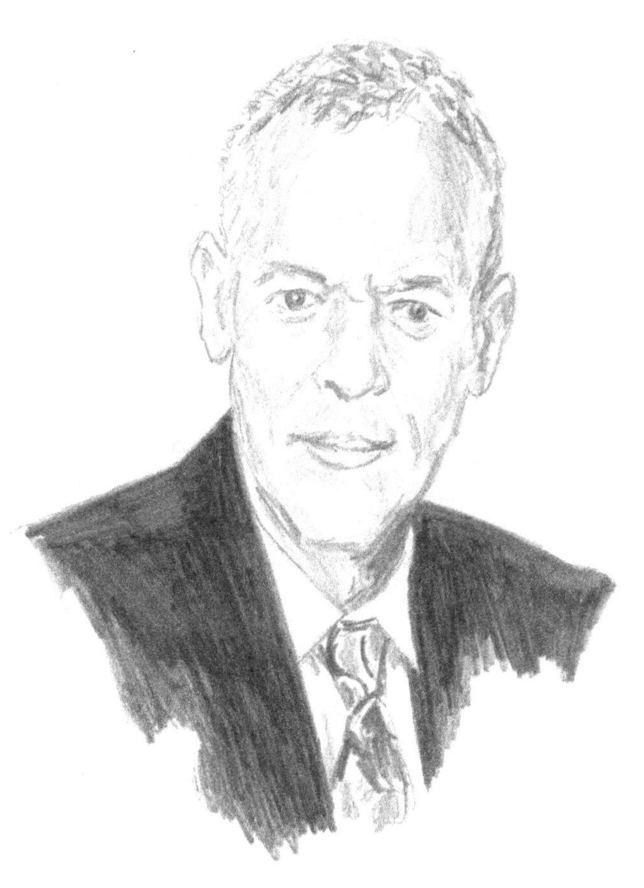

HORACE JULIAN
BOND
American social activist, civil rights leader
politician, professor and writer

1940-

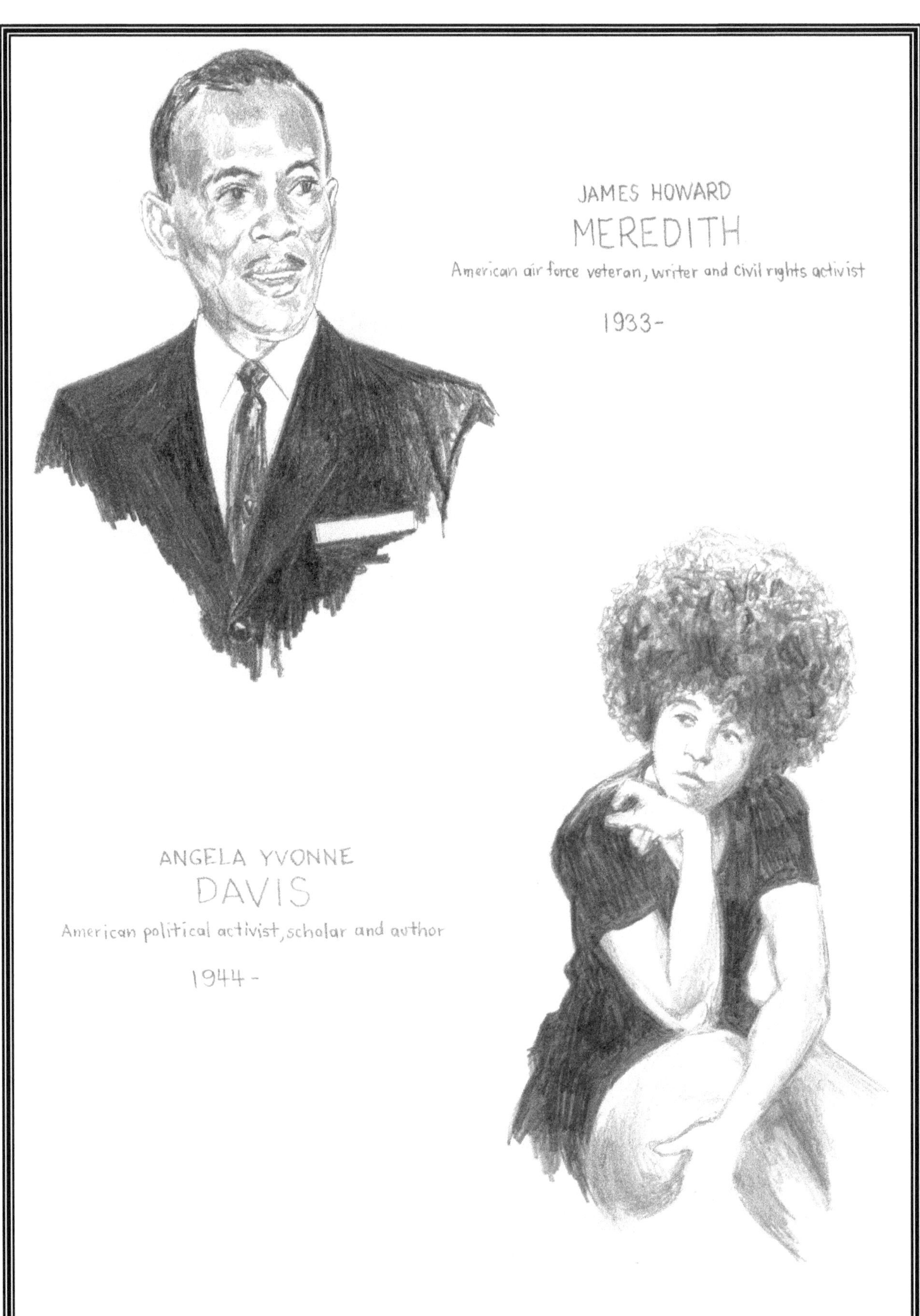

JAMES HOWARD
MEREDITH
American air force veteran, writer and civil rights activist

1933–

ANGELA YVONNE
DAVIS
American political activist, scholar and author

1944–

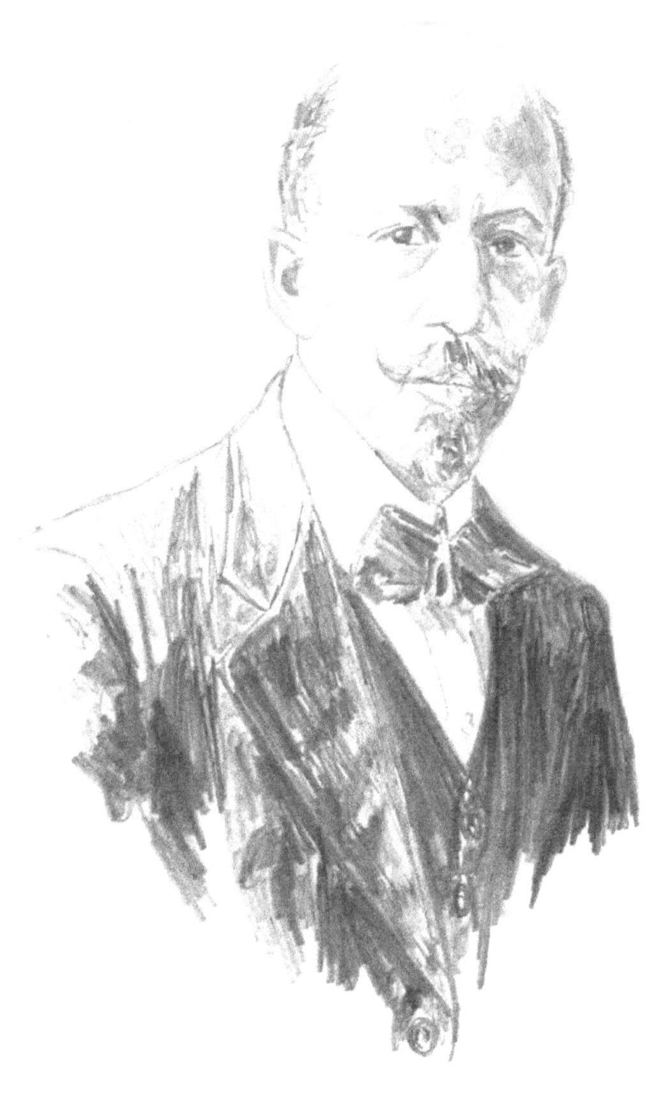

WILLIAM EDWARD BURGHARDT
DuBOIS
American sociologist, author and editor

1868 - 1963

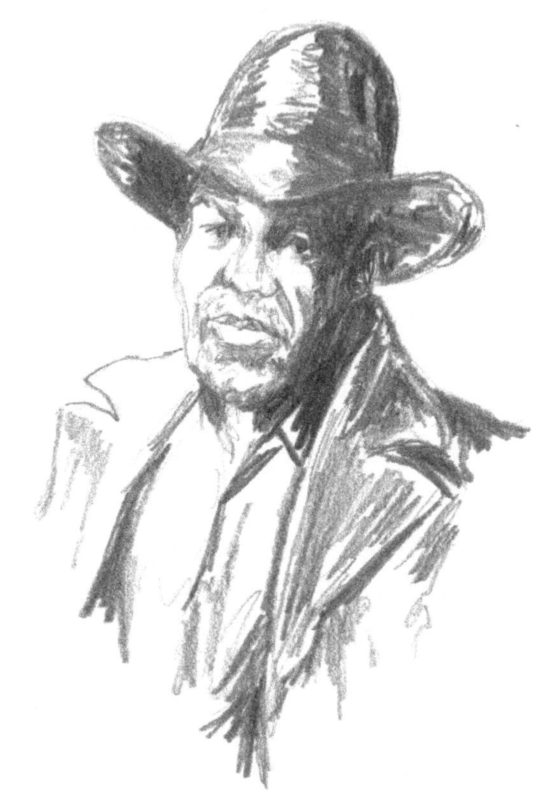

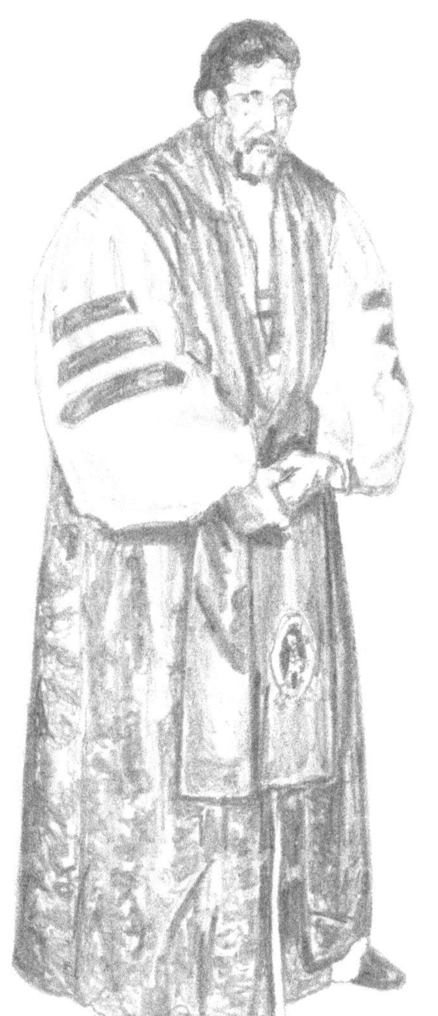

TURNER

African American slave revolutionary

1800-1831

WILLIAM J.

BARBER II

American Protestant minister and social activist

1963-

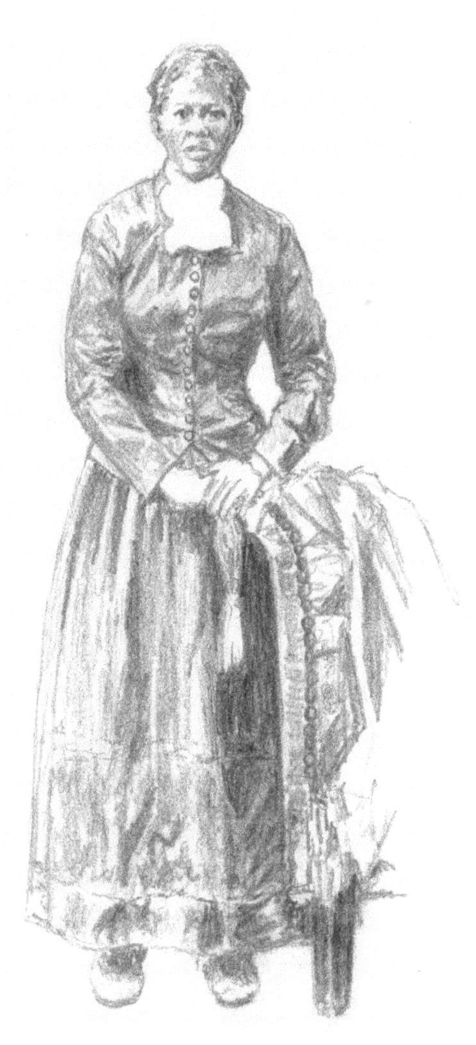

HARRIET
TUBMAN
American (escaped slave) abolitionist and political activist

1822-1913

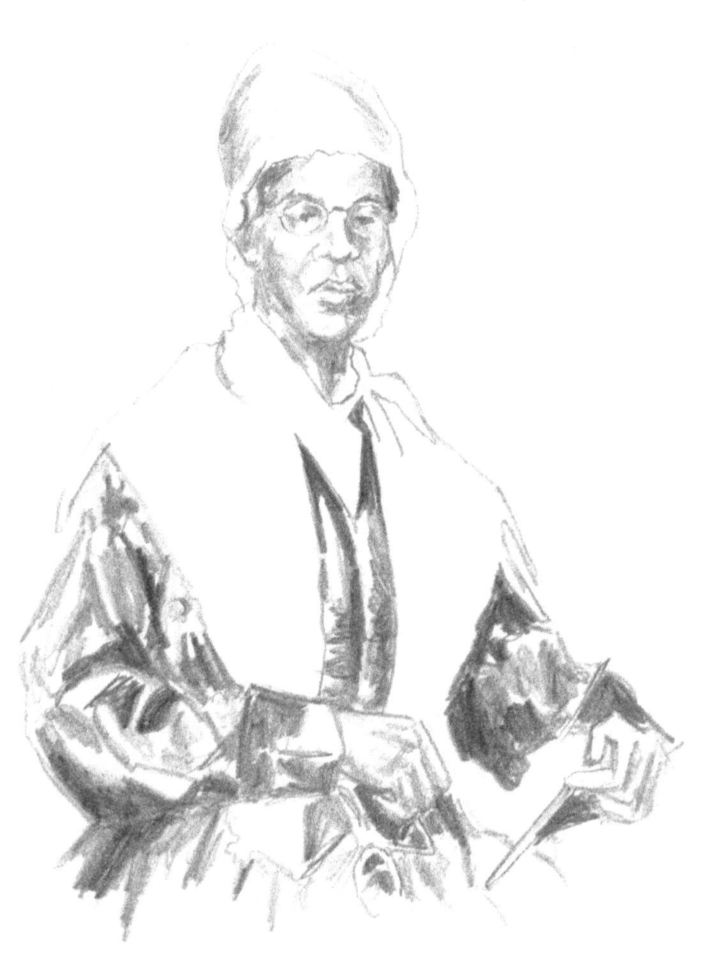

(ISABELLE BAUMFREE)
SOJOURNER
TRUTH
American (escaped slave) abolitionist
and women's rights activist

1797 - 1883

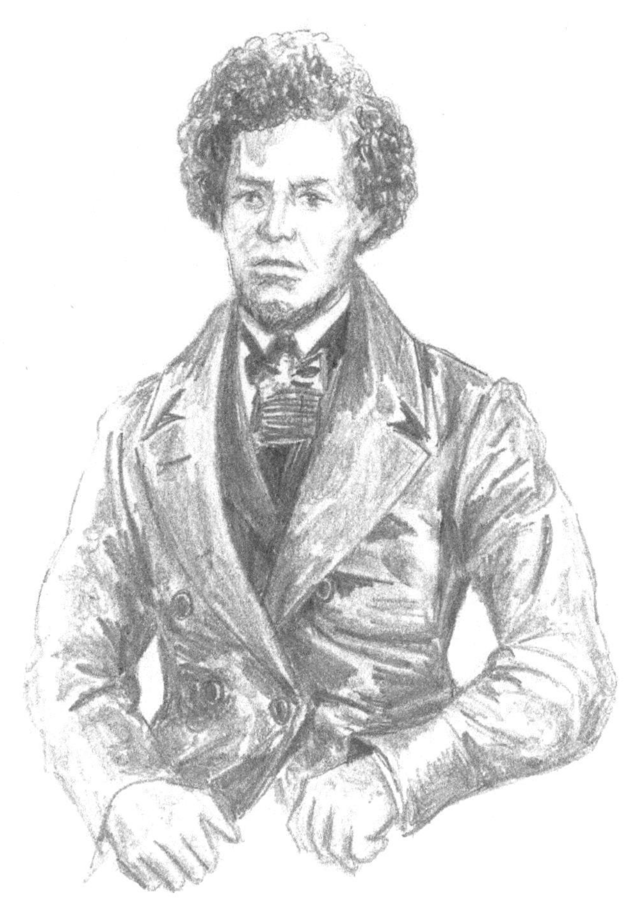

(FREDERICK AUGUSTUS WASHINGTON BAILEY)
FREDERICK
DOUGLASS
American (escaped slavery) abolitionist
orator, writer, social reformer and statesman

1818 - 1895

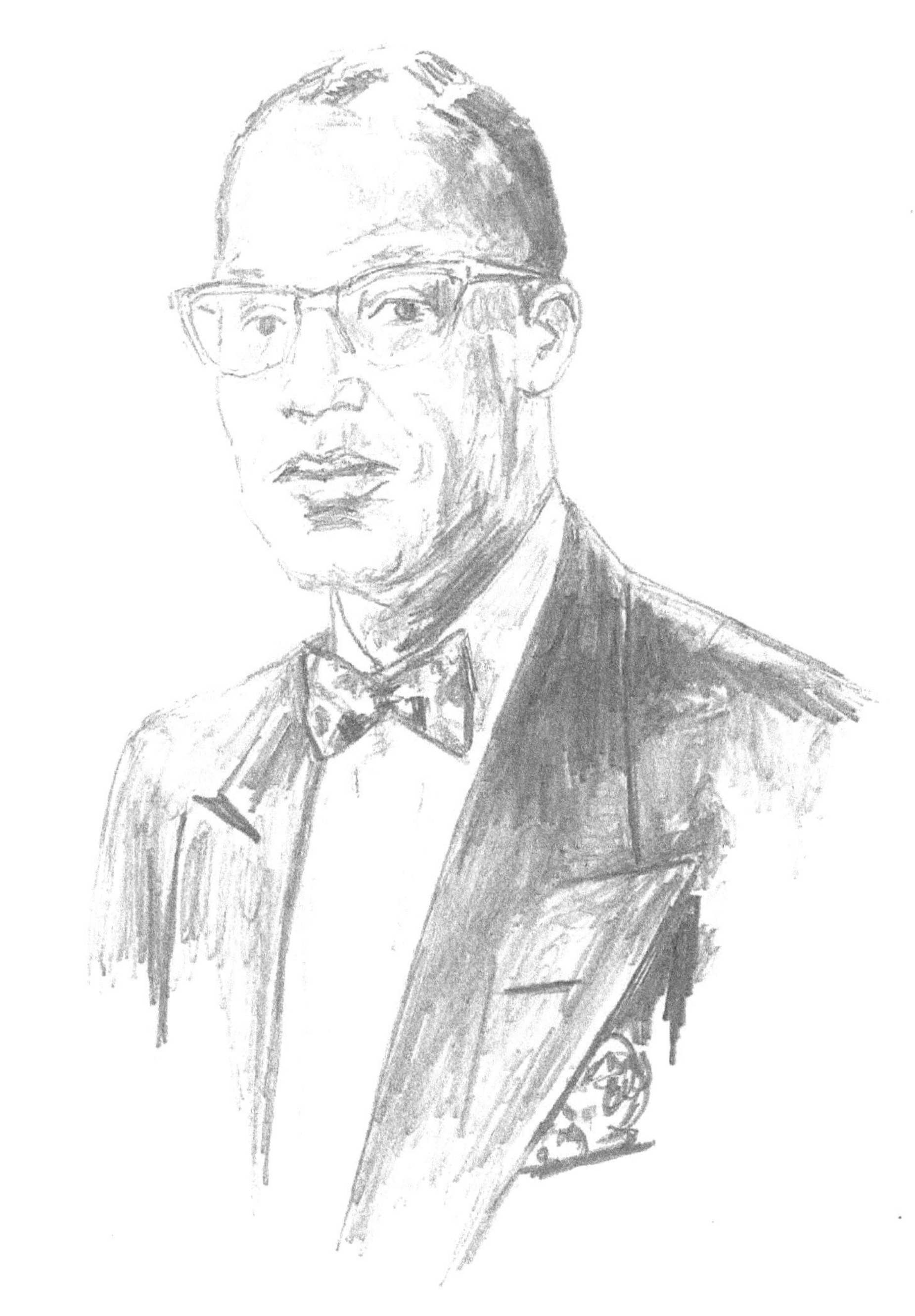

(LOUIS EUGENE WALCOTT) (LOUIS X)
LOUIS
FARRAKHAN
American violinist, religius leader and social activist

1933-

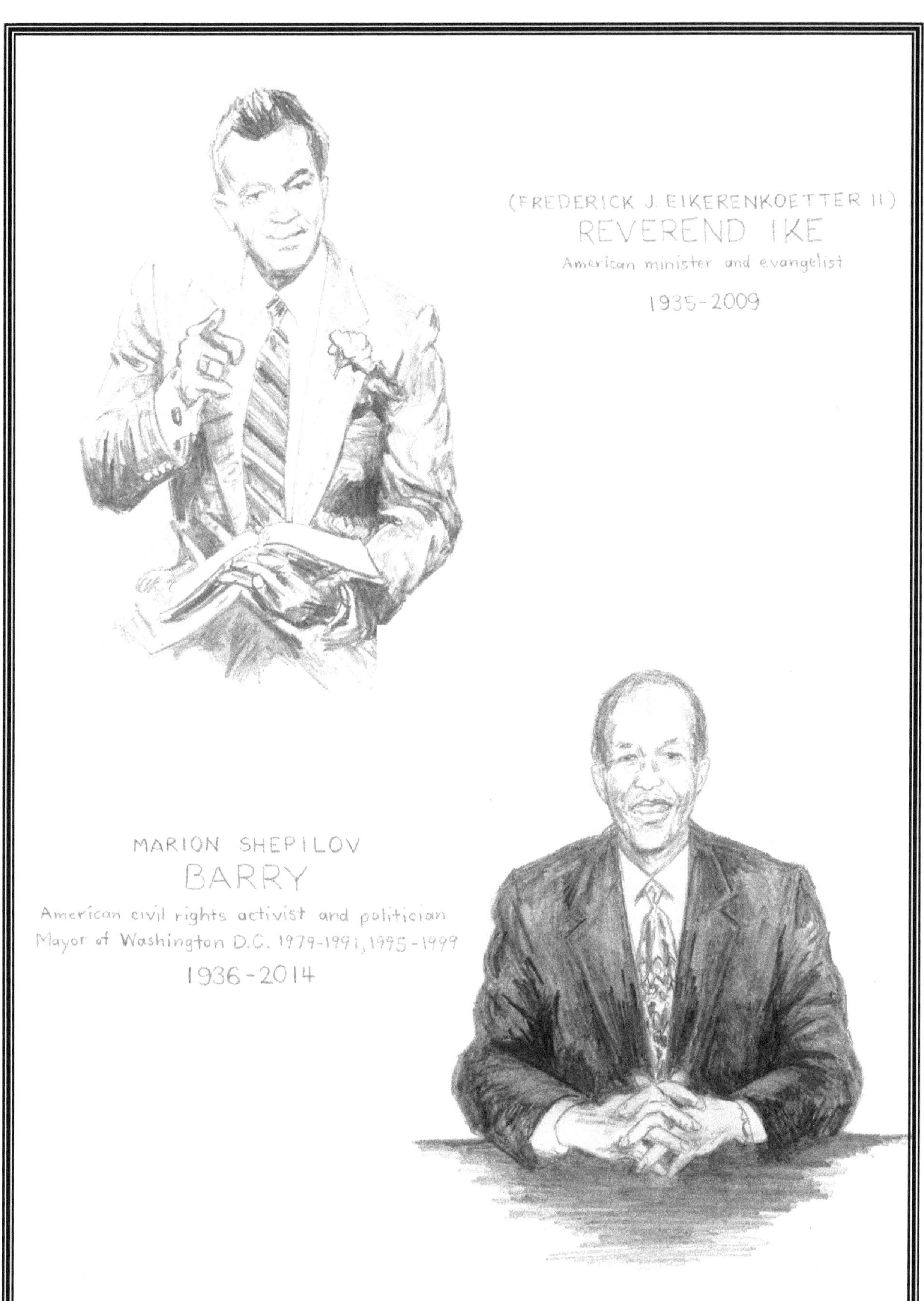

(FREDERICK J. EIKERENKOETTER II)
REVEREND IKE
American minister and evangelist

1935-2009

MARION SHEPILOV
BARRY
American civil rights activist and politician
Mayor of Washington D.C. 1979-1991, 1995-1999

1936-2014

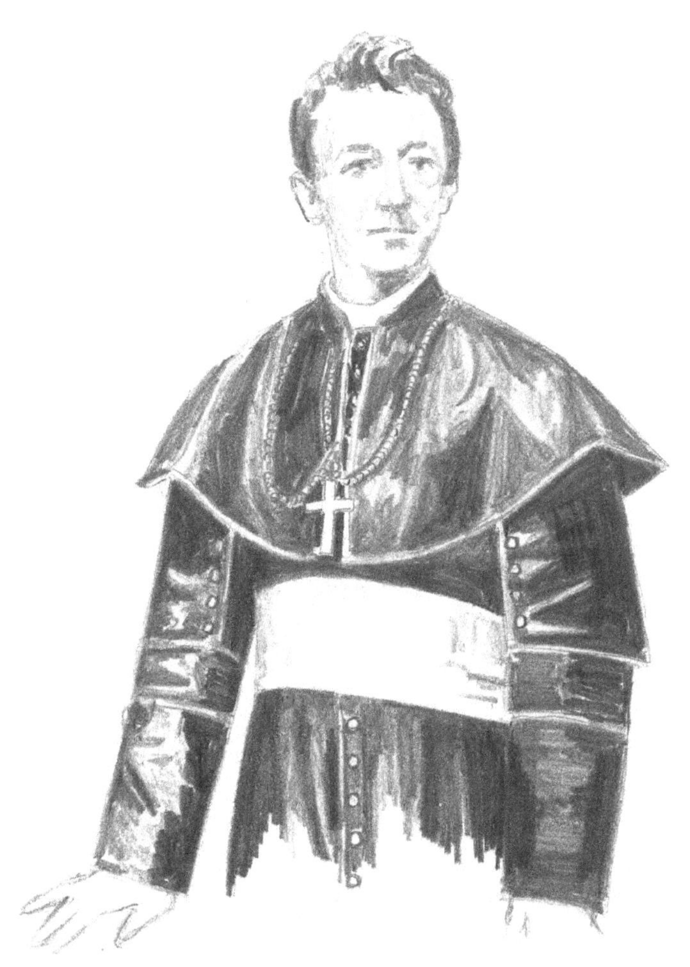

JAMES AUGUSTINE
HEALY
American Roman Catholic bishop

1830 - 1900

Historians and Scholars

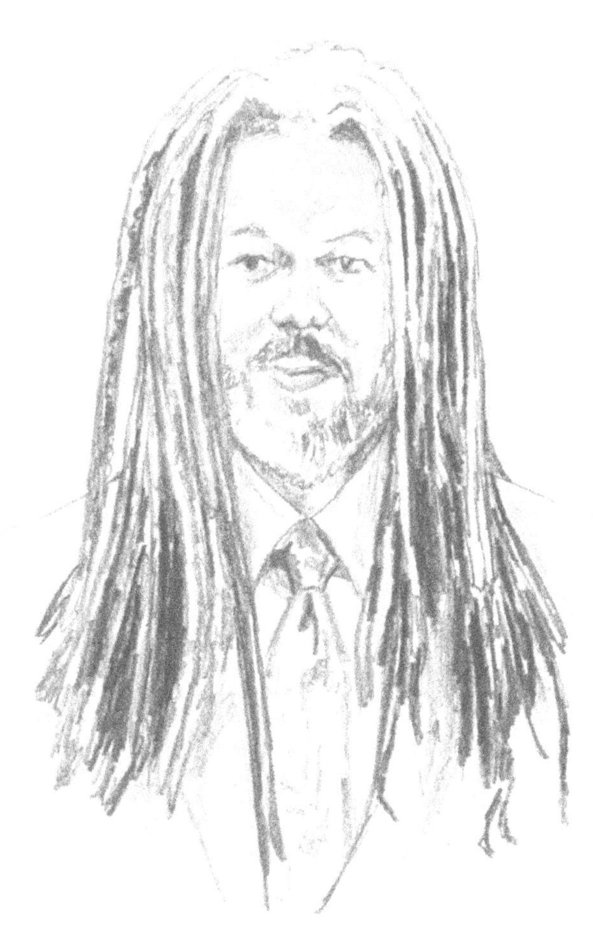

VINCENT
BROWN
American historian

1967-

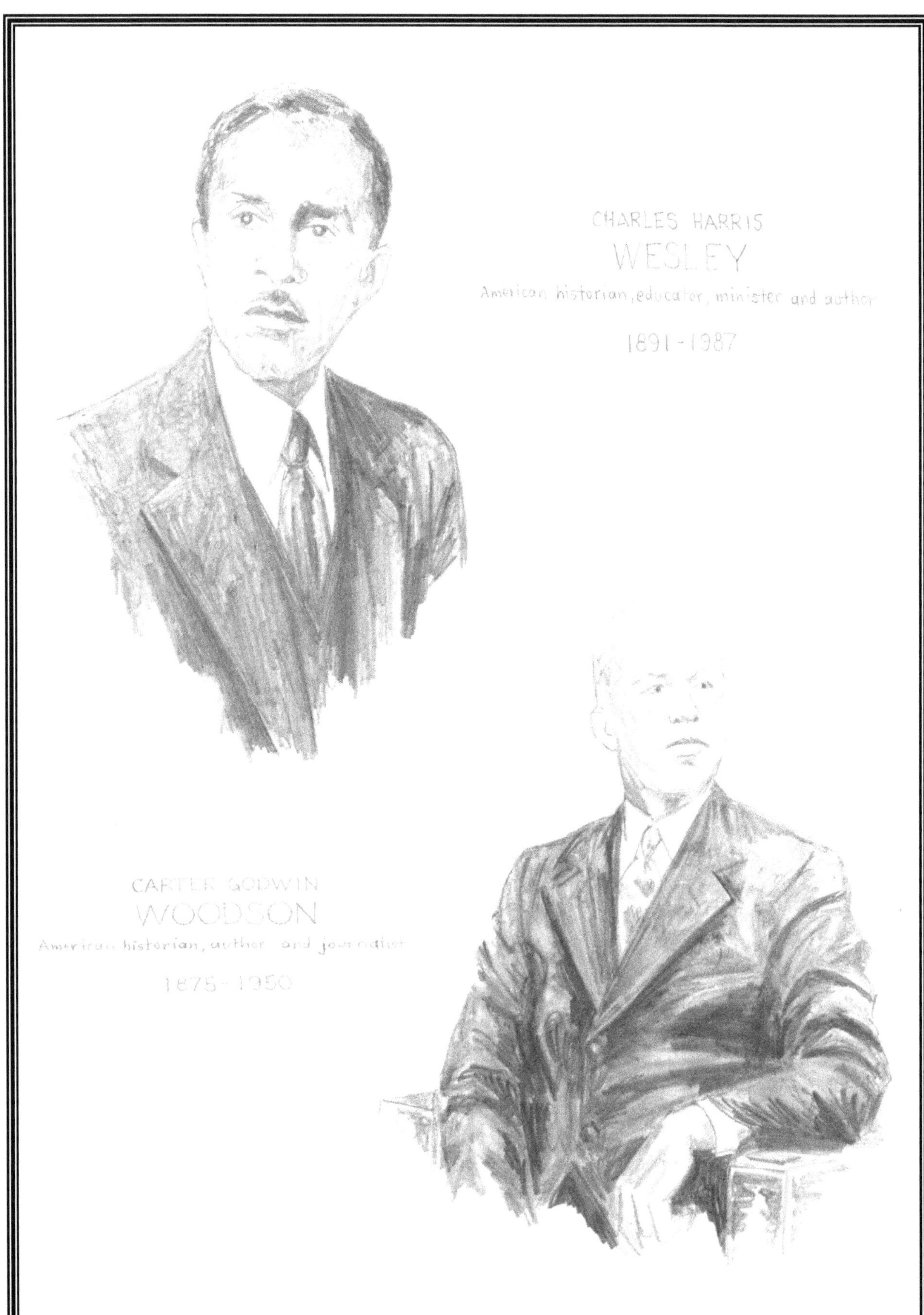

CHARLES HARRIS
WESLEY
American historian, educator, minister and author
1891 - 1987

CARTER GODWIN
WOODSON
American historian, author and journalist
1875 - 1950

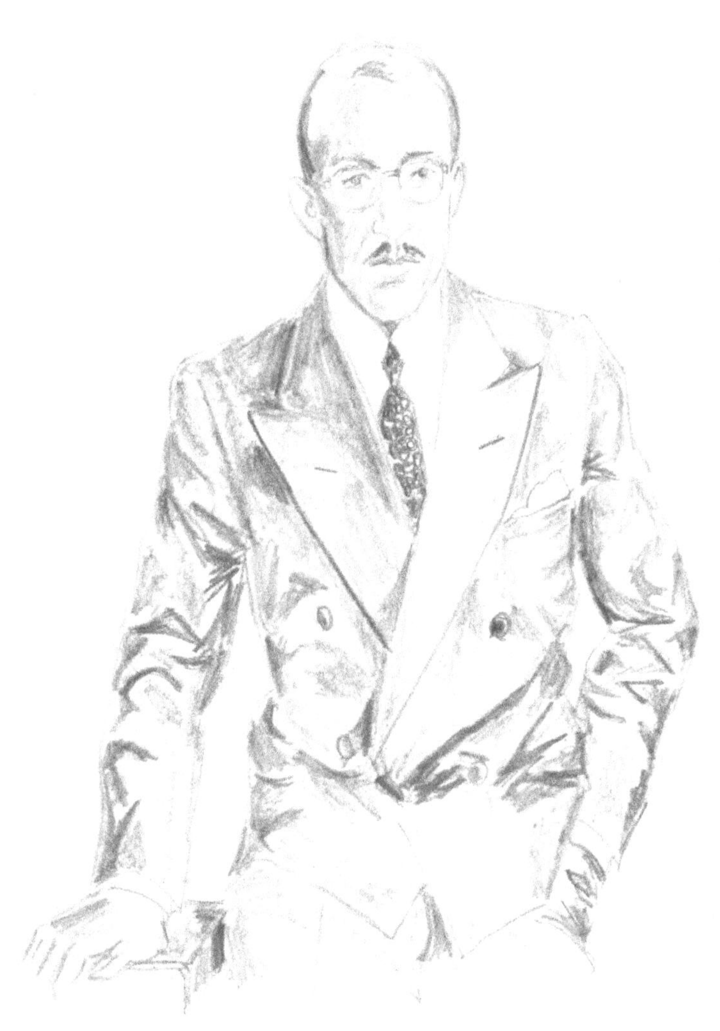

CHARLES SPURGEON

JOHNSON

American sociologist, reformer and scholar

1893 - 1956

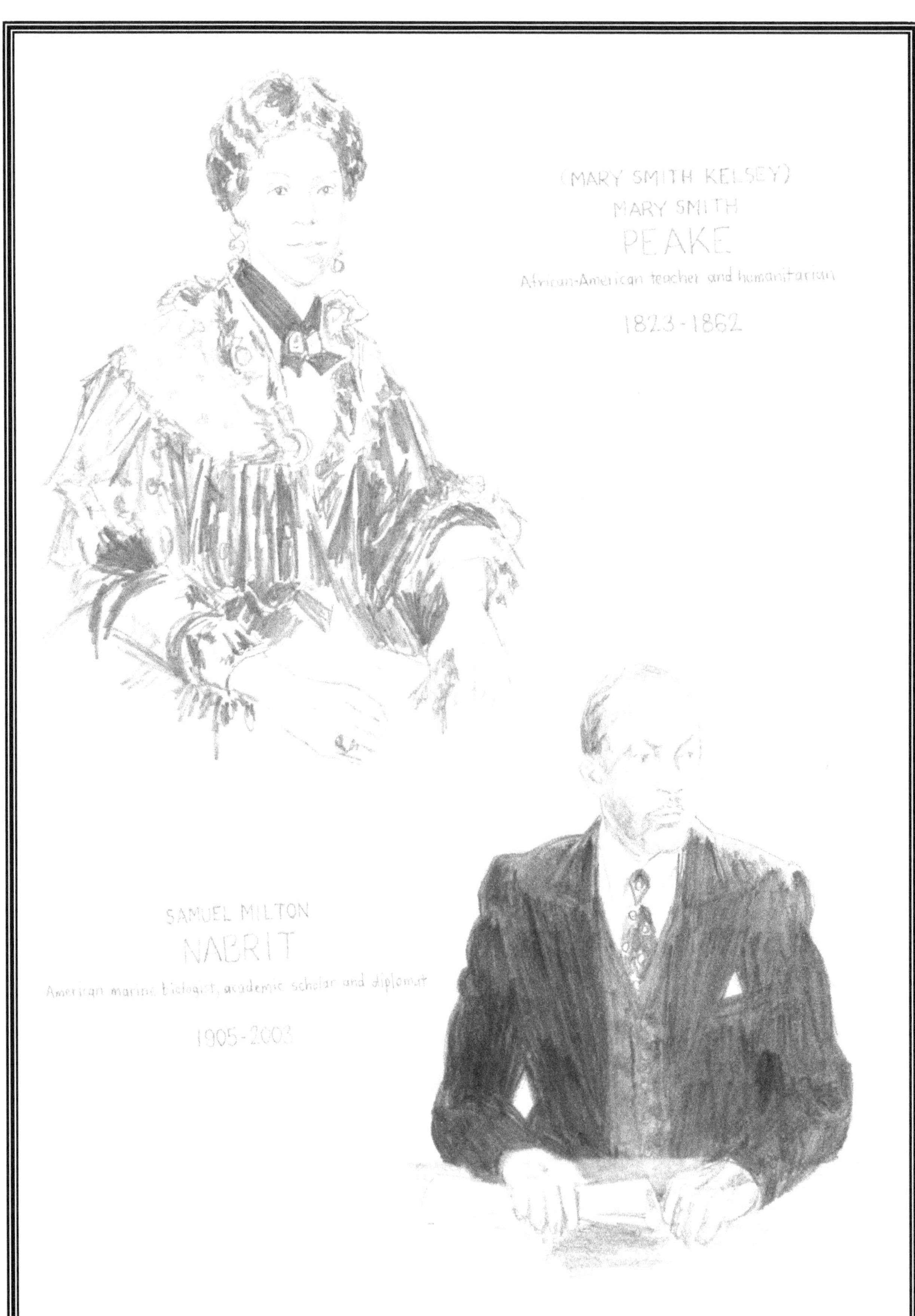
(MARY SMITH KELSEY)
MARY SMITH
PEAKE
African-American teacher and humanitarian

1823-1862

SAMUEL MILTON
NABRIT
American marine biologist, academic scholar and diplomat

1905-2003

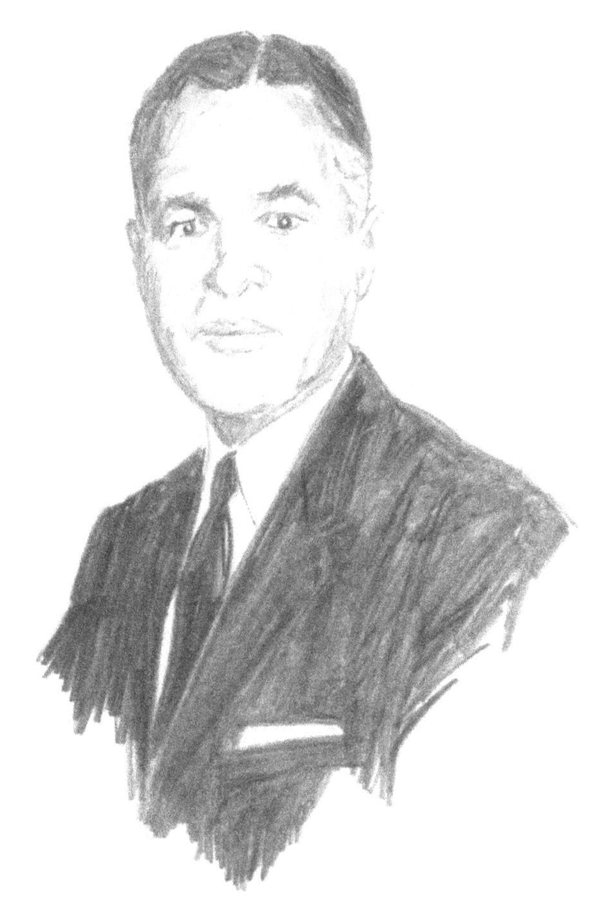

RALPH JOHNSON
BUNCHE
American political scientist and diplomat,
winner of Nobel Peace Prize (1950)

1903-1971

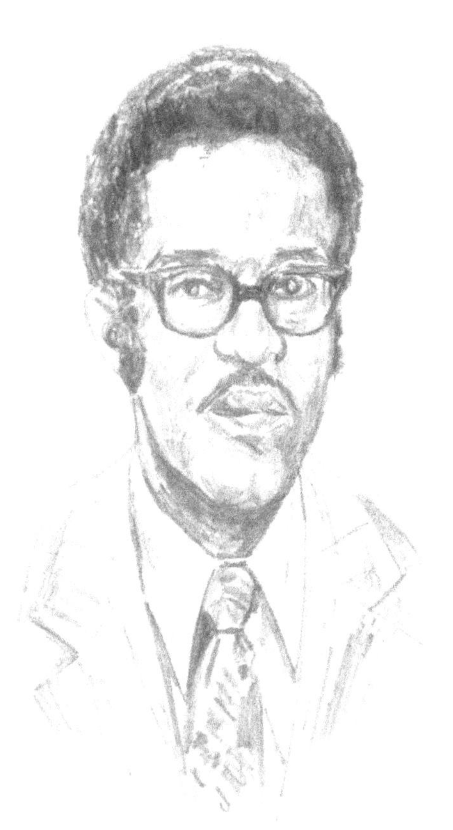

JOHN WESLEY
BLASSINGAME
American historian

1940 - 2000

VIRGINIA ESTELLE
RANDOLPH
American schoolteacher

1870 - 1958

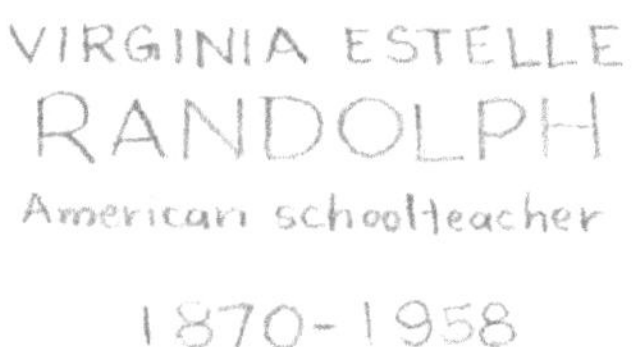

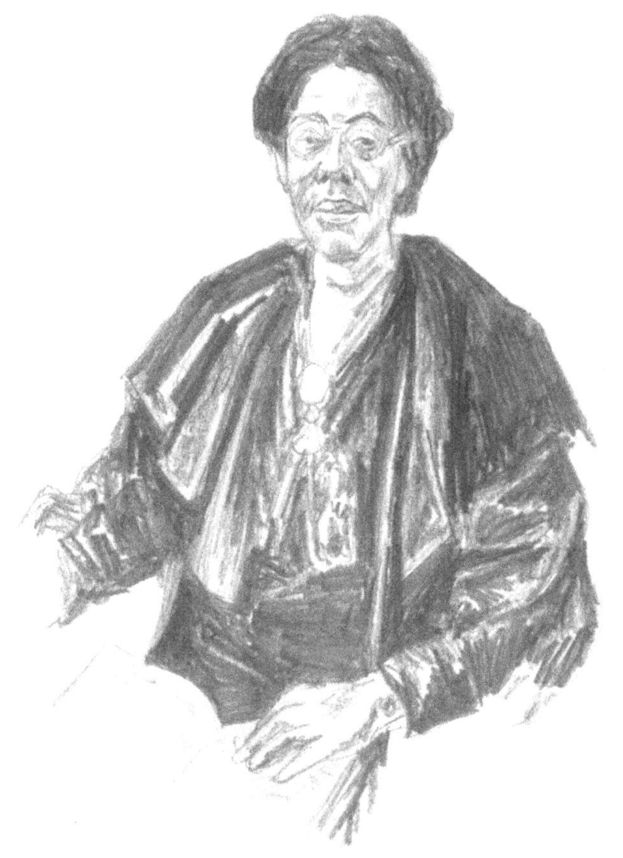

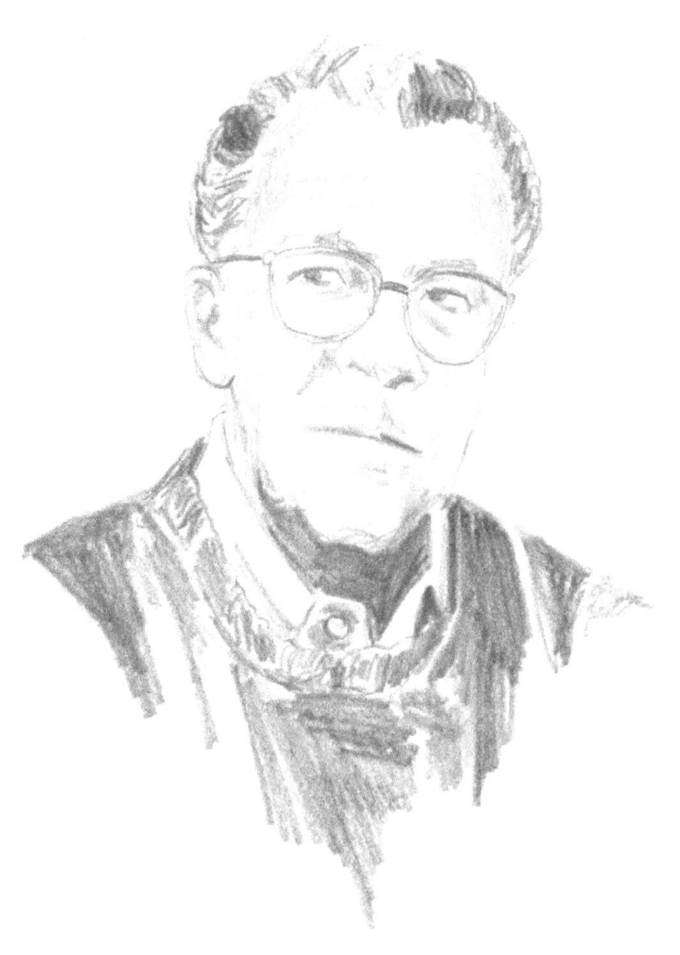

DAVID LEVERING
LEWIS
American historian

1936 -

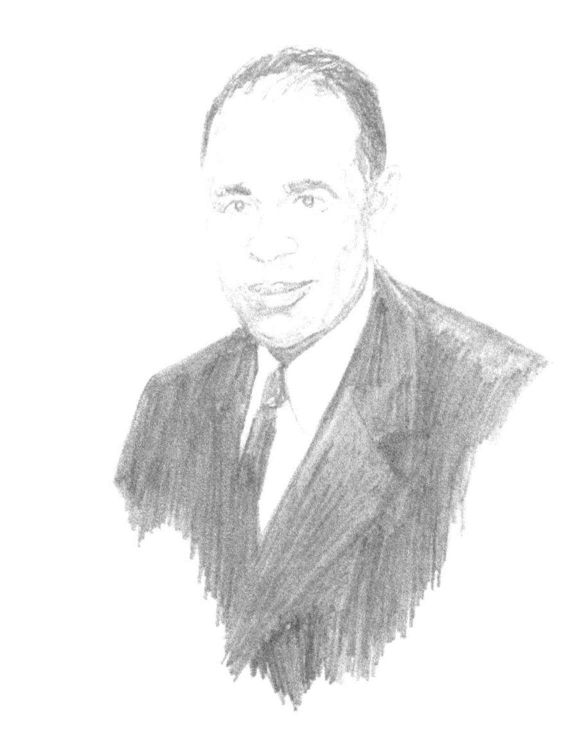

BENJAMIN ARTHUR
QUARLES
American historian, educator, writer and administrator

1904-1996

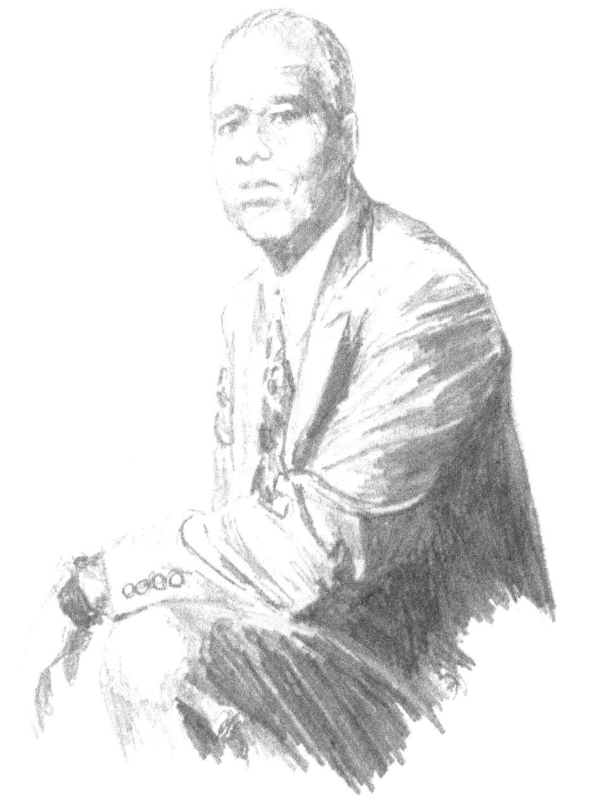

(JOHN HENRY CLARKE)
JOHN HENRIK
CLARKE
American historian and educator

1915-1998

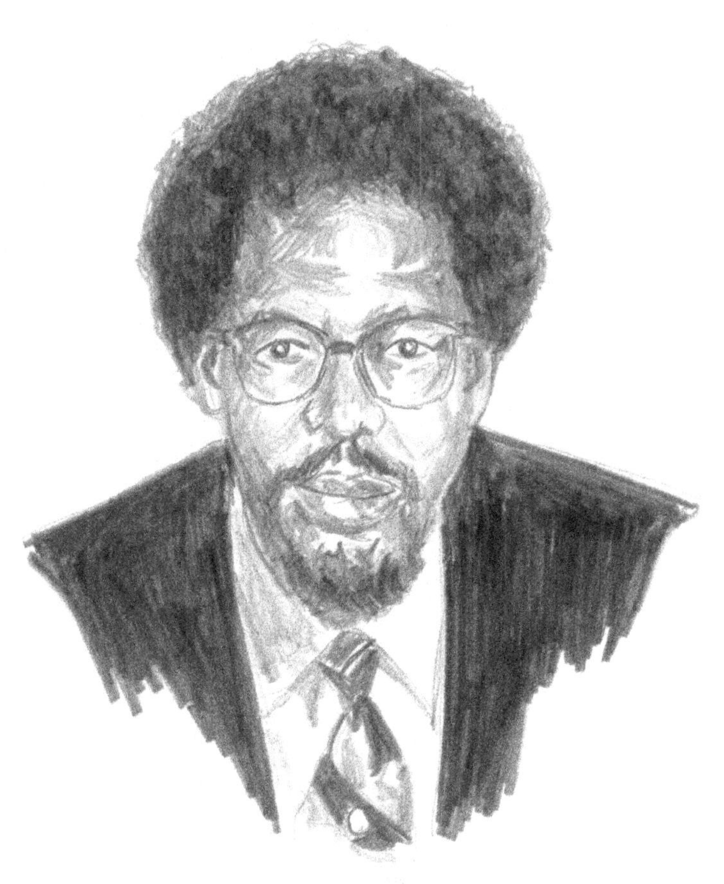

CORNEL RONALD
WEST
American philosopher, political,
activist, social critic and author

1953 -

Lawyers and Judges

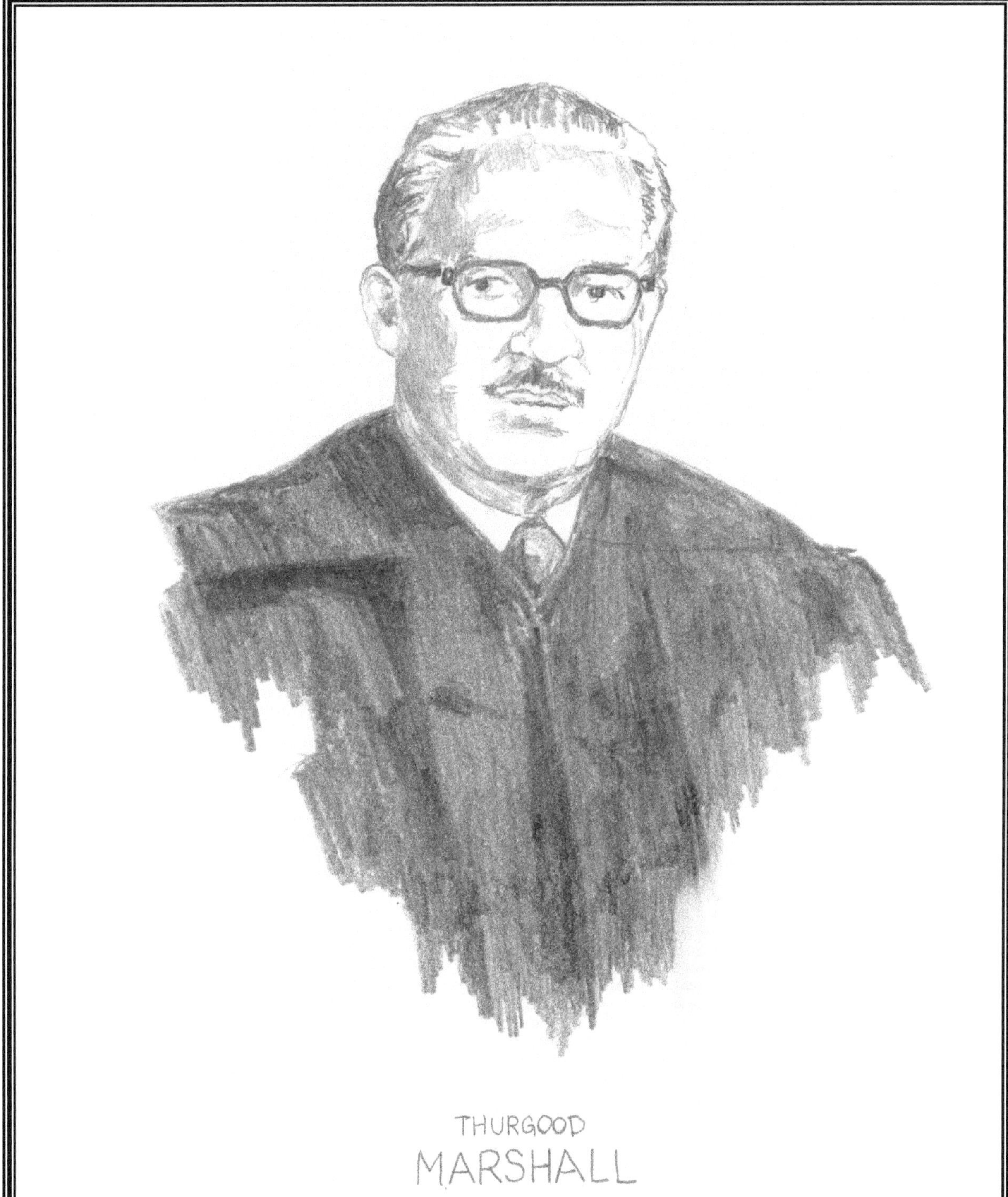

THURGOOD
MARSHALL
American civil rights lawyer
U.S. Supreme Court Justice 1968-1991
1908-1993

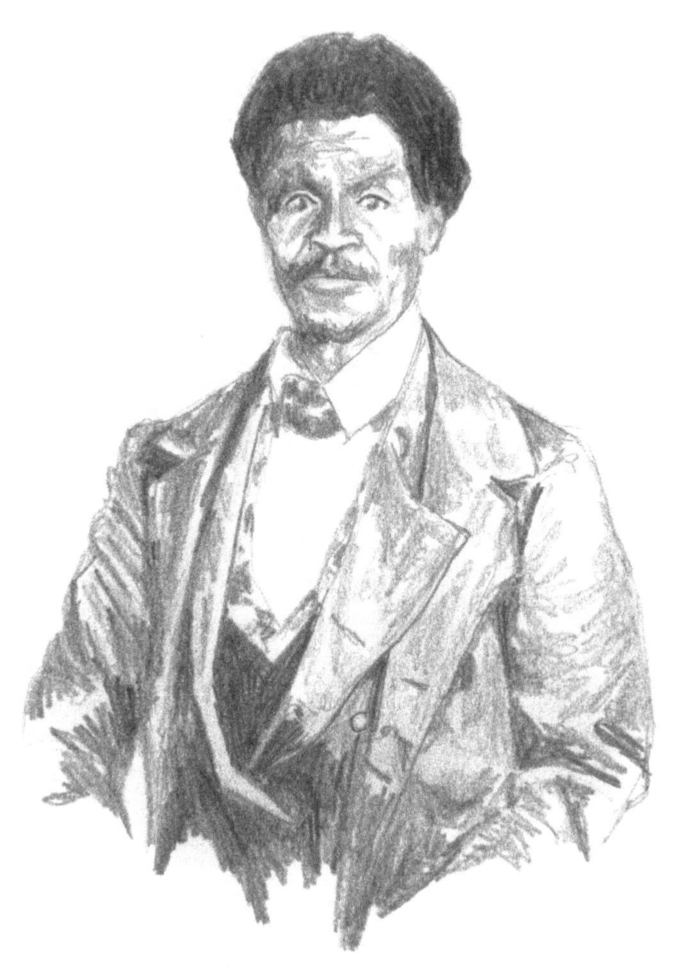

DRED
SCOTT
African-American slave and U.S. supreme court litigate

1799-1858

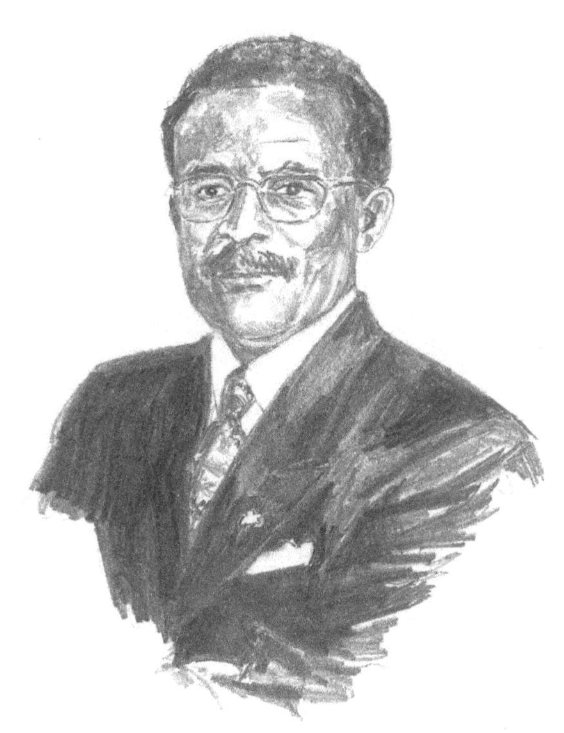

JOHNNIE LEE
COCHRAN Jr.
American lawyer

1937-2005

MARIAN WRIGHT
EDELMAN
American lawyer and social activist
founder of the Children's Defense Fund
1939-

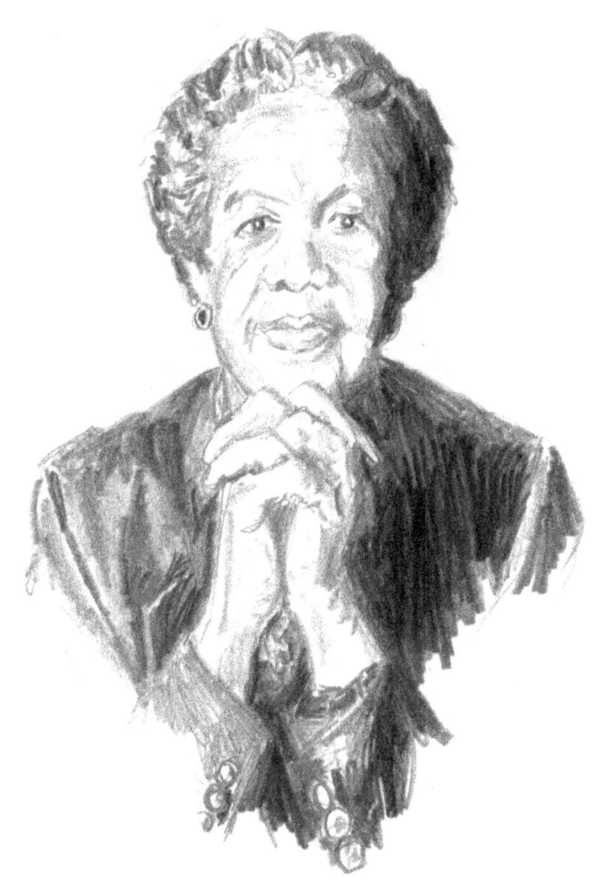

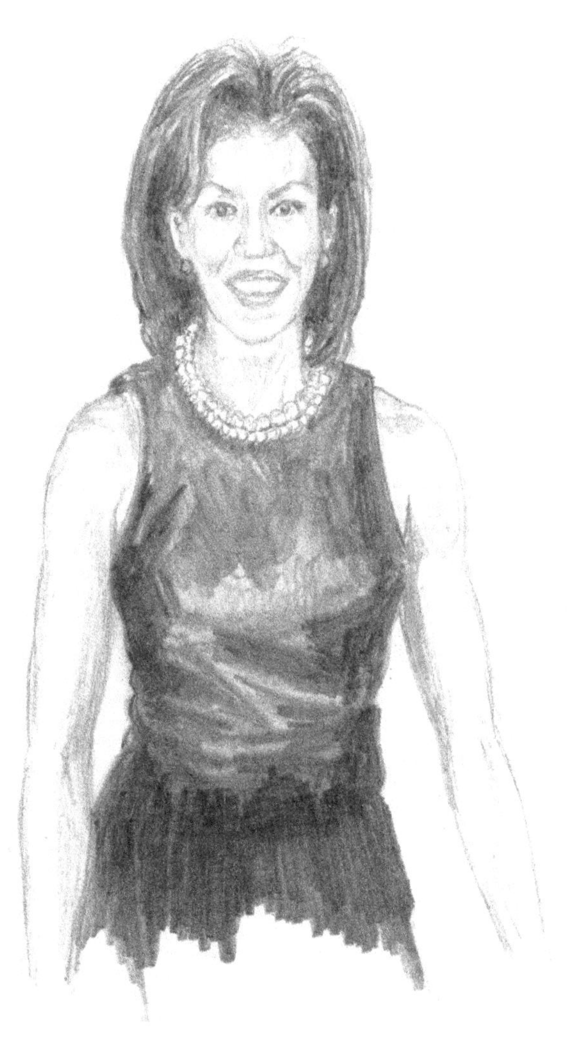

MICHELLE LaVAUGHN ROBINSON
OBAMA
American lawyer and writer,
First Lady and wife of President Barack Obama

1964 –

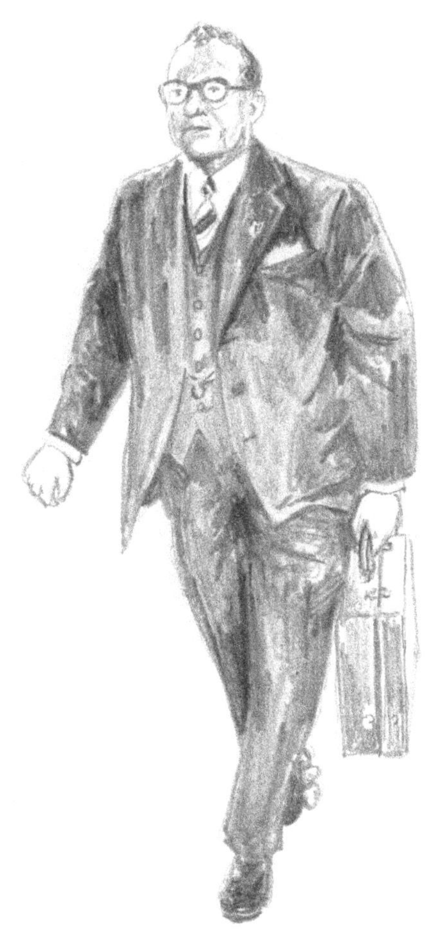

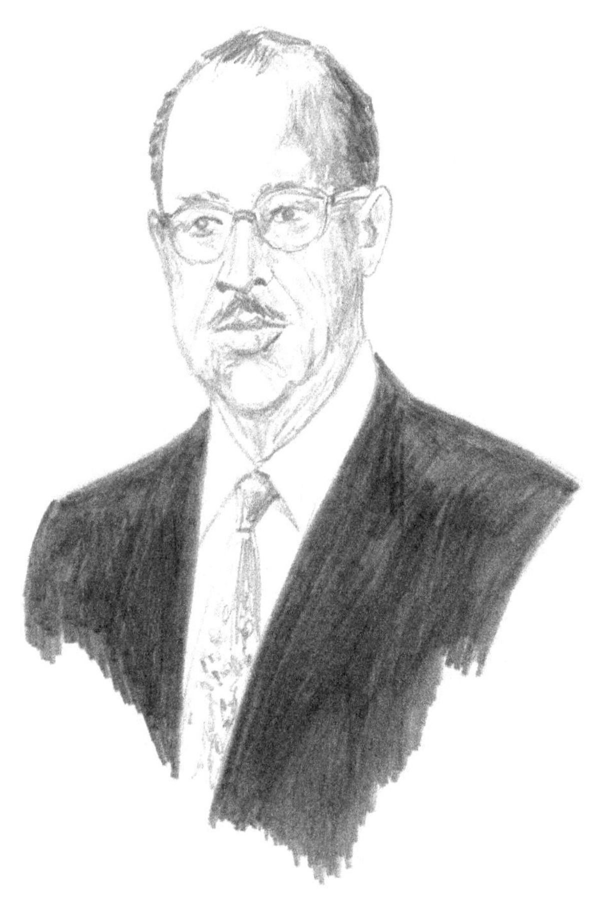

WILLIAM THADDEUS
COLEMAN Jr.

American lawyer, politician and judge
US Secretary of Transportation 1975-1977

1920-2017

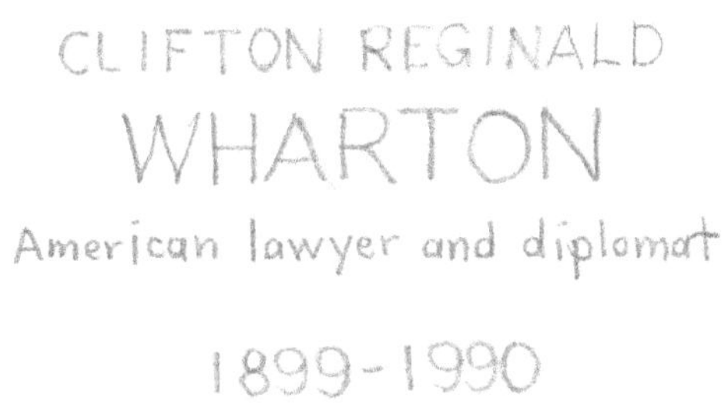

CLIFTON REGINALD
WHARTON

American lawyer and diplomat

1899-1990

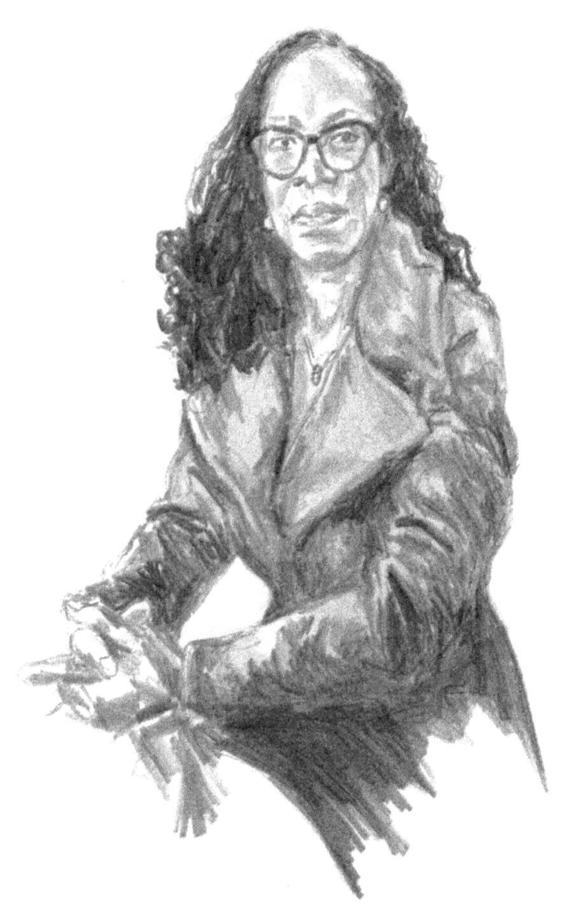

KETANJI ONYIKA BROWN
JACKSON
American lawyer, jurist and
U.S. Supreme Court Justice 2022–

1970–

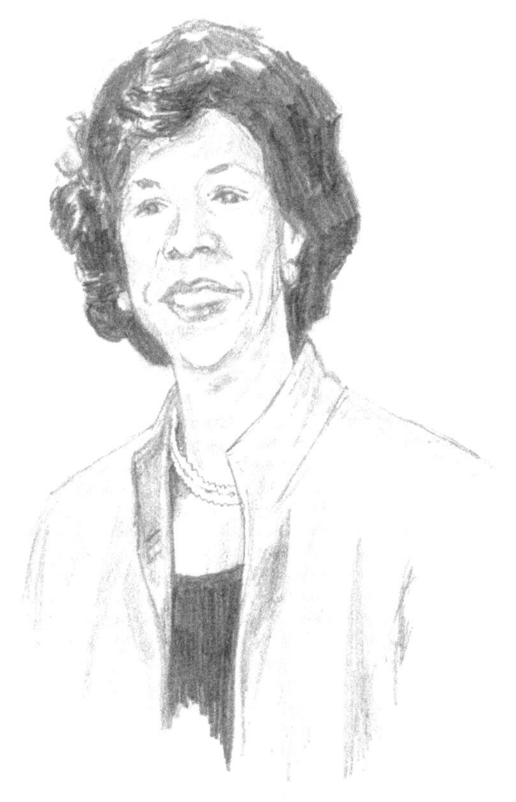

GABRIELLE ANNE KIRK
McDONALD
American lawyer and judge

1942–

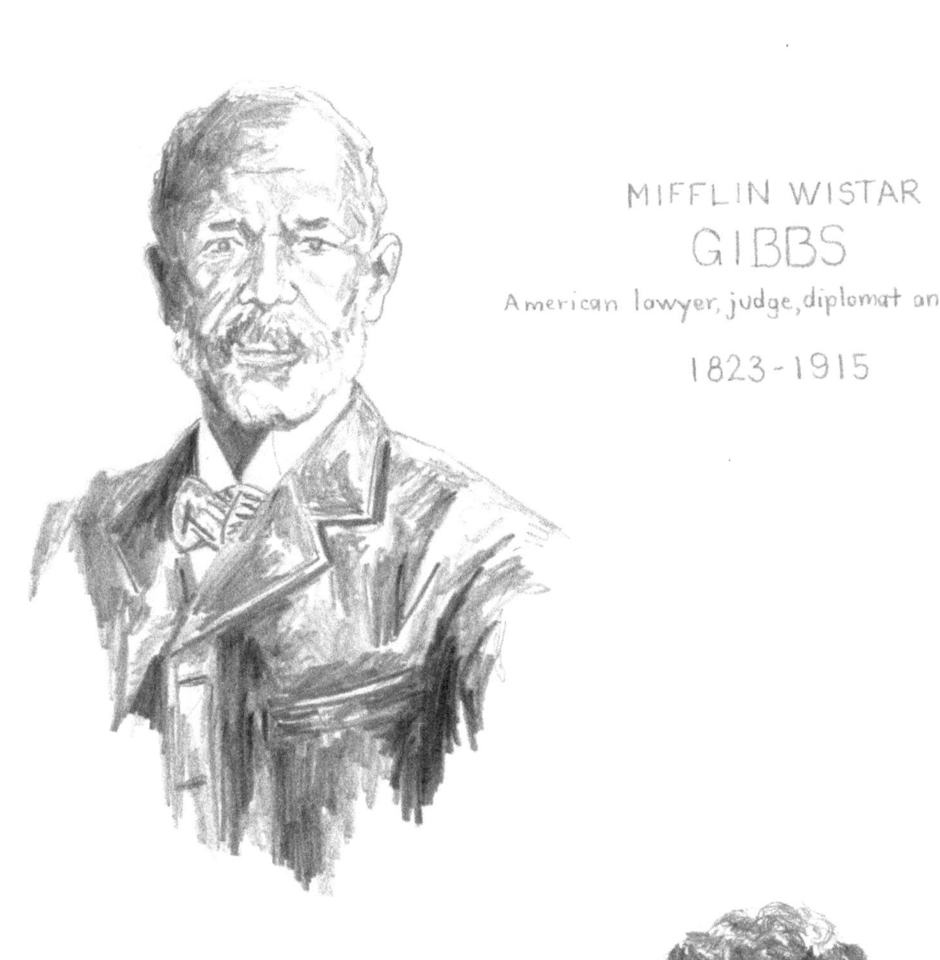

MIFFLIN WISTAR
GIBBS
American lawyer, judge, diplomat and banker

1823-1915

BARBARA CHARLINE
JORDAN
American lawyer, educator, politician and U.S. congresswoman

1936-1996

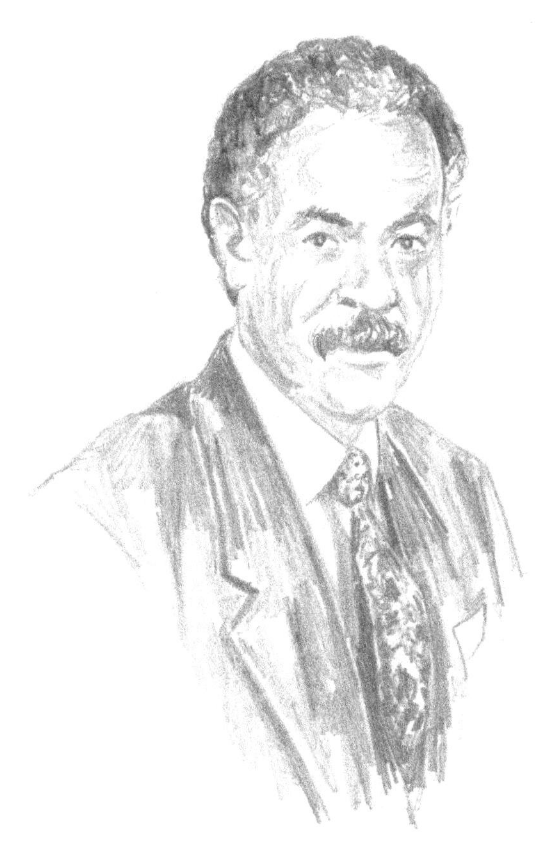

"RON" RONALD HARMON

BROWN

American politician
U.S. Secretary of Commerce 1993-1996

1941-1996

Military Leaders

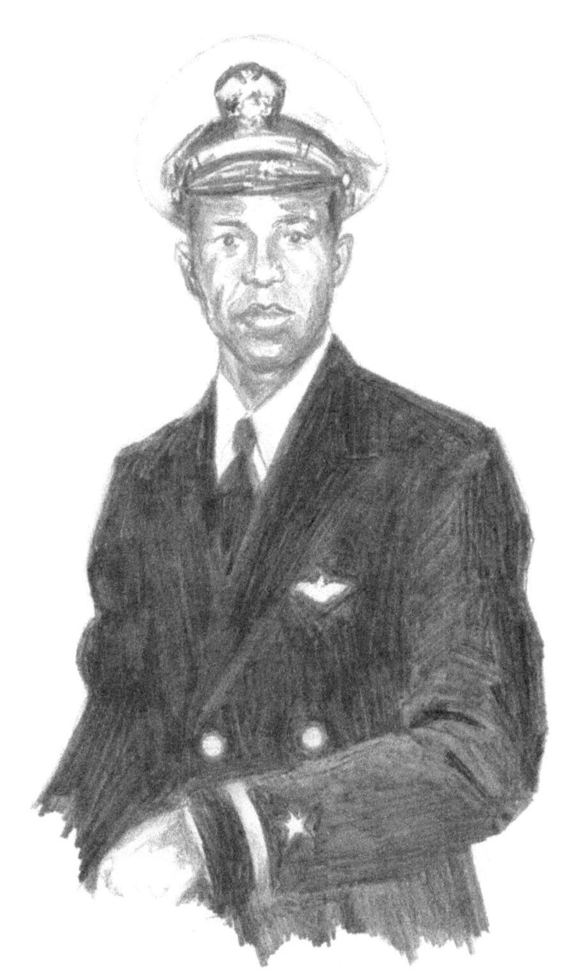

JESSE LEROY
BROWN
American naval officer and pilot during the Korean War

1926 - 1950

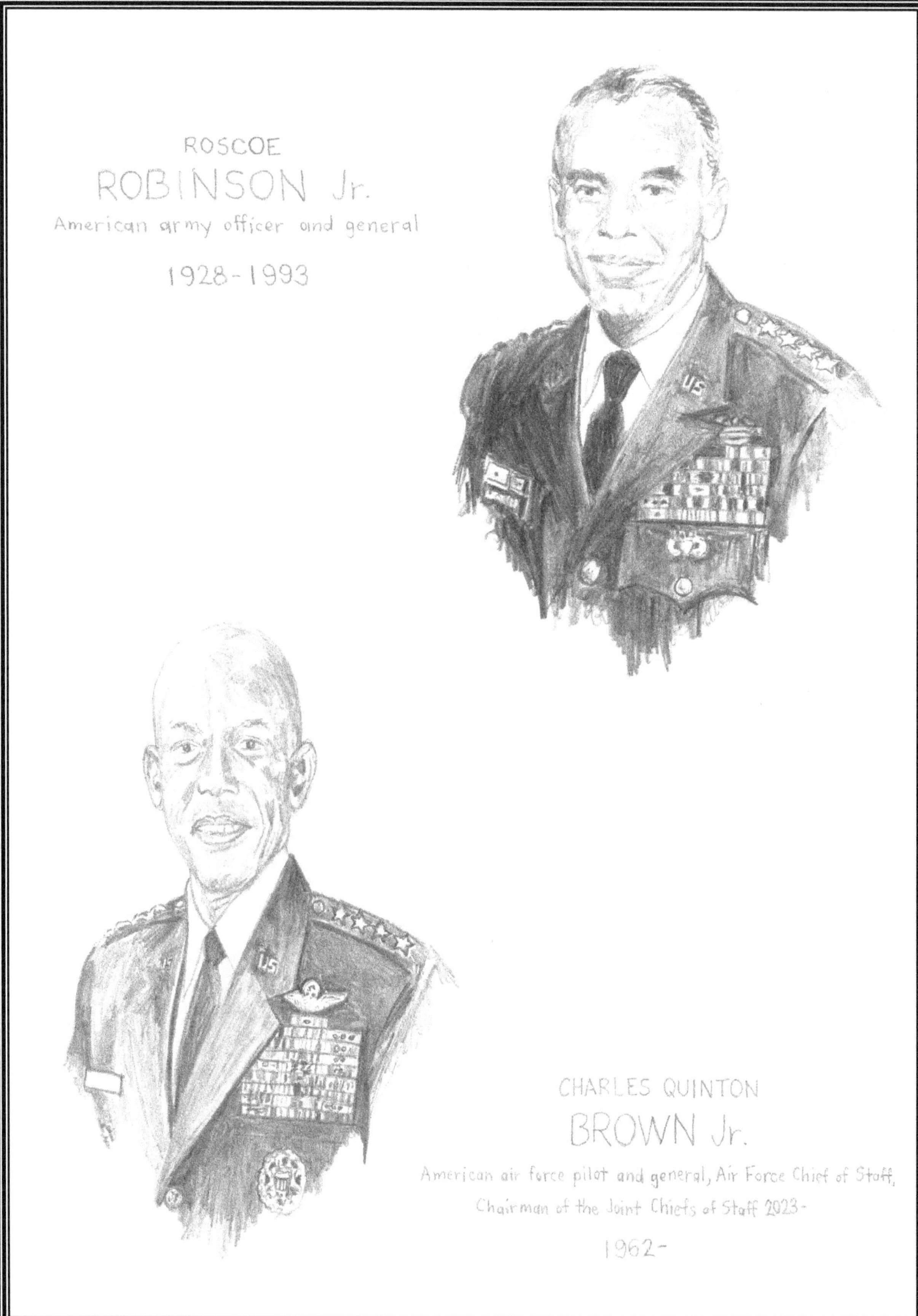

ROSCOE
ROBINSON Jr.
American army officer and general

1928-1993

CHARLES QUINTON
BROWN Jr.
American air force pilot and general, Air Force Chief of Staff,
Chairman of the Joint Chiefs of Staff 2023-

1962-

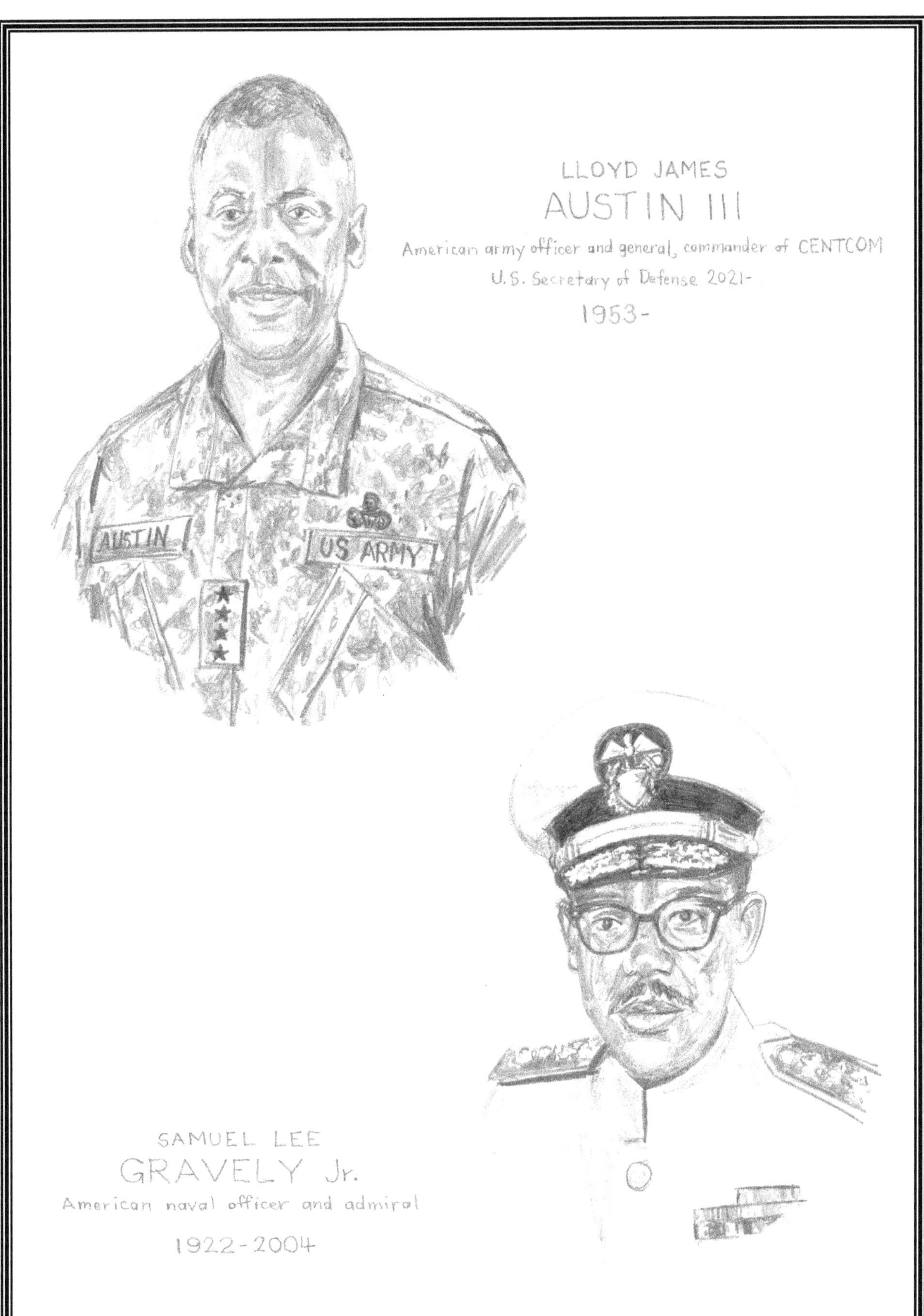

LLOYD JAMES
AUSTIN III
American army officer and general, commander of CENTCOM
U.S. Secretary of Defense 2021-
1953-

SAMUEL LEE
GRAVELY Jr.
American naval officer and admiral
1922-2004

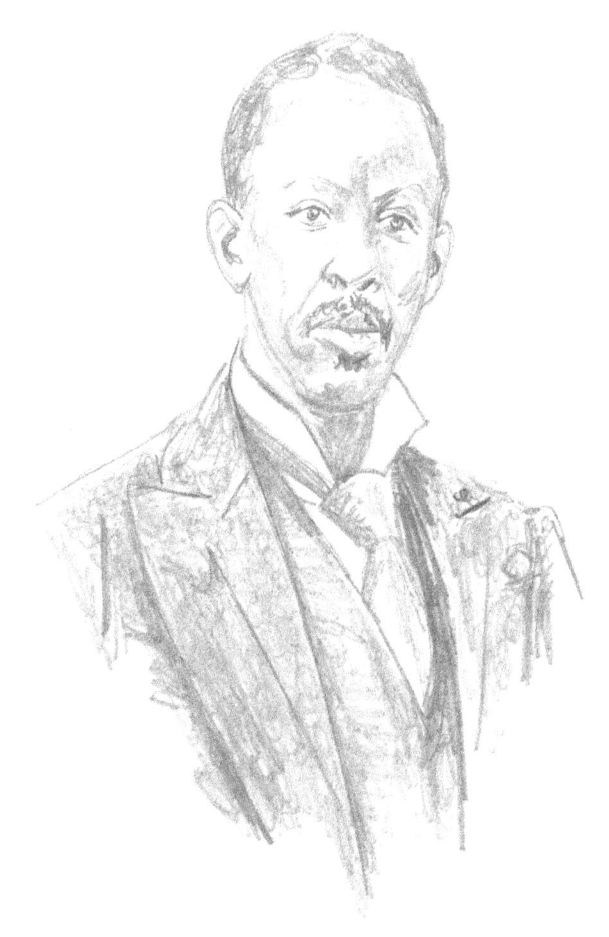

RICHARD ROBERT
WRIGHT
American army officer, educator, administrator,
politician, civil rights advocate and banking entrepreneur
1855 - 1947

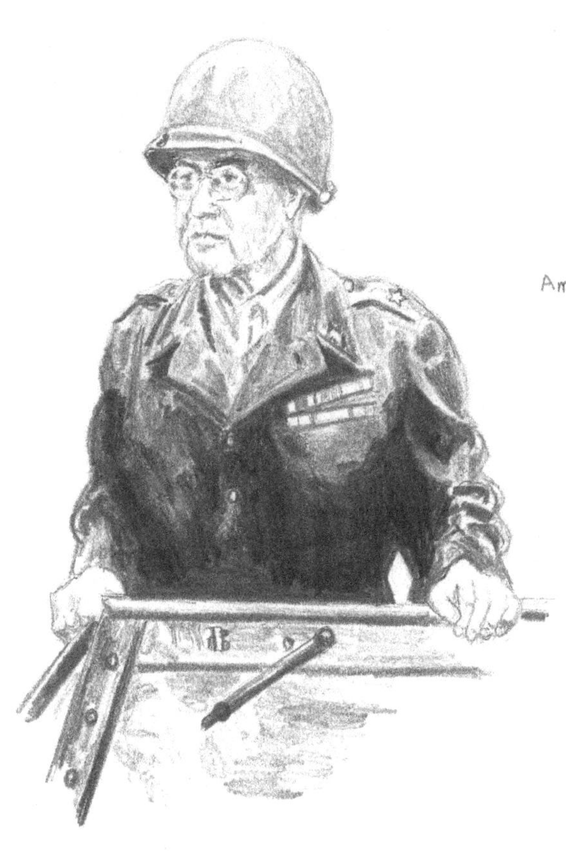

BENJAMIN OLIVER
DAVIS
American soldier, army officer and general

1877-1970

BENJAMIN OLIVER
DAVIS Jr.
American (Tuskegee Airman) fighter pilot
during World War II and the Korean War, air force officer,
general and civil servant, son of Benjamin O Davis

1912-2002

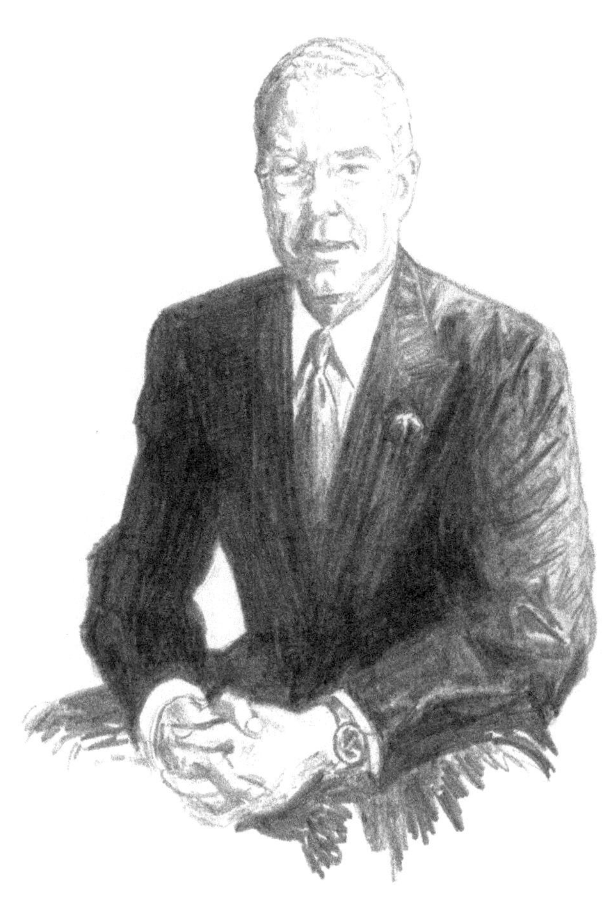

COLIN LUTHER
POWELL

American army officer and general, statesman and
diplomat, Chairman of the Joint Chiefs of Staff 1989-1993
U.S. Secretary of State 2001-2005

1937-2021

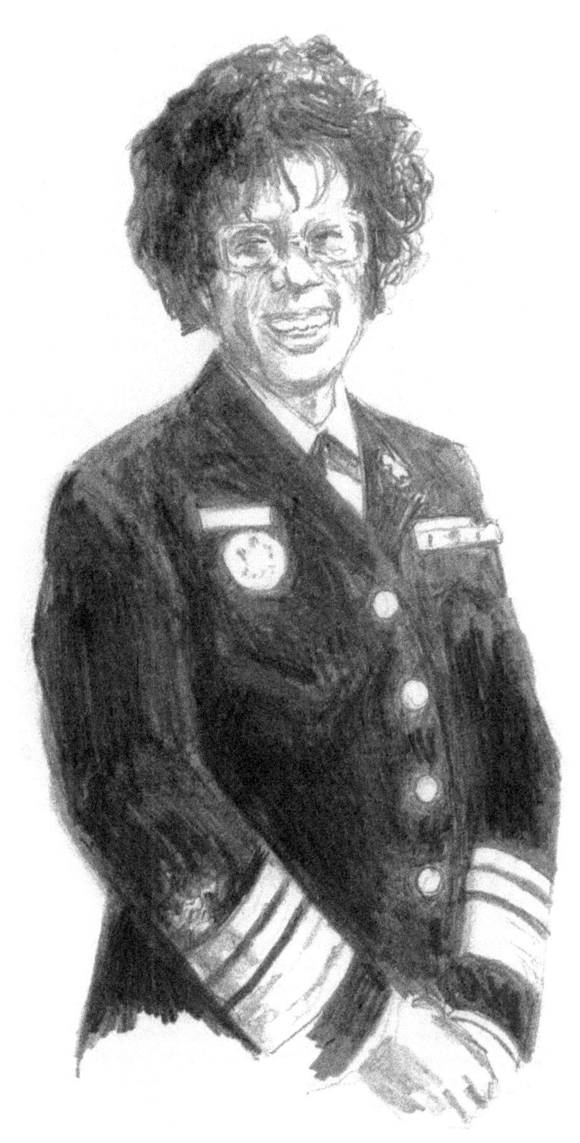

MINNIE JOYCELYN
ELDERS

American pediatrician, vice-admiral in the Public Health Service
Commissional Corps and surgeon-general of the U.S. 1993-1994

1933-

Diverse Careers

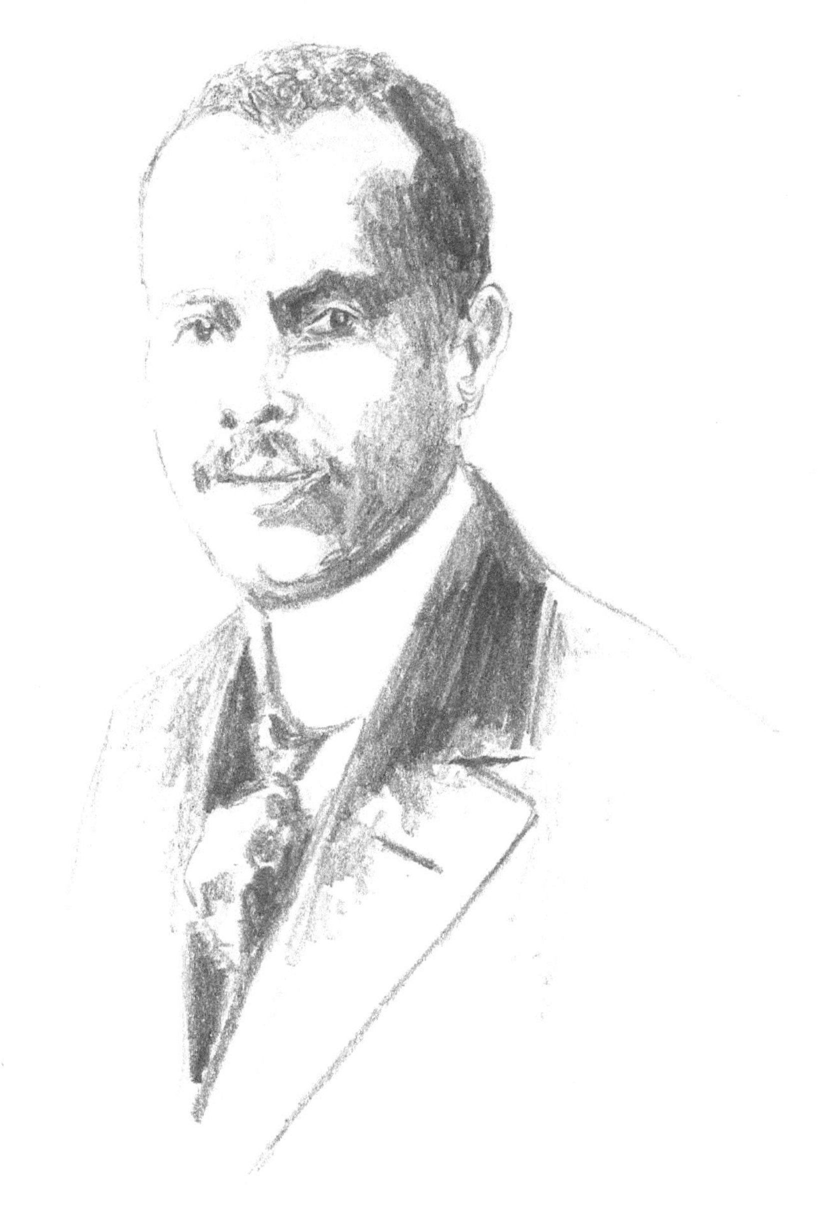

JAMES WELDON

JOHNSON

American author, educator, lawyer, diplomat,
songwriter and civil rights activist

1871 - 1938

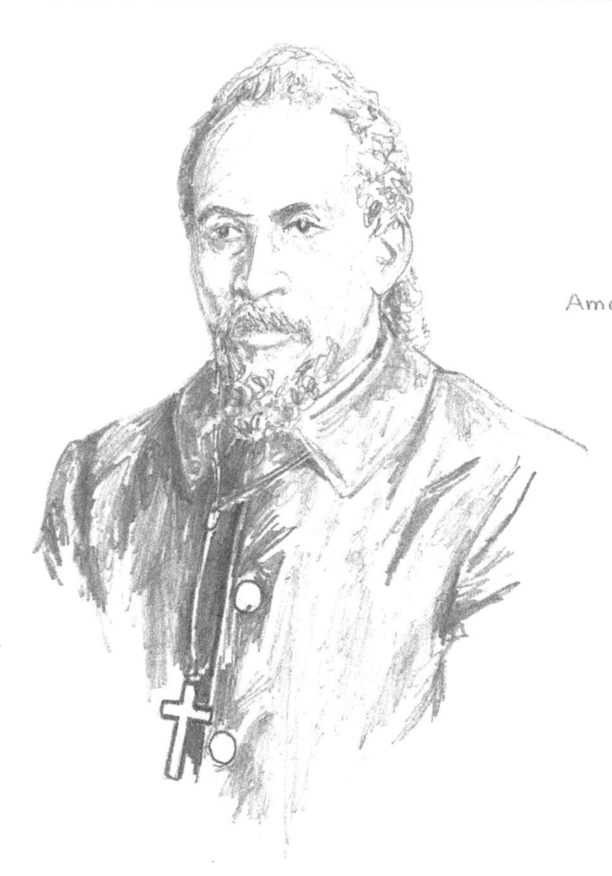

BENJAMIN TUCKER
TANNER
American African Methodist Episcopal
clergyman and editor
1835-1923

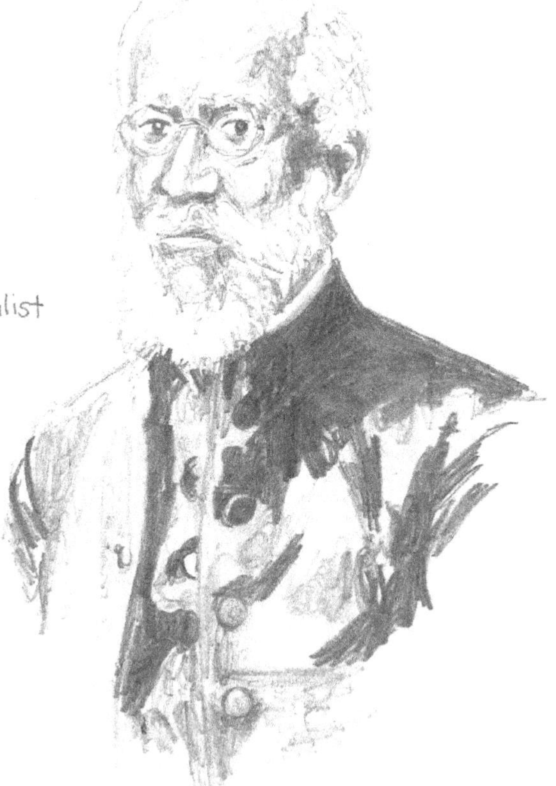

ALEXANDER
CRUMMELL
American Episcopal priest and African nationalist
1819-1898

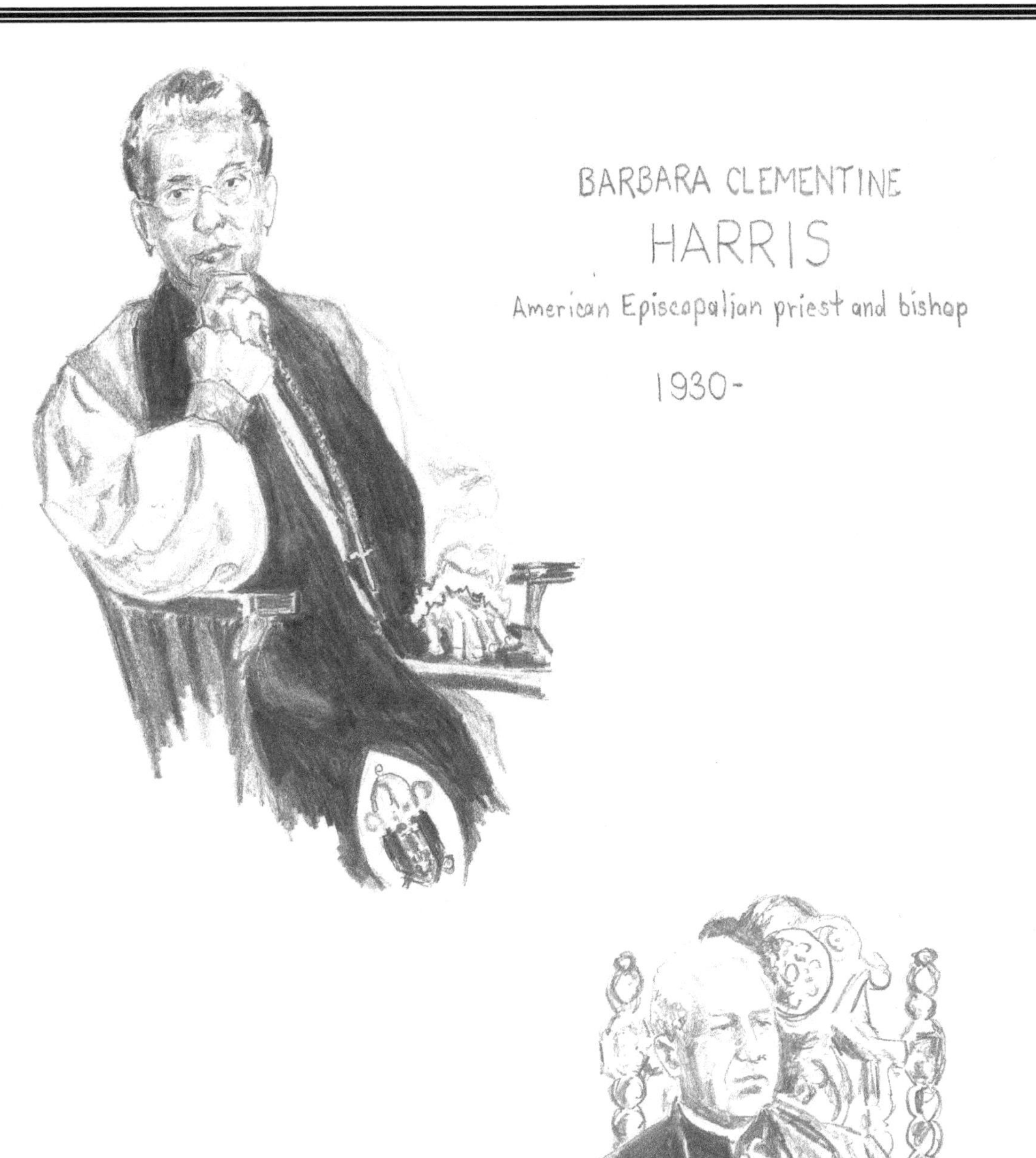

BARBARA CLEMENTINE
HARRIS
American Episcopalian priest and bishop

1930-

HENRY McNEAL
TURNER
American AME bishop and politician

1834-1915

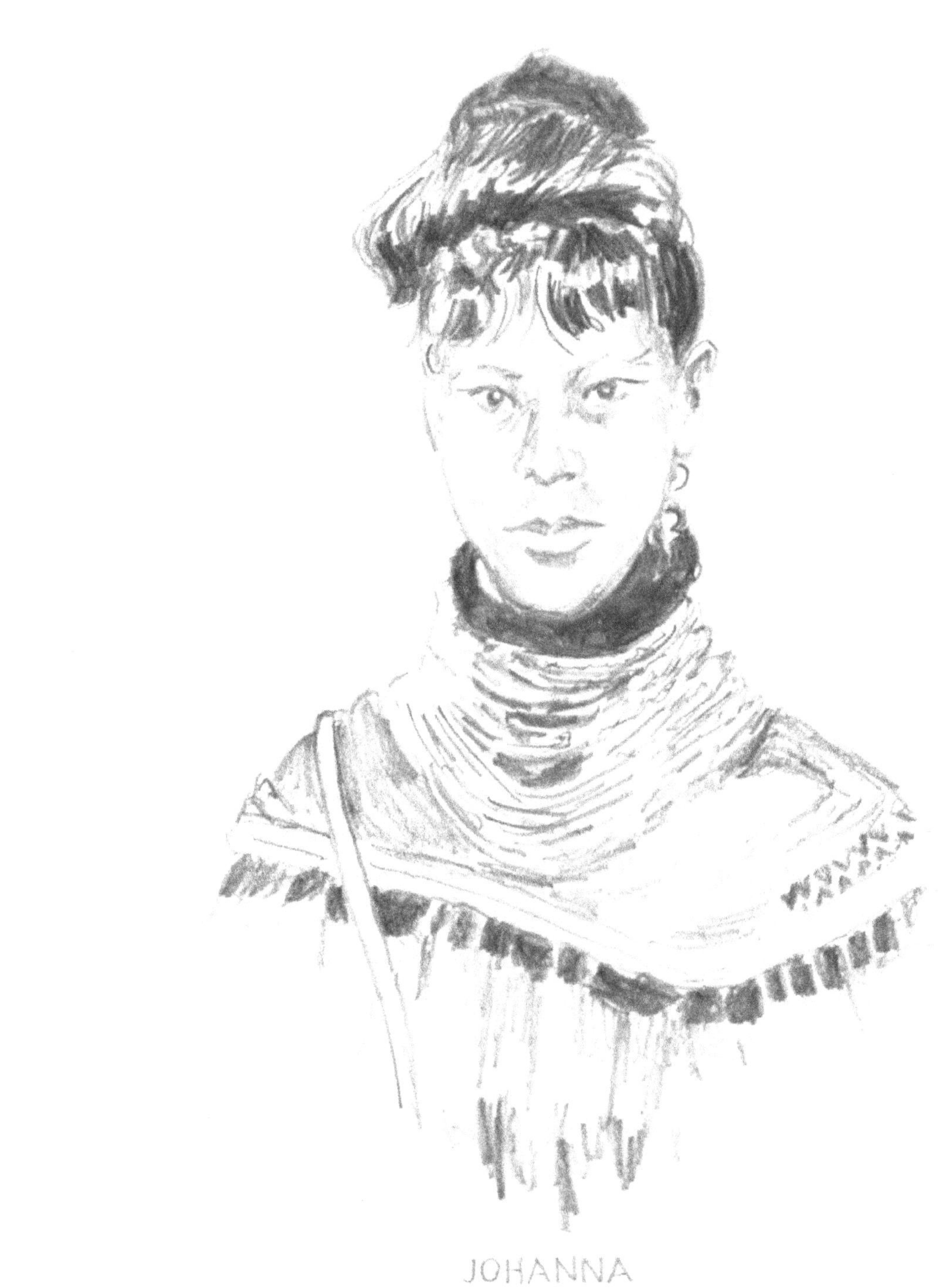

JOHANNA
JULY

Black-Seminole (native-American) cowgirl and horse tamer

1857? - 1946?